FRANCIS STUART
face to face: a critical study

Photograph by J. and S. Harsch, Dublin, 1972, reproduced by kind permission of the University of Ulster.

Francis Stuart
1902–2000

FRANCIS STUART
face to face: a critical study
ANNE McCARTNEY

THE INSTITUTE OF IRISH STUDIES
QUEEN'S UNIVERSITY BELFAST

The Institute of Irish Studies
Queen's University Belfast
8 Fitzwilliam Street
Belfast BT9 6AW
www.qub.ac.uk/iis/publications.html

British Library Cataloguing-in-Publication Data
A catalogue record for this book is available from the British Library.

ISBN 0 85389 768 9

Typeset in Garamond 11 pt

Printed by ColourBooks Ltd, Dublin
Cover design by Dunbar Design

Contents

Acknowledgements

This book is the outcome of prolonged and sustained research into the works of Francis Stuart and as a result many have provided help, support and encouragement.

I am indebted, first, to Finola Graham, Francis Stuart's widow, and Paul Durcan, his literary executor, for granting me copyright permission. I would also like to record my profound gratitude to Professor Robert Welch, Dean of the Arts at the University of Ulster, his wisdom, guidance and generosity as research supervisor, colleague and friend have been, and continue to be, an inspiration. His support, and that of his wife Angela, has been an important element in the production of this book and for that I thank them both. Also Bob's vision and foresight in securing the Francis Stuart Collection for the University of Ulster not only made my task much easier, it created a unique resource in Ireland for Stuart's work. I wish to acknowledge the helpful assistance of the staff of the library at the University of Ulster, in particular, Kay Ballantine, Sub-Librarian in Humanities, Frank Reynolds and Joe McLaughlin. Also my thanks go to the librarian of the Morris Library at the Southern Illinois University at Carbondale who provided me with an annotated inventory of their Francis

Stuart Collection. I am also grateful for help and assistance extended at the National Library of Ireland and the British Library. This book was completed while I enjoyed the facilities of a Visiting Scholarship to St John's College, Oxford and I would like to extend my thanks to the Trustees of the College and especially to Dr John Pitcher. Publication of this book was made possible, in part, by grants from the Arts Council of Northern Ireland and the Research Committee of the University of Ulster for which I am grateful and would thank in particular, Dr John Gillespie, Head of the Research Committee, Professor Gerry McKenna, Vice Chancellor of University of Ulster, and Professor Terence O'Keeffe, former Dean of Arts, Design and Humanities. I would also like to thank my colleagues at the Centre for Irish Literature and Bibliography for all their help and support, especially Dr Frank Sewell, Wendy Taulbautt, and Maeve Patton; also Professor Brian Walker of the Institute of Irish Studies, and Margaret McNulty and Catherine McColgan, also of the Institute, for their help with the production of this book.

A very special thank you goes to my sons Michael and David, whose love and friendship light up my life, and to my daughter-in-law Jolanta for her magical vision. Most importantly, to my very special daughter and friend Caroline, who provided me with the crucial experience necessary to write this book. Finally, my utmost thanks go to the late Francis Stuart who was generous with his time and who responded with complete honesty to my questions. Suaimhneas ar a anam, ceart is cóir dá shaothar.

Anne McCartney
November 2000

For Robert Welch
who acted as mentor
and midwife for this book.

Abbreviations

The following abbreviations of the titles of Stuart's works are used in the text of this book.

ACOL	*A Compendium of Lovers*
AHH	*A Hole in the Head*
BLSH	*Black List, Section H*
F	*Faillandia*
GFD	*Good Friday's Daughter*
M	*Memorial*
PI	*Pigeon Irish*
R	*Redemption*
TAOP	*The Angel of Pity*
TASS	*The Abandoned Snail Shell*
TCD	*The Coloured Dome*
THC	*The High Consistory*
TPOC	*The Pillar of Cloud*
TTLF	*Things to Live For*
TTS	*Try the Sky*
TWH	*The White Hare*
VV	*Victors and Vanquished*
WG	*Women and God*

Introduction

Ní bhíonn saoi gan locht.
(There is no saoi without fault)

The obituaries published on the death of Francis Stuart on 2 February 2000 followed the pattern of the criticism that dogged him in his later life. Even though he was a Saoi of Aosdána, an honour which recognised his outstanding contribution to the arts in Ireland, the main focus of interest was the controversy of his life rather than his writing. Despite the fact that his writing provides a unique nexus between the Yeatsian mysticism which marks his early work and the postmodernism of his recent novels, thereby illustrating the many changes which have occurred in the genre of the novel and of storytelling in particular, in the twentieth century, little credit was given to his success as a writer. His work is also a fascinating record of one man's commitment to writing and of his determination, despite all the odds, to make a living out of words. Above all though, his work charts the journey Stuart undertook in his search for truth. In the cynical climate of the late twentieth century this journey must have seemed somewhat misguided and dated, but from the perspective of the millennium, in fact

1

reveals much that is relevant to contemporary thinking in the areas of theology, gender studies, narratology and reading practices. Stuart's work has always been ahead of its time but this is not the reason for his comparative neglect and the fact that most of his novels, even those published in the 1970s and 1980s, are now out of print. This neglect has occurred precisely because the interest in Stuart has, since the publication of *The Pillar of Cloud* in 1948, been aimed at his life rather than his work.

Stuart himself was partly to blame since he always mined his own life to create his fiction and while in Japan there is a form of novel, *watakushi-shōsetsu* or 'I-novel',[1] where the fiction is based on the lived experience of the writer but is not strictly speaking autobiography. There is no category of Western fiction which encompasses this blend of fact and fiction. Stuart coined his own category for *Black List, Section H*, when he called it 'autobiographical fiction'[2] but this does not really encompass the interrogation of the self that forms the basis of his later work.

Stuart's life is the stuff that novels are made of. His birth, for instance, was marked by tragedy and mystery. Born on 29 April 1902 in Townsville, Australia, Henry Francis Stuart was the son of Henry Irwin Stuart and his wife Elizabeth nee Montgomery. Stuart's parents had married the previous year in Dervock, County Antrim in the North of Ireland where both their families had moderate-sized estates, the Stuart's at Ballyhivistock and the Montgomery's at Benvarden.[3] As the youngest sons in a family of eight, Henry and his twin brother James went to Australia in 1874 with very little capital but by 1882 they had earned enough to buy a sheep station which they developed into a prosperous town. Henry returned to Ballyhivistock at the end of the century, then aged 45, to seek a bride. His choice was the youngest sister of his near neighbour John Montgomery. Lily Montgomery was twenty-five years old when they married two years later. She and her more unconventional sister Janet, who was an ardent nationalist despite her family's long British military tradition, ran the household at Benvarden for their brother. Following the wedding the couple departed immediately for Australia.

Less than four months after Francis's birth, on 14 August 1902, his father killed himself. The circumstances that surrounded the death were shrouded in mystery for Stuart, since his mother never spoke of them to him. The result was that he filled the gap imaginatively and convinced himself that his father had died as an alcoholic.[4] Stuart's biographer, Geoffrey Elborn,[5] to some extent fills in some of the gaps in his study of the writer published in 1990, in which he chronicles Henry's mental illness, his repeated suicide attempts and his commitment to a private asylum in Sydney, where he finally succeeded in ending his life by hanging himself with a rope made from a bed sheet. Even he, though, cannot resist adding to the sense of mystery by speculating that Henry's rapid decline into insanity may have been brought about by sunstroke due to a severe drought, or 'that Lily, who was attracted by younger men, had an affair which the older Henry discovered'.[6] Whatever the reason, this dramatic start to his life haunted Stuart and his fiction is marked by attempts to exorcise and appease the ghost of his father.

Stuart's marriage to Iseult Gonne also provided its own dramas, not least of which was its effect of catapulting him from insecure and isolated schoolboy to the very centre of the Irish literary community. On leaving Rugby, the English public school where he had been an unhappy and unsuccessful scholar, Stuart, then aged sixteen, went to Dublin to be tutored for the Trinity College Entrance examination. Within six months he had encountered Iseult at one of George Russell's literary gatherings, Stuart having decided by that time that he wanted to be a poet. Introduced to him as Miss Gonne, Stuart at first was transfixed by Iseult, thinking that he was looking at the Maud Gonne who had inspired the love poetry of W.B. Yeats. On their second meeting Stuart brought along a volume of Yeats's poetry and asked her to read from it. Their initial attraction was enhanced by their mutual love of poetry, and despite her mother's disapproval, the pair eloped to London in January 1920. Stuart was then seventeen and Iseult twenty-five. On their return to Dublin a marriage was arranged for 6 April, a few weeks before Stuart's birthday, with Stuart converting to Catholicism for the ceremony.

The early years of the marriage were difficult; money was scarce and Maud Gonne proved a difficult mother-in-law, rows ensued and Yeats himself was at one stage brought in to negotiate between the couple.[7] The situation was not improved by the sudden death of their first daughter, Dolores. The outbreak of the Irish Civil War provided a distraction and while Iseult and her mother were busy setting up a hospital for the wounded in their home in St Stephen's Green, Stuart volunteered, on the republican side, to go to Belgium for the IRA and brought back two guns. Although not fully committed to the cause, he became increasingly involved and while attempting to highjack an armoured car he was arrested and interned for almost eighteen months in various camps. During this time he continued to write poetry and even attempted a novel which he sent to Edward Garnett, an editor at the publisher Jonathan Cape, who returned it noting that it showed some promise.[8] His poetry had more success and some verses Iseult had sent to the American magazine *Poetry*, won a prize of $100.[9] Iseult then gathered all the poetry Stuart had written in prison and F.R. Higgins, who was later to become director of the Abbey Theatre, arranged to have the poems published. *We Have Kept the Faith* by H. Stuart, appeared in January 1924, a few weeks after Stuart was released. It was published privately, the only publication of the Oak Leaf Press.[10] So began Stuart's writing career.

The second publication followed swiftly in the form of a small pamphlet produced by the Sinn Féin Árd-Chomhairle in March 1924 and based on a lecture he had delivered on nationalism and culture. Strangely, given his later views, in this pamphlet Stuart advocates a form of censorship against 'cheap English novels and magazines' in order to increase the demand for 'Irish poets and writers', and 'what is best in foreign literature'.[11] But Stuart's concern was with what he saw as the new state's lack of any commitment to a national culture. Because of this he agreed to Con Leventhal's[12] suggestion that, along with Liam O'Flaherty and Cecil Salkeld,[13] they should launch a monthly literary magazine, *To-morrow*, which would stir things up a bit.[14] As well as using the new magazine as an outlet for their own work they solicited contributions from Margaret Barrington, Joseph Campbell and Lennox Robinson. Yeats was also approached and enthusiastically gave them the poem 'Leda and the Swan', and also provided an unnamed editorial.[15] The magazine ran into trouble even before it was produced. Robinson's story about a young girl named Mary who, having been seduced by a tramp, dreams she will give birth to the Christ Child in his second coming, only to give birth to a girl and die in childbirth, was thought blasphemous by the Dublin printers. The magazine was eventually printed in Manchester and *To-morrow* ran for two issues in August and September 1924 before the controversy it aroused forced its young editors to discontinue.[16]

This first venture into publishing confirmed Stuart in his assertion in the second editorial that his was 'a voice in the wilderness in the hour before dawn'.[17] Rather than encourage him in the enterprise Stuart's experience with *To-morrow* seems to have convinced him that he would never make any impact, or perhaps more importantly, money, as a poet. For several years he retreated to Glencree, County Wicklow, and concentrated on chicken farming, racing, and reading the mystics. A son, Ion, was born on 5 August 1926 and a daughter Catherine on 21 May 1931 but the period from 1924 to 1931 was a barren time creatively for Stuart who published only a few poems and a pamphlet issued by the Catholic Truth Society, *Mystics and Mysticism* (1929). But Stuart had not completely given up the dream of being a writer and, following a summer working as a stretcher-bearer in Lourdes, he turned his mind to writing a novel about the experience, in which he was encouraged by Iseult and Liam O'Flaherty who persuaded Edward Garnett and Jonathan Cape[18] to publish it. *Women and God* was published in 1931 with a print run of 1500 of which 600 were wasted[19] so it was not an economic success. Neither was it a critical success but Stuart, caught up in a flurry of writing activity that lasted for the next eight years, was already well into his next novel, loosely-based on his recollections of the Civil War.

Not surprisingly, given the low sales of *Women and God*, Cape turned down the new novel, *Pigeon Irish*, but Stuart soon found another publisher in Victor Gollancz who was then building up his list. Yeats was approached for publicity material and he praised its 'cold exciting strangeness'.[20] This time the reviews were more favourable and Stuart found himself being praised on the cover of *The New York Times Book Review*.[21] He also came to the attention of the writer, Compton Mackenzie, whose glowing reviews for the *Daily Mail* did much to make Stuart's reputation at this time.[22] Over the next few years Stuart settled into a pattern of writing at home in Laragh Castle, County Wicklow, punctuated by trips to London with O'Flaherty, ostensibly to visit his publisher but more often than not to provide opportunities for drinking and womanising.[23] Three more novels followed in quick succession, all published by Gollancz in London and simultaneously by Macmillan in New York, *The Coloured Dome* in 1932 and *Try the Sky* and *Glory* in 1933. The latter two novels take as their subject matter Stuart's new interest in flying and reflect his changing attitude to this pursuit, at first seeing it as an alternative to the mystical journey, but then realising that it was another form of mechanisation which offered only an unsatisfactory escapism.

Despite his now prolific output Stuart still was not making much money from his writing and was keen to try his hand at writing for films, despite the fact that his Abbey play *Men Crowd Me Round* was heavily criticised for its lack of stagecraft.[24] The film script for *Riders to the Sea* was also unsuccessful and was never used.[25] But whatever the economic success of his work, Stuart was gaining acceptance as an established writer and was deemed sufficiently distinguished for Jonathan Cape to commission his memoirs which were published in 1934 under the title *Things to Live For*. By 1935 his visits to London were becoming more and more prolonged and Stuart found himself, for the first time, writing specifically for money. He wrote *In Search of Love*, a satirical look at the film industry, in six weeks. It was published by Collins who was Compton Mackenzie's publisher, but without great success despite its topical theme.

The novel which followed this light-hearted effort, only a few months later, was very different. *The Angel of Pity* (1935) was a serious work, a philosophical treatise on the need for spiritual values. Knowingly at odds with the contemporary literary fashion for social realism, Stuart looks towards to the aftermath of a future war and presents a powerful portrayal of Christ as Woman in the torn and raped heroine Sonia. The work had a cold reception from the critics and from the public and even Iseult, to whom it was dedicated, thought that it 'was all wrong'.[26] The work is notable in that it anticipates many of the themes that run through Stuart's post-war work and also the philosophy that drove him to seek out ostracism.

By this time his marriage was in difficulty and Stuart went so far as to consult a solicitor to find out whether or not an annulment was possible, but despite the emotional turmoil, he continued writing and the following year saw the publication of *The White Hare* (1936) again by Collins, who was to publish the remainder of Stuart's pre-war novels. This novel has a strange mythic quality and tells of the love of one woman for two brothers, and was the only one of Stuart's novels to fulfil his early dream that his work would be made into films; however it took some sixty years before it was produced under the title of Moondance. His novel *Glory* (1933) made an earlier transfer to the visual media, being the stage of the Arts Theatre in London at the beginning of 1936.[27]

Stuart's love of horse-racing led, in 1937, to a commission by Talbot Press of Dublin, for a small book on the subject, *Racing for Pleasure* and *Profit In Ireland and Elsewhere*. In the same year *The Bridge* (1937) was published by Collins. Set in a small community in the west of Ireland, the novel questions the morality of such places, contrasting the deadness of conventional marriage with the passion of an adulterous affair. *Julie* (1938), a romance between a young South African girl and a Jewish fraudster who is ultimately redeemed by her love, followed this. Stuart's only foray into historical narrative, *The Great Squire*, was set in eighteenth-century Ireland, and published in 1939 shortly before he departed for Germany. Stuart had eleven novels published in eight years, but despite this remarkable output he did not make a great deal of money from it so when Helmut Clissman, Head of the German Academic Exchange Service, told Iseult that he could arrange for a lecturing tour for Francis in Germany, she was enthusiastic.

Stuart arrived in Berlin in April 1939, employed on a short contract, but when he returned to Ireland that July he had arranged to go back to take up a lecturing post after Christmas. Whatever the long-term effect that the decision to go to Germany had on Stuart's subsequent writing career, the immediate result was a nine-year gap in Stuart's publishing, the only exception being the publication in 1940 of a German translation of William J. Maloney's *The Forged Diaries of Casement*, which had been published by the Talbot Press in 1936, in which the Irish-American academic argues that diaries used to condemn Roger Casement had been published by the British authorities; an Abbey production of one of his plays, *The Strange Guest*, arranged by Iseult again in 1940[28]; and Hungarian and Spanish translations of *The Great Squire* (1945) breaking the silence. During the war the only outlet for his creative energies apart from the broadcasts he made, from 1942 to 1944, to Ireland for Irland-Redaktion, the Irish service of German Radio set up in 1939 to broadcast talks encouraging Irish neutrality, were his diaries.

However, throughout the war Stuart continued to plan his writing career. The diaries he kept at this time are full of comments on the progress of his writing. On 16 October 1942, for instance, he contemplates his earlier novels and considers his recent writing.

> Looking back I can now value my work in a balanced way. All my books
> are very imperfect, all are fragmentary, confused and much marred. I had
> not found the way to the Truth and had not found myself. I was submitting
> to all experience, letting thought and sensation go through me. Only when
> I become a complete being (or begin to) shall I be capable of a more or less
> complete and satisfying utterance.[29]

He describes too the physical and emotional energy demanded by the work
and records the difficulties he experiences in his writing.

> SEPTEMBER 25. Believe I have got the book going at last. How long! But it
> must be as good as I can possibly make it. No time or patience need be
> spared. I begin at last to 'feel' it a bit. That mysterious, secret exciting
> 'sense'. But no wonder it is not easy seeing that I am trying to write in an
> entirely new way. Both as to aim, or theme and also as to technique. [30]

Even as he writes Stuart knows that publication will be a problem.

> AUGUST 20. This morning a letter from Scherl saying the Propaganda
> Ministry had refused permission for *Winter Song*'s publication in German.
> The Propaganda Ministry has neither interest in nor knowledge of the
> truth. This book could not now be published in England or America either,
> though it is in no way political. At least that is something – to know I have
> written what would please none of the Propaganda Ministries. Later I may
> publish it at home.[31]

Despite this setback Stuart feels driven to write, seeing it as 'part of [his]
destiny',[32] and indeed even plans a solution for the post-war period.

> I would like to have a small publishing concern in Dublin where I could
> publish my books – *Winter Song* first, my poems and then the one I am
> now writing. Then I would be independent of America and England where
> in any case it is doubtful if they would be taken.[33]

Stuart never doubts that after the war he would return to Ireland, though
not necessarily to Iseult.

> I must not go back to a permanent living at Laragh because, no matter how
> I may long for much of it after two and a half years, I do not believe that

I would have that minimum of peace and fulfilment from such a life that is the basis of everything. To live in Dublin? Or in Meath? To leave Ireland altogether and live here in Germany? I don't think I could bear that or in America? Where I would certainly not be very welcome! Anyhow I feel such a desire for Ireland that I want to be there for a long time as soon as I can.[34]

One of the main barriers to the likelihood of this ever happening was his relationship with Gertrud Meissner. Stuart met Gertrud (or Madeleine as she became known when they moved to London in 1950) when he arrived in Berlin in January 1940 and she took the job of typing the translations he did for the English Redaktion, the English section of German Radio. They quickly became friends and in September 1941 they became lovers. Again the diaries provide a fascinating insight into their relationship, their quarrels over Gertrud's jealousy when Stuart withdrew into his writing, but most of all their shared joy in reading together, particularly the Gospels. More significantly, though, the diaries record their last days in a Berlin that was being reduced to rubble, and his fear of being forced to separate from Madeleine which led them in September 1944 to become, effectively, homeless refugees, a situation which lasted until well after the end of the war. Much of these chronicles of survival will be familiar to those who have read Stuart's post-war work, for he has used them to great effect in novels such as *The Pillar of Cloud* (1948), *Redemption* (1949) and *The Flowering Cross* (1950).

Those looking for a document that politicises the historical events would be disappointed; instead Stuart notes the small domestic details of their lives, recording each meagre slice of bread that they have been able to obtain each day, worrying over each squabble with other refugees in case they will be informed on, dreaming of being back in Ireland, then filled with remorse by thoughts of abandoning Madeleine. The intensity of the situation is marked by the writing itself which, in the manuscript becomes smaller, more compacted and illegible; and by an increasing tendency to copy out prayers and extracts from the Gospels. Yet even at this time Stuart's thoughts turn to the nature of his own writing.

… all suffering in its simplicity, in its primitiveness. Death by bombs… And hunger… The humiliation of the outcast, the thing of having literally

9

nowhere to lay one's head… All this must be in the ground work so that the book has a new taste, a new slant.[35]

But the novel he began at this time was interrupted when the French occupying forces in the Austrian town of Dornbirn imprisoned Madeleine and himself in November 1945. Although no charges were ever made against them, they were not released until the following July, and Stuart was again detained for a short time in October 1946. It was therefore January 1947 before he sent off his first post-war novel, *The Pillar of Fire*, to Victor Gollancz.

There has been some speculation that Gollancz had fallen out with Stuart and refused to publish *In Search of Love* (1935) because of the unflattering portrayal of Sam Salmon, the agent, who although not overtly defined as Jewish, is described in a way deemed by some, rather dubiously, to be anti-Semitic.[36] Certainly there is no evidence of animosity in Gollancz's correspondence after the war when he writes warmly to Stuart about the 'vision' of his work and how proud he is to be his publisher.[37] This did not preclude him from turning down *The Pillar of Fire* (which was later redrafted as *Victors and Vanquished*, (1958)) on the grounds that Stuart was too close to his subject matter, but six months later Gollancz was able to write that he was accepting the new novel, *The Pillar of Cloud*, without reservation,[38] thereby renewing the partnership that was to continue throughout what was essentially the second phase of Stuart's writing career.

By the time *The Pillar of Cloud* was published in 1948, Stuart had already completed *Redemption* and started on *The Flowering Cross*, the fourth novel to draw on his war-time notes for material. Advised by his critics that he was running out of steam on this topic, he turns again to racing for inspiration. *Danny Boy* is a slight story of chance relationships and casual partings into which Stuart attempts to inject a sense of the comic absurdity of life, Gollancz's reader judging that he fails to achieve this because 'the sad poetry of life is his true vein'.[39] Refusing to publish *Danny Boy*, Sheila Hodge writes to Stuart that given the poor reviews of *The Flowering Cross* 'to put out a rather slight novel at this time would have a disastrous effect on your future'.[40]

At this time Stuart and Madeleine were living in Paris awaiting the documentation that would allow her to leave. Early in 1951 Stuart returned to Laragh to visit his mother who was ill. Iseult had by this time accepted the situation with Madeleine but the two were still in dispute over money and property.[41] Realising that it would not be possible for him to return to Ireland, Stuart and Madeleine moved to London later that year. Stuart's various jobs, whether as an attendant at the Geological Museum (now part of the Natural History Museum) or as a temporary sorter at the Post Office, limited the time available for writing, but nevertheless he managed to produce *Good Friday's Daughter* in 1952 and *The Chariot* in 1953. Iseult's death on 22 March 1954 left the way clear for Stuart to marry Madeleine, the wedding taking place on 28 April. Stuart was then working at the National Science Museum and finding time when on nightshift to write *The Pilgrimage* (1955) and *Victors And Vanquished* (1958). In the latter novel Stuart returns to a thinly-disguised account of his experiences in Berlin and Dornbirn. On the day it was published, 28 April 1958, Stuart returned to Ireland, he and Madeleine moving into The Reask, a small cottage they bought in Meath. His next novel *The Angel of Providence* was the last to be published by Gollancz, the partnership coming to an end when Gollancz refused *A Trip Down the River*, a book which remains unpublished.[42]

In 1961 Stuart began work on a new novel the working title of which was *We The Condemned*. More than any of his other novels the work went very slowly, needing repeated drafts, and was not completed until 1967. Stuart sent the manuscript to numerous publishers and agents but the next five years were marked by repeated rejection. No-one, it seemed, wanted to take a chance on the work, some worrying about the threat of libel in a work so recognisably autobiographical, others on its literary merits.[43] Timothy O'Keeffe, then with McGibbon & Kee, dismissed it on the grounds that 'you seem to be hinting at more than you actually convey'.[44] The book went though various re-writes. One of them, suggested by the novelist and playwright, Tom MacIntyre, was that Stuart used the real names of those concerned rather than fictional ones.

During this difficult time for Stuart the Abbey Theatre rejected *Who Dares to Speak?*, a play Stuart wrote for the Terence MacSwiney Commemoration in 1970. Eventually though, as a result of Stuart meeting Jerry Natterstad, an American who was undertaking a doctoral thesis on him, *Black List, Section H* was published by The Southern Illinois

University Press, Carbondale in January 1972, but it was not until 1974 that Timothy O'Keeffe, then with Martin Brian & O'Keeffe, agreed to publish it in London. The previous year the same firm had published *Memorial* (1973), the novel that effectively marks the beginning of the third phase of Stuart's career, the phase where he experiments with the formal strategies of narrative in an attempt to get across his vision.

His seventy-fifth birthday was marked by the launch of *A Festschrift* in his honour edited by W.J. McCormack and by the publication of *A Hole in the Head* (1977). The Stuarts were by this time settled in Dublin and enjoying the support of the literary community there and for the first time some limited financial security, the Arts Council of Ireland having awarded him a three-year grant in 1979.[45] This funding was effectively continued when, in 1981, under the recommendation of Anthony Cronin, the government set up Aosdána, a body of writers to whom an annual income would be paid, and Stuart was on the first list of members. This year also saw the publication of *The High Consistory* (1981), a novel which, in essence, is a collage of extracts from his notebooks, diaries, letters and news clippings.

Dermot Bolger who had just set up his own publishing company, Raven Arts Press, organised the celebration for Stuart's eightieth birthday in 1982. Bolger re-issued Stuart's *We have Kept the Faith* (1982) with new additions for the occasion and also commissioned Paul Durcan to write a long poem, *The Ark of the North*. Raven Arts Press took over from O'Keeffe as Stuart's publisher, bringing out *States of Mind* in 1984 and *Faillandia* in 1985.

In 1986 Madeleine became ill following a trip to Canada and was diagnosed with liver cancer. Stuart nursed her until she died on 18 August. He marked her death with the publication of *The Abandoned Snail Shell* in 1987, dedicating to her this thoughtful piece on his creative enterprise. Among those who consoled Stuart following Madeleine's death was Finola Graham, an artist who had worked with her in St Kilian's German School in Dublin. Drawn together by a mutual understanding of loss, the relationship deepened, and they were married in the church of St Francis Xavier, Dublin, on 29 December 1987. Stuart's writing continued apace and later that year he published a short collection of poetry *Night Pilot* and in 1990 a novel which centred around the arrival of a comet, *A Compendium of Lovers*.

Stuart's ninetieth birthday in 1992 brought about renewed media interest: Fintan O'Toole in the *Irish Times* giving an excellent critique of his career and RTÉ broadcasting a celebratory programme called 'Stuart at 90', but he continued to have his critics; Kevin Myers could not allow the occasion to pass without an attacking Stuart because he had broadcast from Germany during the war. Raven Arts Press reissued *We Have Kept the Faith* (1992) for the occasion and, in response to the upsurge in interest, brought out a new edition of *The Pillar of Cloud* and *Redemption* in 1994. Further editions of *Black List, Section H* were produced by Lilliput Press, Dublin, in 1994 and Penguin in 1995. A collection of new poems, *Arrows of Anguish* appeared in 1996 and a short novel, *King David Dances* in 1998, both published by New Island Books. In 1996 a Francis Stuart Special Issue of *Writing Ulster*, edited by Bill Lazenbatt, was published by The University of Ulster.

Stuart's standing as a writer was finally acknowledged when in 1996 the Arts Council elected him as Saoi of Aosdána, the highest literary honour available in Ireland, but the decision to honour him evoked a vitriolic response in some quarters. Further controversy arose over a broadcast at the end of 1997 which resulted in an open session of Aosdána to consider the proposal laid before it that Stuart should be arraigned for his allegedly anti-Semitic views. The motion was overwhelmingly rejected and in 1999 Stuart successfully sued the *Irish Times* for libellous comments printed at the time of the arraignment. Stuart's increasing fame remained focused on the controversy of his war-time activities rather than his writing.

From this brief account of Stuart's life and writing career it will be obvious that there is a body of work worthy of recognition and study but before that can happen a barrier of prejudice needs to be broken. This present study therefore is not just a critical analysis of the literature but also a guide to the philosophical outlook and creative motivations that underpin Stuart's work. I feel that this approach is justified by the fact that Stuart himself knew that conventional criticism would fail to get to the heart of his work, the purpose of which he always claimed was to reveal the revelations he had glimpsed of what he initially called truth or God, but later 'a working model of reality' (*TASS*, p.7). Stuart's novels are, in one way or another, testimonies to his desire to express what he felt to be one of the truths of human existence: that there is a reality beyond that one normally

13

accepted, the world of power, moral codes and commerce. Initially Stuart circles this reality, glimpsing his goal from afar then eventually, from the insights he gained through his war-time experiences, he realises that before he can allow his imagination to take flight, he must burrow underground.

To encourage the reader to follow his example of delving into the inner consciousness, Stuart at first shocks the reader out of complacent ways of thinking. He uses incidents from his own life, particularly his decision to remain in Germany during the war, to entice the reader to judge him critically, he then turns the tables to question the grounds on which such a judgement is made. By questioning accepted modes of thought Stuart forces the reader into a process of self-analysis which parallels the state of his own mind and, by repeated textual inferences, the mind of Christ on the cross. This network of relationships provides experiential proof of Stuart's vision of reality.

Taking a lead from Stuart's narrative techniques and from feminist criticism, it becomes clear that his work demands a personal response since the proof of his insights lies within the realm of the individual reader's own experience and so I end the volume with an account of my own experience of working with Stuart's texts. The purpose of this approach is to encourage readers to look beyond the controversy, to see a writer committed to his craft and to finding an appropriate narrative form to frame his perception of human experience. From this perspective it is possible the better to appreciate the skilful way in which he employs and advances novelistic techniques to create an innovative and unique style, a style which requires a deeply personal form of criticism. By focusing on Stuart's writing, its underlying philosophical motivation and its provocative approach, it is hoped that readers will come to an understanding of Stuart and begin to see beyond his life to his work for only then will the full impact of both be felt.

1

The Reality of Unreality

Given that his writing career spanned more than seventy-five years, it is inevitable that Francis Stuart's novels should have developed in style and form in keeping with literary trends. However, the stylistic and formal changes in Stuart's writing not only stem from a narrative evolution, they also developed as a result of a life-long obsession with the nature of reality, an obsession which he claims lies at the heart of all human reflection. 'The most constant and intense need of mankind throughout history has been to achieve a working model of reality'. (*TASS*, p.7)

Over the years his quest to understand the subject led him to read accounts of various saints, philosophers, poets and scientists,[1] all of whose theories and suppositions, in turn, helped to shape and inform his thinking and, as a result, his earlier novels. His growing conviction that the experience of isolation and suffering was a necessary prerequisite to knowledge of reality was a subliminal motivating factor in his decision to go Berlin in 1939, and it was the realisation of this conviction that energises the powerful trilogy written in the immediate aftermath of the war. In the later novels, however, Stuart's reflections on reality not only inform the subject matter but become an integral part of the narrative process, so that, as Samuel Beckett said of James Joyce's work, 'his writing is not about something, it is that something itself'.[2] Stuart's writing, or more precisely, a combination of the writing and the reading of his work, becomes a practical demonstration of the interconnections that he deems to be reality. Stuart therefore finally 'achieves a working model of reality'(*TASS*, p.7), one that is the culmination of changing formulations and strategies, and one that is best understood by retracing the steps he followed on his journey towards this realisation.

An early story, 'The Pond', later published in *Things to Live For,* reveals much about the origin of Stuart's obsession. It describes the epiphany of a child who, on staring deep into the water of the pond, catches a glimpse of a fish in the shadows and realises that he is 'on the fringe of reality'. (*TTLF,* p.9)

> My feet were then set on that quest, that pilgrimage that, with so much straying from the way, they are still bent on. I had started in search of that reality that cannot be counterfeited, that is stark and cold and harsh like the smell of water and the noise of leaves. (*TTLF,* p.10)

The pilgrimage undertaken is essentially a Platonic one since it mirrors the journey undertaken in the cave allegory with which Plato charts the various stages of human enlightenment from appearances to the real world.[3] Where Plato has his prisoners in the cave move from a contemplation of shadows to the objects which form the shadows, Stuart has the boy move from the 'shadow of a shadow' (*TTLF,* p.8) of half-formed memories in which 'the essential moods, thought, and feelings, are forgotten' (*TTLF,* p.7) into a dim cave-like light.

> Under the rhododendron bushes were dark leafy caves smelling damp and sweet with an exciting fragrance. I picked up the gossamer skeletons of leaves and put them in a little box… (*TTLF,* p.8)

He then progresses to a world which resembles that outside the cave, by peering closely into the pond which becomes 'transparent with the sunlight', revealing a world 'strange and remote'. (*TTLF,* p.9) Breaking through the illusions of a shadow-bound consciousness the boy glimpses the world as if for the first time.

> ... a door had been opened to me, a secret revealed. I could not have said what that secret was, and I cannot say now. But I know that it was the first glimpse I had into life, beautiful in its terrible passivity, delicate and intricate with a savage strength. (*TTLF*, p.10)

So just as Plato's pilgrims 'attempt to pierce the veil of selfish consciousness and join the world as it really is', [4] the boy's experience merges the world of the senses and the world of objects.

> In my ears there was the whisper of the leaves in the summer breeze, and in my nostrils the smell of the water, cold and slightly bitter in the sweet warm air. The stones on which I knelt were hurting my knees, but I did not move. A leaf floated past curved at the tip like the bow of a picture book boat. (*TTLF*, p.9)

But, for Plato, this is still the world of appearances, not reality, which is epitomised by the sun; 'the Good'. When the prisoners escape into the outside world they become aware of a world bathed in the light of the sun, but the ultimate goal of the quest, the sun itself, remains inaccessible.[5] The sun is not viewed directly in Stuart's story either, being present only as a reflection in the pool, but its absence is noted by the need to continue with the search. 'And although I had a secret joy, from then that seed of discontent was perhaps sown in me.' (*TTLF*, p.10)

Here then Stuart sees reality as something hidden and beyond normal sensual perception, so there is no clear definition of its nature, only a recognition of its existence. Again this is in keeping with Plato's doctrine of *recollection* or *anamnesis*[6] which maintains that at birth the soul is cast from the 'real' world of the forms which is no longer seen in the temporal world, but is not forgotten altogether as it remains as a shadow. But, apart from sharing this veiled presence, Stuart's transcendental reality would seem to have little in common with Plato's ideal world in which beauty was to be found in abstract rational thought, 'not in the complexities of organic nature, but in geometry... in straight lines, circles, and squares'.[7] In contrast, Stuart's early novels are extremely critical of the cold rationalism of materialistic society and centre around his desire to show a reality in which spirituality plays an important role.

Pigeon Irish, for instance, depicts Ireland as 'the last stronghold of Western culture against the expansion of over-civilization' (*PI*, p.73), holding out against a surging tide of materialism from the continent. The novel equates the rationality of scientific thought with mindless sterility 'Science controlling life. Hygiene. Hygienic love. A psychotherapic religion'. (*PI*, p.58) Set in the future the novel voices the fear, prevalent in the mid-war period, that the growing confidence in the primacy of scientific knowledge with the consequent negation of the spirit, feelings and imagination was leading to what Karl Jaspers diagnosed as 'the great modern drift towards a standardized mass society'.[8] Despite the optimism brought about by the technological advances there was a tendency in the 1930s to envisage the universe as a machine on the verge of collapse, an image Stuart utilises to good effect in this novel.

> ... time turned like a cogged, invisible wheel, geared to the wheel of the earth. But already a tooth in that huge cogged wheel had broken. Slowly it turned towards the broken tooth in the silence of that latest war. (*PI*, p.19)

The sense of pessimism which envelopes *Pigeon Irish* stems not only from the belief that scientific 'genius had developed machinery to a perfection of destructive intensity' (*PI*, p.17) but also from the conviction that society was itself corrupted. 'We're not just fighting an army on the Continent, we're fighting a civilization that has been refined to rottenness. It's swamping the world like a second flood.' (*PI*, p.37)

This, it is suggested within the novel, is due to the repression of human spirituality by the institutionalised values of mass industrial society and although the plot centres on an embattled Irish force providing 'a sort of sanctuary from this super-civilization' (*PI*, p.37) their defeat is always inevitable.

The structure of the novel reflects its concern with projecting a reality in which matter and spirit attempt to co-exist, since it yokes together a realist text about the war and a symbolic allegory about carrier pigeons. In the first the conflict between body and spirit is revealed not only in the opposition between the materialistic threat from the Continent and the romanticism of ancient Ireland but also in the characterisation of Brigid Allen and Catherine Arigho. For the male protagonist, Frank Allen, his wife Brigid is representative of a sensuality that remains linked to the physical world.

... and beneath the tense curve of her short hair I saw her neck which had
the new, smooth look of a branch peeled of bark... I could smell the warm
scent of her sleep-bathed flesh, part of the early morning smell of the
world. (*PI*, p.24)

On the other hand his lover, Catherine Arigho, like her namesake, St
Catherine of Sienna, represents an ascetic, world-denying religious spirit.
Throughout the novel Catherine promotes the virtues of the mystical love
of God over the sensual love of marriage, pointedly telling Brigid that
'there's no marriage in heaven. Angels don't marry' (*PI*, p.29). Trying to
persuade Frank that Ireland can only be saved through their martyrdom
she echoes the words of St Catherine when she promises him a spiritual
union, saying that she will 'await him at the holy place of execution' (*PI*,
p.78). Brigid, of course, sees Catherine's complete denial of the self as a
fanatical and excessive form of spirituality, and argues instead that 'the
wildest lust and obscenity is better than this morbid, spiritual perversion'
(*PI*, p.91). In Frank Allen therefore, Stuart creates a character torn between
sensual and spiritual goals. At times he feels enticed by Catherine's ideals,
especially when they are linked to an image of Ireland as a sanctuary of the
spirit.

... standing in the ruins of Refearta Church I might believe in something
like that too: in Ireland's destiny as the saviour of humanity; for there was
in me too a root of fanaticism that was sensitive to surroundings. (*PI*, p.57)

But he also recognises that her suppression of sexuality is a 'transmutation'
of physical desire into 'a more dangerous passion' (*PI*, p.94). What Frank
actually seeks is the unification of both passions, but at this stage of his
career, Stuart can only symbolically suggest the possibility of such a union.

The more imaginative account of the pigeons gives Stuart greater scope
to represent a reality in which body and spirit co-exist harmoniously. The
carrier pigeons with their intuitive homing instinct provide a suitable
representation of the crossover between the natural and the transcendental
worlds.

She was feeling. She was conscious of a sea of sensations. Not in her brain
which was only used for the practical, material things of life; but in that
deep, mystical breast of hers, beneath the steel-grey feathers, she was

conscious of the flow of sub-human emotions. Passion burned there high up in the icy air, unfreudianised. (*PI*, p.21)

The image opens out quite logically to serve as an illustration of an interconnecting web of experiences linking past, present and future.

> So a memory had persisted through thousands of bird-generations up to this. The memory born in the breast of a dove returning spent and desolate over a waste of water to a big wooden boat… Fading, getting fainter, until now, in the breast of Buttercup, suddenly as though another wave had caught it in a new emotion, the two experiences, separate many thousand years, united. And this blending, this bridging of an eternity sent a quiver through her body beneath the close feathers, a fearful tremble. (*PI*, p.50)

The parable therefore provides Stuart with a better means of expressing his vision and it also serves as a narrative strategy. The continual shifting between the allegorical and the realist text disturbs conventional reading expectations and prevents readers from settling into mundane patterns of thought and thereby encourages them to become more receptive to the possibility of non-ration experience. 'He didn't think in words, not in thoughts. In a forest of sensations. New emotions washed the staleness from outworn phrases.' (*PI*, p.20)

But although successful in opening the reader's mind to the possibility of an intuitive form of knowledge, the novel does not really convince, primarily due to its failure to fully reconcile the symbolic and the realist modes. This breakdown is most noticeable in the device of a parallel martyrdom in the two sections of the novel. In the pigeon section, Stuart is able to allow his imagination to take full flight and express a mystical union in death.

> Not satisfied with the unmingling contact of flesh, but with wild longing for the undisentanglable blending of blood in death. A mystical union. Very physical, very spiritual. Because she did not think that this shedding of their blood would be the only consummation. Beyond that, like the one shadow thrown by two embracing figures, was a vaguer, but vivid image. As though the archangels swooping down, remoulded the shed blood, the shining feathers into one vivid and immaterial bridge between earth and heaven. A rainbow over the receded flood. (*PI*, p.99)

But, in the realist section, Frank's martyrdom for the soul of Ireland is foiled when Catherine's dying father steps in to take his place so, rather than the climactical sacrifice of the pigeons, Frank's destiny is one of social condemnation as he is shunned by all except Catherine. Indeed the only glimmer of hope the novel offers its human characters lies in the deepening understanding between these two as they struggle to uphold the traditional values in a world crumbling about them.

> She had a spiritual faith, a mystical faith that believed in spite of all human reason.
>
> But that tenderness, that I suddenly felt in Catherine would not give out for a long time. It was drawn from somewhere very deep. Cool dark depths of tenderness that I had not glimpsed before. (*PI*, p.275)

Stuart's concept of a symbolic redemption through martyrdom cannot be sustained in his realist text, primarily because of his pessimistic view of modern society, so the two strands of the novel therefore run parallel to each other rather than integrating fully. The effect of this is to make evident an underlying belief that spirituality can only survive in isolation from society, behind the convent walls, or in some lonely spot in rural Ireland.

Such a view is hardly surprising given Stuart's fascination with mysticism at the time. In *Mystics and Mysticism*, published by the Catholic Truth Society in 1929 he argues that 'the goal of our life is union with a personal god' (*MM*, p.1) and stresses the importance of both physical and mental suffering for the mystical life.

> And this suffering, so longed for, so bitter, and yet so cherished by the mystic, is a power for good in the world quite immeasurable. The life of the contemplative orders, one of severe penance and mortification is surely secondary only to the perpetual sacrifice of the Mass in securing forgiveness and mercy for a world so dark with sin and rebellion. (*MM*, p.3)

He goes on to assert that in order to attain mystical knowledge, which he describes as 'a love that draws the soul towards God and unites it to Him in a union surpassing words to express' (*MM*, p.20), it is necessary to undertake a reclusive introspective quest. The personal nature of this type of redemptive journeying offers little hope for the salvation of society as a whole and in his early novels Stuart's concern is certainly to show the redemption of the individual rather than social reform, but he also makes it clear, in *The Angel of Pity* for example, that such individuals offer the only hope to a civilization hurtling towards chaos.

> The Brothers Karamazov fulfilled no social problems but it inspires thousands of beings separately by its grasp of a particle of that truth that has nothing to do with the conduct of a state or the betterment of material conditions, but has everything to do with the conduct of a man's secret, personal life. (*TAOP*, p.44)

Stuart was later to realise that in these novels he was searching for the truth using the intellect rather than the emotions and, writing in his diary during the war, he recognised this had had a detrimental effect on his fiction.

> How well I see now what was wrong with the structure of my early books. All that mental obscurity which was in all the books. 'Ideas'. Complicated ideas; groping after the Truth with the mind and only finding sterility instead of going towards it with the heart, which is the only true way and in which there can be no obscurity.[9]

It is clear from this that Stuart was later to recognise the flaw of his early novels is that while they strive towards a transcendental truth or reality, he can only at this stage intellectualise it, with the result that he constantly finds himself trapped within logical frameworks that make it impossible for him to fully realise his vision. Instead, time and time again, he is forced into a position where the only place that revelation of the spiritual can occur is outside the corrupted norms of society. Such a position therefore leads Stuart to see the experience of isolation as a necessary prerequisite for the writer, since, as he shows in *The Angel of Pity*, if the artist was to gain an insight into the nature of reality he must, in effect, be like the saint and follow an isolated path.

> Show me the being who has suffered most... I would know beyond doubt that he had gone further towards finding the eternal truth than anyone else whether as an artist, a lover, a saint or in some other more obscure capacity... Lovers and saints remain for the most part unknown to the world. It is only artists of whom one can say: He is the greatest because he suffered most... it may be known from the quality of the artist's work. (*TAOP*, p.72)

It is not difficult to see how this, either consciously or subconsciously, must have influenced Stuart a few years later when he decided, just prior to the outbreak of the war, to take up a lecturing post in Berlin. Certainly recollecting this move in *Black List: Section H* Stuart again evokes this view of the writer.

> If he was ever to have experience, in his ordained degree, of what he thought of as the nature of reality, he had to be in the exposed place where such could reach him. (*BLSH*, p.234)

By taking this decision Stuart not only faced the danger of living in wartime Berlin, he also knew that he would be reviled and indeed, at the end of the war, he also experienced hunger and imprisonment. However, more importantly, he knew it would probably lead to the kind of experiences he saw as paramount to the writer and indeed this period of his life did have a vital effect on his writing.

> Of course my war experience – the fact that I was in Germany and so forth – were a great disadvantage, understandably so, I think. Yet, if I had stayed quietly in Ireland I would have gone on writing mediocre novels… it was essential for me as a writer, and perhaps even as a person, to go through what I did go through… but I wouldn't have it otherwise because I see it as a very, very valuable experience.[10]

If Stuart was driven by the need to place himself in precarious and isolating situations in order to live out the role model of the writer he had created imaginatively in his novels the actuality of living *in extremis* led him to a new understanding of the nature of reality, one which was rooted in human frailty.

> Mysticism was the life of the world and must be so again if the world is to have any life. But a mysticism with its roots in life and not in 'ideas', above all not in moralistic conceptions.[11]

In his work this change in perspective is marked by a movement away from depictions of sacrifice and martyrdom to an examination of the unique bond that arises among those who have endured the horrors of the world in some form and survived. This idea is most strikingly conveyed in Stuart's description of the fall of Berlin in *The Pillar of Cloud*.

> Because they had passed through the night of dungeons and prisons, of prison-cellars in which time stagnated and air-raid shelters which trembled and filled with smoke and glower with reflected fire, they could be together in this room, happy in a singular fraternity… Outside were the ruins, the hunger, the suspicion and hopelessness, but in their room high up above the street there was another mode of living. All was new, intense and tender. (*TPOC*, p.66)

The novel exposes the illusion of Stuart's previous vision of reality with its comforting metaphysical order and final reward most effectively in the character of Petrov, a Rumanian refugee. He voices a belief in the redemptive power of suffering which echoes that held in *Pigeon Irish*.

> Once he had believed that all those who had suffered and died were martyrs from whose wounds and blood the seed of a new wisdom and love would be nourished. And this faith had touched him inwardly with life. (*TPOC*, p.170)

He also articulates the part such a faith plays in the human capacity to withstand such pain and anguish.

> As long as he had lived in the glow of a vision of a mysteriously ordered world, where all had its hidden reason and purpose, where whosoever sowed in tears would reap with joy… then all could be borne. (*TPOC*, p.172)

The complacency of such a comfort is torn away as Petrov is ultimately brought face to face with 'all the signs of materialism and blind self-seeking' and is forced to see that 'his faith had been an illusion' (*TPOC*, p.172). In this way the reader is also made to contemplate a world in which there is only 'chaos and blindness and torment'. (*TPOC*, p.170)

> … he was face to face with another vision of the world, in which all was betrayed for a few good meals and a pair of silk stockings, where not only a sparrow but a few million men could perish, many of them in torment, without there being the slightest sign of any paternal spirit in the whole empty cosmos. (*TPOC*, p.173)

This nihilistic vision is further reinforced in the character of Halka who has been tortured, both physically and mentally, first in a prison camp and consequently in an asylum, and it is through her eyes that Stuart's new vision of reality begins to takes shape.

> There is no resurrection. In the whole world, there is only pain, there are
> only victims and executioners... It's not even necessary to fall into the
> hands of men. There's disease and accidents, famine and cold. That is the
> great reality. (*TPOC*, p.105)

While suffering still plays an important role in this new conception of
reality it is no longer just a means to an end, it is the end in itself. It is an
unmitigated fact of existence.

> ... she could not believe in a great, universal equity in which those who
> wept would laugh and the hungry would be filled with good things. For
> others it might be a matter of indifference. They might console themselves
> with believing in the possibility of an earthly equity. But for her there was
> no escape. (*TPOC*, p.106)

The only glimmer of hope that breaks through this bleak picture is in the
recognition of common humanity that binds together those who have
come face to face with this dark reality.

> Ah, how small we are, this little band of the living! When one sits here and
> thinks of all the hosts and hosts of the dead! Then we who happen to be
> alive are so few, and we should be able to love each other and comfort each
> other before we are separated forever. But we don't. Only here and there,
> by a miracle, does someone discover what it is to have fraternity with some
> other being. (*TPOC*, p.106)

This representation of reality has its grounding in a Dantean view of the
wretchedness and arbitrary nature of existence, but Stuart's main concern
is not the tragic fate of mankind. His interest lies in the effect this has on
those who come to recognise this fact through their own experiences. Like
T.S. Eliot who claimed that 'human kind/Cannot bear very much reality'[12]
Stuart believes that everyday existence with 'all the make-believes, the
kissing and coupling and gorging and cinema-going' (*TPOC*, p.105), is just
an avoidance of reality. In *The Abandoned Snail Shell* he argues that it is
those 'who have experienced extremes of inner or mental suffering' and not
been 'destroyed by it through insanity, suicide or by escape into criminality'
(*TASS*, p.34), but who have instead found a common bond with other

victims, who have really experienced reality. But it is not just the experience of pain that Stuart feels is the key to this experience but the intermingling of pain and love, and this again is given a religious dimension but this time one which is related to the figure of Jesus rather than mystics and saints.

> ... He was the one prophet who did not promise peace on earth, but destruction and desolation, from the razing of Jerusalem to the end of the world... He did not preach any revolution or counter-measures. He said: these things must be, and remember that I have told you. But above all: 'Love one another as I have loved you', that is, through all these things, even through passion and death. And that is our fraternity, and the only true fraternity.' (*TPOC*, p.131)

In *The Pillar of Cloud* Stuart hints at a link between the suffering of the crucifixion and that of all other victims but it is only tentatively implied when Dominic and Halka read the Bible together.

> ... and sometimes in reading they could come on some passage that seemed to refer to this that had happened to them, and these passages they re-read and marked, but even then they did not definitely compare their own state to what they read. That was something that they did not dare to do; they had both an instinct against trying to speak of it. (*TPOC*, p.232)

The suggestion of such a link, although veiled, succeeds in conferring a quasi-mystical dimension on this model of reality since it infers that even the most mundane incident of suffering plays a part in a wider scheme which includes the suffering of Jesus. So the novels written immediately after the war continue to show the remnants of the religious quest and it is only with *Black List, Section H* that the search begins to take on an aesthetic focus.

The character of H in this 'autobiographical fiction'[13] explains his interest in the mystics and the figure of Jesus Christ, not in religious terms, but as part of a search to overcome the solipsism of 'being alone in the haunted room of (his) mind' (*BLSH*, p.253). Jesus also becomes '... a kind of super-spirit crossing the otherwise barred threshold of the combined wonderland and cesspool of my consciousness' (*BLSH*, p.253). What interests H is the psychological make-up of those 'in the grip of new kinds of perception and emotion' (*BLSH*, p.133), and in the figure of Christ he sees someone who seems to have a similar fascination with delving into extremes of consciousness.

> ... with a neurological makeup so receptive and vulnerable who seems to have gone deliberately as far into the depths with the expressed purpose of gaining admission into other minds and hearts. (*BLSH*, p.253)

This interest in the communion of 'minds and hearts' brought about by shared suffering would seem yet again to suggest an embracing of orthodox Christianity but H's rejection of the conventional interpretations of the Church precludes any religious solution to his solipsism.

> What I need, Father, isn't the Christ at present preached by the Church but intimations of a spirit more (at least imaginatively and potentially) perverse than myself, one that has had the experiences I can only guess and tremble at... I shall always need, and to that extent believe in, the possibility of the companionship of such a spirit, but if there is such now and in the future, it will be, for those like me, an occasional great artist. (*BLSH*, p.254)

Stuart's quest for reality therefore turns inwards to the psyche itself and by focusing the search in the depths of consciousness he is, in effect, reflecting the changes which had occurred in the intellectual climate over the first half of the twentieth century when philosophers, scientists and artists gradually broke down the barriers between subject and object and exposed the difficulty of maintaining a rigid differentiation between external and internal realities. It is of course difficult to isolate changes in collective modes of perception, but as Ortega y Gasset points out in *The Modern Theme* (1951) these are most likely to appear first in pure science and in art.[14] Scientific developments such as those of quantum physics, wave mechanics and chaos theory have combined to dispel any remnants of the mechanical model of reality and have tended to accentuate the part human consciousness plays in scientific theories. As early as 1930, Sir James Jeans speculated on the supremacy of consciousness over matter.

> The old dualism of mind and matter seems likely to disappear, not through matter becoming in any way more shadowy or insubstantial than heretofore, or through mind becoming resolved into a function of the working of matter, but through substantial matter resolving itself into a creation and manifestation of mind.[15]

Although modern astro-physicists and cosmologists would tend to dismiss this rather crude speculation, many of their theories recognise the complex interrelationship between mental and physical space.[16] The introduction of consciousness into the scientific world picture has had, Stuart believes, a profound effect on the task of the creative writer.

> People's assumptions were superseded by the work of Einstein and others. Similarly the whole basis of early literature has been superseded. We can't continue to live in the old way, nor can we continue to write in the old way, because everything has changed out of recognition. Literature now can perceive things which were never brought into focus before.[17]

Literature has always questioned its relationship to reality with ontologies such as the mimetic theory asserting that the literary work mirrors the real world,[18] in which case both are mutually independent and mutually implicated.

> For the real world to be reflected in the mirror of literary mimesis, the imitation must be distinguishable from the imitated: the work of art must stand apart from and opposite to the nature to be mirrored. A mimetic relation is one of similarity, not identity, and similarity implies difference – the difference between the original object and its reflection between the real world and the fictional heterocosm.[19]

Other theorists claim that literature is not just a passive reflection of the status quo but an active intervention;[20] as Octavio Paz has observed, 'if art mirrors the world, then the mirror is magical; it changes the world'.[21] Both theories, of course, are dependent upon the concept of a knowable external reality which stands in opposition to a fictional world. However, for Stuart, scientific and social reality is in itself a form of fiction. Stuart's belief in the social construction of reality is therefore similar to that of sociologists such as Peter Berger and Thomas Luckmann.

> (Reality is) a kind of collective fiction, constructed and sustained by the processes of socialization, institutionalization, and everyday social interaction.. (which) are relatively permanent (although subject to historical change) and opaque, that is, accepted as 'the' reality... [22]

Stuart sees scientific theories, such as the Big Bang theory or the theory of relativity, as fictions which have been constructed within the limits of the consciousness of individual scientists and which can be discarded as human consciousness is extended.

> This planet from which we regard the universe is too limited in time and space for us to have any direct experience of the universal laws. The local measurements and observations have probably little relevance beyond the solar system. What goes on 'out there' is only limited in getting into the local news by our imaginative capabilities, or by what proportion of events are on this side of the barrier of unthinkability. (*TASS*, p.52)

The problem facing the writer then, given an awareness of the fictionality of the shared social reality of everyday life and of scientific models of reality, is how to write anything at all.

Doubts cast on the 'reality' of external reality caused Modernist writers such as Joyce, Proust, Woolf and Gide to substitute an inner world of subjectivity and imagination but, even in this subjective inner realm, external reality still had an important part to play. Richard Kearney in his critique of Joyce's *Ulysses*[23] argues that this work is an exploration of the limits of the creative imagination, and a final recognition of the illusion of the artistic aspiration for a creatio ex nihilo. The cul de sac in which Joyce places Stephen and Bloom at the end of their journey was meant to reflect, Kearney believes, the ultimate sterility of such a quest.

> The sheer encyclopaedic abstruseness of their dialogue or what Joyce referred to as the 'dry rocks of mathematical catechism' belies the dream of an exclusively aesthetic alliance. The auto-creative imagination proves to be sterile, devoid of all genuine creativity, all intimacy and life. [24]

The point being made is that the only valid form of imagination is one which incorporates temporal reality and in Molly's soliloquy temporal reality is revealed to be an integral part of the imagination, not a separate entity.

> In the final soliloquy, we may say that imagination which seeks to lead the mind beyond reality and memory which seeks to lead the mind back to reality become one and the same... Molly's mind moves in circles; it allows for no journey from one point to another... For once the two poles of the

journey – the subjective pole of the ordering imagination and the objective pole of disordering reality – are superimposed.[25]

Joyce therefore exposes the need for reality in the creation of fiction and also the fictionality of our conception of reality. Paul de Mann, in his essay on Nietzsche's *The Will to Power*, has shown that Nietzsche also found reality to be the most necessary of all fictions.

> … a fiction of our deepest need for a stable and permanent substratum, a context of constancy, regularity, and similarity, and of the entity which is identical with itself.[26]

In other words, the classical conception of reality has been created out of our will to survive. To affirm the objectivity of the real is to affirm that there can be unmediated knowledge of it and this, Nietzsche claims, is not the case. 'Because we have to be stable in our beliefs if we are to prosper, we have made the 'real' world a world not of change, but one of being.'[27] Therefore, by undermining any possibility of a solid standpoint from which the novel can be interrogated, Joyce created a crisis of identity for the writers who followed him.

One such writer was Samuel Beckett who, Kearney argues, saw the merging of imagination and reality as a victory of the former over the latter. The key to Beckett's preoccupation with an imaginative reality lies in his favourite quotation which is Democritus's 'Nothing is more real than nothing'.[28] In his essay on Proust, Beckett very clearly states that '… the only world that has reality and significance is the world of our own latent consciousness'.[29] Given this then, the only world the writer can know is the one that exists inside his own head, the otherness of reality being only a figment of imagination, and so Beckett sees the writer's attempt to write his way out of the labyrinth of self-representation as a doomed project.

> … there is nothing to express, nothing with which to express, nothing from which to express, no power to express, no desire to express, together with the obligation to express.[30]

This obligation drove Beckett to make a virtue out of necessity by writing about the impossibility of writing.

To be an artist is to fail, as no other dare fail, that failure is his world and

> to shrink from it desertion... I know that all that is required now... is to make of this submission, this admission, this fidelity to failure a new term of relation, and of the act which, unable to act, obliged to act, he makes, an expressive act, even if only of itself, of its impossibility, of its obligation.[31]

Because of this Beckett's novels question their own possibility and the characters are shown to be nothing more than inner voices so that by the conclusion to *The Unnamable* these voices become autonomous and ultimately assimilate narrator, author and the temporal world to themselves.

> Perhaps it is a dream, all a dream... I don't know, that's all words, never wake, all words, there's nothing else, you must go on, that's all I know... you must go on, perhaps it's done already perhaps they have said me already, perhaps they have carried me to the threshold of my story, before the door that opens on my story, that would surprise me, if it opens, never know, in the silence you don't know, you must go on, I can't go on, I'll go on.[32]

Trapped within this solipsistic world of the imagination the writer is condemned to write about himself alone.

As we have already seen, Stuart, like Beckett, believes that 'consciousness is at the foundation of things' (*TASS*, p.23), and that this can ultimately lead to solipsism since at times he is aware of 'being alone in the haunted room of my mind'. (*BLSH*, p.253) In contrast to Beckett though, he does not dwell on this but instead turns to the unexplored nature of that consciousness. 'Inner space (as Rilke called it), the area in which psychic events – thoughts, dreams, imaginings take place, remains dark and largely unexplored'. (*TASS*, p.13) Stuart therefore sees the task of the writer to be to undertake 'an all-obsessive and perilous inward journey' into this vast, unexplored area, the consciousness.

> ... fiction is now forced to do the one thing it can do supremely well, better than science and better than any of the other art forms: to delve deeper and deeper into the human system, and also to develop that outwardly.[33]

So rather than see consciousness as a prison-house Stuart envisages it as an unknown world, one whose workings hold the key to a new model of reality, so, while Beckett pictures the writer caught in a never-ending circle of self-generating fictions, Stuart's writer undertakes a pioneering role.

> ...the true purpose of fiction was the moving in on unoccupied areas by the imagination and their incorporation into small new aspects of reality. (*BLSH*, p.273)

Stuart's writing begins by clearing away the comfortable assumptions at the surface level of consciousness which accepts, unthinkingly, the consensus views of society.

> Jung found from a wide experience that most people live unconscious of their psyche, distracted and outward – turned and smoothly blended into a consortium of inertia. (*TASS*, p.18)

The narrative strategies Stuart uses to achieve this breakthrough involve both form and content. His later novels have a fractured form with frequent authorial interjections and chronological disruptions, all of which attempt to disorientate the reader. The unreliability of the narrator is often emphasised by the traumatised consciousness through which the action occurs. The narrative of *Memorial*, for example, takes the form of a self-reflective meditation by an almost forgotten novelist, to the ghost of a young girl with whom he had been romantically involved and who had been killed in a terrorist ambush.

> Yes, I'm back at the cottage and whatever there is to tell about the last day at the Laggan I'll insert into the report from here. What among the memories unshared with you from up there should be recorded? Perhaps that from your grave there's a view of the estuary. (*M*, p.255)

In *The High Consistory* the structure takes the form of the misplaced pages of various manuscripts and diaries which allegedly have been mixed randomly in an aeroplane crash. The narrative therefore jumps from first person narrator to a diary concerning Stuart's own life and back again.

> The record of a lifetime has been lightly shuffled by chance, as is the past, more thoroughly and repeatedly, by memory. In neither case can the imposition of a strict chronological design improve the general picture. (*THC*, p.7)

However, Stuart achieves his most disorientating effect in *A Hole in the Head* as the novelist-narrator struggles to come to terms with mental and political derangement. In the first part of the novel the narrator's actions and thoughts are depicted through a haze of insanity and drugs, all 'reality' being questioned by an inability to discriminate between fantasy and fact. 'What was dream-within-dream, what plain dream, what drug-induced hallucination, and what the reality at the heart of imagination?' (*AHH*, p.20)

Stuart magnifies the instability of the text by the disjointedness of the narrative structure with its shifting location and disruption of normal temporal pattern. The narrative switches from a clinic in Dublin to one in Paris; from Belbury to Haworth Rectory without any clear indication as to whether the character is fantasizing or not. All chronological order is undermined by the character's distrust of his memory and by merging past and present events.

> A blank had set in over my consciousness soon after leaving Le Bourget until about an hour ago. It is true this had happened before when I'd been dosing myself... Perhaps all would become clear and prove quite normal when the effect of drugs wore away, or when I took others. (*AHH*, p.11)

As the narrative drifts from the character's psychotic obsessions to a drug-induced hallucination or an attempt at realism the reader struggles to gain a firm foothold from which to make sense of the text, only to find a myriad of fictions. In this way Stuart draws the reader into the labyrinth of fictionality in which the writer dwells, creating a sense of frisson which ultimately casts a seed of doubt on the stability of the reader's own experience of reality. This doubt is magnified in *A Hole in the Head* when the main character flatly discounts the psychiatrist's distinction between interior and exterior reality, claiming instead that 'nothing of any moment could happen outside of my own imagination'. (*AHH*, p.34) Form and content therefore combine to undermine preconceived assumptions about the nature of reality and to open the reader's mind to other possibilities.

Stuart also compounds this strategy in his novels by breaking down the religious and moral attitudes of conventional society,

> ... who remake the untamed world into the image of the mediocrity in their hearts, diminishing the wild wonder to a mean morality! Incapable of true, self-forgetting passion, there's no compassion possible. (*THC*, p.77)

Textually this breakdown is achieved by reversing the sacred/profane opposition so that in *Memorial*, for instance, a car is given the status of a sacred object by its metamorphosis into a hearse. 'Better the mobile cell in which I'd prayed, speeded, sinned and suffered, being driven soberly in its latter years than desecrated by cigar-smoke and ribald laughter.' (*M*, p.144)

In a similar manner activities such as sex, gambling and violence are given all the dignity and sanctity of a religious ceremony.

> Here in the hotel restaurant all was hushed and dimmed, draped, shaded, and perfumed in preparation of body and imagination for the coming night when, all over Paris, in the sanctum of hotel and private rooms, attics, parked cars, the Bois, in any corner where it was possible, the miracle would be performed according to its various rites and accompanied with all kinds of private incantations. H whispered to Iseult a few words of an introductory canticle. (*BLSH*, p.172)

The inversion of the sacred and profane in Stuart's novels is not merely a matter of bestowing a religiosity on profanities, he also succeeds in casting a sexual and human glow over the sacred.

> Jesus had been waiting for hours, tempted to go and suddenly appear in her room; his wounds were still bleeding a little and she'd have gently let her tears fall once more on his sore and aching flesh. They didn't see each other again; she went on working in the night club. (*M*, p.182)

The result of this deconstructive device is two-fold, not only does it shock the reader out of a complacent reading of the text, it also opens up the mind to a new understanding of reality, one in which the consciousness of the artist strives to create '… a synthesis between a God-controlled cosmos and the mathematical molecular one'. (*TASS*, p.66)

In *The Abandoned Snail Shell* Stuart uses the metaphor of 'the seamless garment' (*TASS*, p.65) to capture his sense of an 'homogeneous overall molecular reality' (*TASS*, p.27) and it is this form of reality which is described by Stuart in *Black List, Section H* when he hints at an interconnection between an outer and an inner reality.

> Looking up at the night sky above the park and gazing into the black gaps in the pale shoal that ran across it, they glimpsed depths that weren't completely strange to me, and they were conscious of contemplating reflections of abysses in themselves. (*BLSH*, p.384)

This image of the night sky filled with stars is an ideal one to choose to reflect the network of correspondences which links objects of perception and the human consciousness. The stars as we know them, in their familiar groupings are often situated many thousands of light years apart, so that the relation between them, which we identify as somehow 'necessary' and self-evident, is in fact merely an accident of point of view. So the patterns which the human mind perceives in outer space can be said to be dependent of that mind, and a relationship across space established in an act of consciousness.

Stuart's model of reality as an intuition of an incorporeal web of correspondences is one that is evident in the work of French writers like Pierre Revardy.

> One no longer perceives a thing in isolation, but its relations with other things, and these relations between things, amongst themselves as well as with us, form the web, at once highly tenuous and solid, of an immense, profound and fragrant reality.[34]

Gerard de Nerval, too, envisaged such a network in terms of a magnetic field embracing the totality of the universe.

> All things live, all things act, all things correspond; the magnetic rays which emanate from me or others travel without hindrance across the infinite chain of created things; the world is embraced by a transparent network.[35]

By removing the distinctions normally made between the religious and the profane; the sensual and the pious; fact and fantasy; and objectivity and subjectivity, Stuart is able to establish links and extract connections, thereby providing a textual manifestation of the principal of interconnectedness which marks this model of reality. For Stuart though, the 'network of correspondences' in which 'outspread phenomena and infolded images... all belonged together' (*TASS*, p.65), moves far beyond the confines of the text, providing the writer with a means of escape from solipsism. The premise that all reality is linked by such an invisible intertwined thread, just as the 'bunches of grapes ripening with others on the common vine stock' (*TASS*, p.36) leads inevitably to the perception of a correspondence between that network and the mind of the one who perceives it. This is the ultimate fusion dreamed of earlier by the

Romantics who felt that 'the system of Nature is at the same time the system of our mind'. [36]

More recently, social anthropologists, drawing on concepts derived from psychology and linguistics, have arrived at a view of the mental processes of so-called primitive peoples which would tend to substantiate such a thesis. Claude Levi-Strauss describes the process of 'bricolage' through which the primitive mind makes sense of its surroundings. The process is one of making sense of the teeming impressions from the natural world by identifying them as sets, and forming these into mythical systems. The world picture elaborated by the primitive mind is therefore envisioned as a metaphorical jigsaw puzzle whose pieces are provided by the minutiae of perceptual experience the interlocking shapes of which are fashioned by acts of imaginative interpretation.

> The savage mind deepens its knowledge with the help of 'images mundi'. It builds mental structures which facilitate understanding of the world in as much as they resemble it. In this sense – thought can be described as analogical thought.[37]

This would also tend to substantiate Stuart's contention that the writer's task involves an 'inward journey' since it follows that the writer who desires to make discoveries about reality need only look inside himself, as it is all there, analogically speaking, within himself. To dig into the depths of one's self is an enterprise just as ambitious as exploring the cosmos, and it leads to the same results, intuitive insights of the reciprocal patterning of the microcosm and macrocosm of mind and universe.

The way in which this insight is achieved is perhaps better understood if we consider Kilton Stewart's account of the Negrito people in *Pygmies and Dream Giants*, in which he describes the intuitive approach of the primitive to the problems of physical life.

> … before the Negritos embark on an excursion to collect honey, the shaman falls into a trance and speaks to the group in a song, part of which consists of the bee explaining how he was able to cure the shaman's wounds with his honey. In this way the healing properties of honey are fixed in the collective memory. [38]

It is possible to speculate that the idea of honey having curative power could have come to the shaman by way of an intuited analogy. Sensory memories of the pleasant sweetness of honey on the tongue (possibly heightened by negative associations of the painful stinging of which bees are also capable) could have activated an association of honey with soothing and therefore healing properties. This is essentially an irrational analogy since it leaps from a taste sensation on the tongue to a tactile sensation on the wounded skin, but the soothing nature of both sensations provides a connection, and in this way it can be argued, analogistics have helped the primitive to make an important discovery about the material world. While there is scientific evidence to show that honey does have antibacterial properties, the primitive is prepared to put his trust in intuitions which are never confirmed by scientific testings. Instead, such intuitions are taken as facts simply because they enter consciousness under circumstances of psychological effervescence and the highly charged climate in which such a discovery is made seems to act as a sufficient guarantee of its validity. Stuart too, highlights the role the energised consciousness plays in his model of reality. 'Reality is nothing if not our most intense imaginative concepts of it'. (*BLSH*, p.255)

Reality for Stuart, by this stage, involves a state of perfect osmosis between thinking and its object; between the mind and the world. A state similar to that of which Rilke (whose work Stuart meticulously transcribed in his war-time diaries[39]) was dreaming when he spoke of *Weltinnenraum*, 'world-inner-space'; the undifferentiated oneness of outer and inner being.

> Through all beings stretches the one space:
> World-inner-space. The birds silently fly
> right through us. O, I who wish to grow,
> I look outside, and the tree grows inside me.[40]

Just as Rilke's poem articulates a poetic moment in which the relation of mind to perceived reality has become so intense that subject and object enact a union, so Stuart perceives reality as 'a quantum leap of consciousness' in which 'the separate threads of spirit and matter, outspread phenomena and infolded images' are interwoven to form a 'seamless garment.' (*TASS*, p.11) In the end, Stuart's reality does not lie in the phenomenal world, or in an intuition which transcends the phenomenal world, but in a mode of consciousness which unites the two.

The emphasis is therefore not on 'the seen' but in 'the seeing', a premise also succinctly captured by Octavio Paz.

> The unreality of the seen,
> Makes real the seeing. [41]

Because an integral element of this form of seeing is the creative charge present in an imaginative consciousness, Stuart is able to state with all confidence '... that the creative artist... is the best suited to examine and comment on the sketches of reality that are exhibited'. (*TASS*, p.64) Stuart's reality is therefore identified with the creative imagination to such an extent that it is impossible to disentangle one from the other and any attempt to define the former must, by necessity, examine the latter.

2

Images of Imagination

During an address to the International Writers Conference held in Dublin in 1988, Francis Stuart claimed that 'all great literature is stained with the writer's blood'. This was not some melodramatic assertion on his part about the difficulties of artistic creativity but a deeply-held conviction based on his perception of reality as a network of correspondences which is only recognised by 'an intensely activated consciousness'. (*TASS*, p.70) Given that the writer's mind is constantly being stretched by the imagination it follows that the struggle to write creates the ideal circumstances for such an experience. Further, since he also states that '...the consciousness in which reality is being effectively sought is one in which pain, self-denial and love are involved' (*TASS*, p.68), it is clear that Stuart believes that suffering plays an important role in the creative process.

The link between suffering and the creative imagination has a long history. In *Theogony*,[1] for instance, Hesiod tells how Prometheus stole fire from the gods and bestowed it upon man. As the name suggests, *Prometheus* meaning foresight, the gift of stolen fire or imagination enabled humanity to anticipate the future and project a horizon of possibilities. But by giving mortals the ability to invent imaginary worlds through the various arts, the natural order was disrupted and the gods were so angered they ordered that Prometheus be chained to a rock for eternity and an eagle sent to repeatedly devour his liver. Through this myth of the origins of imagination we can clearly see its ambivalent nature, for while it empowers man to imitate the gods, it does so by an act of rebellion which disrupts the pre-established harmony of nature. In his exploration of the Prometheus myth in *Thieves of Fire*[2] Denis Donoghue acknowledges the underlying tragic nature of the creative imagination.

> Above all Prometheus made possible the imaginative enhancement of experience... No wonder the gift also gave men a sense of the endlessness of possibility arising from the endlessness of knowledge and desire. The power of (imagination) helped men to maintain a relation between themselves and nature, but it did not bring peace between men and gods... The imagination has always been a contentious power... the divine power in men, falsely acquired.[3]

As well as Prometheus, other heroes of Greek mythology are punished by gods angry at the way in which the imagination emulates the divine. Orpheus is dismembered by frenzied Maenads for daring to reconcile man and nature by composing a quasi-divine harmony,[4] while Dedalus, who sculpts figures from rock and gives them the power of speech, is banished into exile.[5] Greek ontology therefore bestows on the imagination the dual attributes of vision and suffering but these myths are not the only source of Stuart's concept of the suffering of the imaginative artist. Christian theology adds a further dimension since he envisages the artist's suffering, not as a punishment but as an enriching experience.

> The two greatest gifts of man are his capacity for love and his religious sense. And these are the sole cause of all deep suffering. It is true that they are also the means by which we come to experience the highest ecstasy that brightens the dark earth. (*TAOP*, p.29)

Throughout his work Stuart's perception of artistic suffering is heavily influenced by his obsessive interest in the mystical experience at that time.

> Show me the being who has suffered most, and I would feel more humble before him or her than in the presence of the greatest geniuses that the

world recognized. I would know beyond doubt that he had gone further towards finding the eternal truth than anyone else, whether as an artist, a lover, a saint… He would be bound to have at least some qualities of these three types, because his being would be developed to the greatest fullness of experience… For me this is the touchstone of great art. (*TAOP*, p.72)

His fascination with the writings of the mystics is evident from repeated references to them throughout his work and in *Black List, Section H* he attempts to rationalise their hold on him.

… he was absorbed by states of mind that appealed to him first because they ran counter to the familiar ones. He began to put his whole heart into trying to share this kind of consciousness, quite strange, in which intense emotion was joined to a daring imagination that seemed natural to him, though it was rare in contemporary literature. (*BLSH*, p.131)

The Angel of Pity provides a useful illustration of the way in which Stuart superimposes the ideals of the solitary, self-denying life of the mystics onto the creative artist.

All great art… springs from minds that have been solitary ones, intensely conscious of their own isolation, experiencing heaven and hell. From the depths of their own often lacerated minds they produce their masterpieces. (*TAOP*, p.43)

Again writing in *Hibernia* in 1975, Stuart paints a portrait of Patrick Kavanagh as the suffering visionary who was '… the first of our writers for a very long time who was the natural enemy of all literary establishments, which, of course, neither Joyce or Yeats had been'.[6] It was, Stuart argues, Kavanagh's isolation and the public ignominy, poverty, illness and rejection which he experienced in the course of his career which enabled him to attain 'earthy and visionary insights'. The nature of these insights is not discussed in relation to Kavanagh but in *The Angel of Pity* the insight which the narrator receives after he has witnessed the brutal rape and death of the heroine is one of compassion and shared humanity.

It is only through a certain solitariness that man can ever come into contact with his fellow man… He must be able to stretch his hand out from his own lonely self towards this other lonely and pitiful being. He must, for a moment anyhow, be able to see them both as two solitary and very vulnerable creatures hastening towards a common destiny which neither can contemplate without a tinge of fear. (*TAOP*, p.37)

The image of the artist as visionary has a long tradition stretching back to the realms of myth and legend but, in the Western world, it reached its pinnacle with German idealism and Romanticism, both of which were greatly influenced by the aesthetic theory of Immanuel Kant. In contrast to his predecessors who saw the imagination as a mimetic mechanism, Kant affirmed its creative powers. The imagination therefore ceased to be merely a mirroring device capable of reproducing some given reality and instead was seen to be a productive device deemed capable of inventing a world out of its human resources. For Kant, the imagination was the precondition of all knowledge since nothing could be known about the world unless it was first performed and transformed by the synthetic power of imagination (*Einbildungskraft*).[7] This radical revision of the status of imagination is intimately related to Kant's overall philosophy of being. According to the tradition of classical and medieval philosophy, to know reality was to rationally judge that the human understanding was in conformity with external reality. Kant's 'Copernican revolution' was to place human consciousness at the centre of the universe and to show that knowledge of the 'objective' world consisted of an imaginative synthesis of sensible intuition (of temporal and spatial objects) and of intellect (or an abiding transcendental ego).[8]

> The affinity of appearances and with it their association, and through this, in turn, their reproduction according to laws, and so experience itself, should only be possible by this transcendental function of imagination… For without this transcendental function no concepts of objects would themselves make up a unitary experience.[9]

However, it is Kant's theory of the sublime which has most relevance for Stuart's philosophy since Kant asserts that the experience of the sublime emanates from the imagination's confrontation with its own limits.

> The feeling of the sublime may appear in point of form to contravene – the ends of our power of judgement, to be ill-adapted to our faculty of presentation, and to be, as it were, an outrage on imagination.[10]

Since the sublime surpasses not only the concepts of understanding but the images of the imagination itself, the pleasure the imagination takes is one of challenge, defiance, risk, excess and shock.[11] In experiencing the sublime, the imagination is expanded to new heights and depths and ventures into dark, unchartered territory.

> We are in awe precisely of the human power to frame ideas which cannot be intuited. Imaginatively we stretch out towards what imagination cannot apprehend. We realize that there is more in what we see than meets or can ever meet even the inner eye.[12]

As we have already seen, Stuart also envisages reality as a confrontation between the phenomenal world and a human consciousness which has been expanded 'by certain intense experiences, particularly of pain' (*TASS*, p.11), and it is this process of expanding the consciousness beyond the limits of the imagination which also lies at the heart of his concept of artistic creativity.

> As in nature, it is the addition of the last few degrees in the expansion of the already almost fully stretched consciousness, that makes it possible to pass a hitherto uncrossable threshold, to think the unthinkable. And this influx of even a few waves of energy to the full-tide of a consciousness can enable... the artist to hit on the unlikely association that furthers the theme. (*TASS*, p.67)

While the belief that creativity stems from an extended consciousness links Stuart with Romantic idealism, the contention that this expansion of the consciousness should occur through the experience of extremes of inner or mental suffering draws on yet another well-established stereotype, that of the artist as madman.

This image of the artist as the demented, possessed soul, unable to distinguish between fantasy and the real inevitably leads us back to Plato, who in the *Ion*, issues his famous polemic against the poet.

> For all good poets... compose their beautiful poems not by art, but because they are inspired and possessed... so the lyric poets are not in their right mind when they are composing their beautiful strains.[13]

Aristotle, too, believed that 'all extraordinary men distinguished in poetry and the arts are evidently melancholic'[14] and indeed it has been recognised that melancholia has been linked to creativity right through to the present day. In the seventeenth century Robert Burton, in *The Anatomy of Melancholy*, described how the sufferer, in the depths of depression would experience '… a most intolerable pain and grief of the heart: to their thinking they are already damned, they suffer the pains of Hell',[15] but at the same time, they would have moments of revelation when 'these vapours move the phantasy to tell strange things of Heaven and Hell'[16] or when the imagination becomes so strong or so confused that it merges with 'reality'.

> (Melancholy) so most specially it rageth in melancholy persons, in keeping the species of objects so long, mistaking amplifying them by continual and strong meditation, at length produceth in some parties real effects.[17]

Dürer's image of the melancholic artist, self-absorbed, distracted, isolated from society, veering from black depression to visionary insight, lost in a world where imagination and reality merge, has found a modern counterpart in the tendency of writers to display neurotic, psychotic or addictive tendencies.

For Stuart the difference between the psychotic and the writer is merely one of degree, since both inhabit a world of fantasy. The similarity in the psychological activity of the artist and that of the psychotic is also noted by Professor Ivor Browne in his article 'The madness of genius'.

> The truly creative writer has to opt out of normality, leave the 'nine-to-five logical brain', to go down into the creative source… When an artist is working in this way he appears to be using the intuitive dimension of the mind, a mode of consciousness akin to dreaming: what has, perhaps over-simplistically, been referred to as right-sided brain activity… This is also the mode of consciousness used by those we term psychotic, those the world calls mad. They, too, predominantly use this dream-like fantasy side of the brain because of a variety of factors, even genetic.[18]

It is this alternative mode of consciousness, in which the imagination is the driving force, which Stuart explores in *A Hole in the Head*. In this novel the first person narrator, Barnaby Shane, is a writer recovering from a head injury caused by a suicide attempt. Through this character the reader is given an insight into a psyche incapable of discriminating between fantasy and fact, and also into the way in which the imagination, once let loose, can become obsessive. During the course of the novel Shane has a relationship with his muse, Emily Brontë, who warns that creative energy can easily degenerate into hysteria.

> 'There's always just one more of anything that we're obsessed and exhausted by.' She too knew on a deeper level of reality than my poor fancies, that the imagination, once aroused to this intensity wanted to roam further and further. (*AHH*, p.91)

Since the creative writer is driven by his imaginative psyche to produce an endless stream of fictions in much the same way as the psychotic creates his world of delusions, both exhibit an obsessional personality whose consciousness is constantly working at an imaginative level, a characteristic which Professor Browne also recognises.

> I have never met an artist who did not work hard. The greater the artist, the more powerful seems to be the drive to work. The true artist is obsessively creative, even when not working, when not producing anything... At a deeper level his mind is working all the time, even when not writing, draining his energy...[19]

The creative process driven by an obsessive desire to create fiction would seem to put the writer in danger of drifting into a state of psychosis but Stuart claims that it is precisely this nature which is necessary for the creative writer. Dismissing as he does the convention of 'medium-mix-fiction' precisely because it lacks all 'passion and obsession' he asserts that the writer needs 'an imaginative, not to say unbalanced temperament': 'A fiction writer with guilt and obsession of his own knows more about secret and shameful passions than the more sober research worker in the literary field'. (*AHH*, p.150)

Despite recognising that the dividing line between aesthetic and pathological fictions is a thin one Stuart argues that it is the fragile division between the two which helps the writer to retain his sanity. 'Imaginative people can resolve inner tensions that keep less gifted ones behind asylum walls'. (*AHH*, p.185) The suggestion in the novel is that unless the imaginative psyche can utilise its energy force by producing fiction it will express itself in mental derangement or even violence: 'A flood of energy with nowhere to go except into fighting or clowning, apart from an occasional one of you who tries his hand at fiction…'. (*AHH*, p.185)

The struggle to create aesthetic form out of the formlessness of the endless possibilities of fiction has paradoxically the effect of relieving the inner tension and, according to Professor Browne, this pathological resolution stems from the way in which the artist makes use of the experience of suffering.

> … the artist will use whatever material and life experience most claim his attention, that upon which he is most forced to focus. It is generally suffering which most acutely claims our attention and focuses our being, more than comfort, joy or even passion.[20]

Browne, like Stuart, also believes that writing should emanate from the writer's own experience.

> Writers… are not autobiographical as such, yet the raw material of their work comes from their own experience, or something that fascinates them so much that they fantasize it as their own experience.[21]

Seen in this light the creative process becomes a form of painful self-analysis in which the writer works through experiences which have been inhibited or repressed by the psyche as being too painful or traumatic to be resolved at the time.

> It seems to me that unresolved situations of this kind are the creative artist's meat. The artist dramatizes them, painfully experiences them and works them through… They are literally living out and experiencing for the first time the shut-off pain and suffering of many years before, albeit in fictional or dramatic forms. In this way resolution, for whatever reason, by the artist is a move towards health, not madness, even if the artist appears to be quite mad at times.[22]

This homeopathic process is also present in Stuart's metaphor for the imagination, the 'hole in the head' of the novel's title. Like the legend it refers to, of the native American Hopi people who perforated the skulls of young children to allow good and evil spirits to enter and escape, the imagination expands the consciousness with endless imaginings but also provides an escape valve by externalising the inner turmoil by shaping these fantasies into the ordered limits of the novel.

Stuart's biographer, Geoffrey Elborn, and critics such as Jerry Natterstad[23] would agree that his work conforms to the pattern of self-analysis described by Professor Browne since both believe that the pattern of his novels stem from unresolved issues surrounding his father's death, particularly the lack of information he had concerning this.

> His father was for him, a hero that justified and validated the notion of the 'outsider', reinforcing some ideas he only half understood about himself and society, which he considered responsible for his misery. Henry had somehow died in disgrace, but his son would both consciously and subconsciously try to atone for the ignominy thrust on his father by an apparently uncaring family.[24]

Stuart himself also recognises that such a traumatic experience was bound to have had an effect on his psychological make-up.

> It's true that during my childhood I didn't know the facts, but I did sense an evasion of the subject of my father, which in my own rather primitive way made me all the more conscious of him and later made me very anxious to learn about him. Evidently he was looked upon as something rather shameful in the family. Well, this has certainly influenced me.[25]

It is tempting therefore to make a crude psychoanalytical interpretation of Stuart's work and to suggest, as Natterstad does, that 'Stuart's art and life reflect a largely unconscious living out of the image or myth of his father'.[26] It is true that his father's life followed the pattern repeated throughout Stuart's work of security, isolation and then ignominy. Henry had left the security of a middle-class life in County Antrim in his early twenties to go to Australia, and while there, isolated from his homeland and his family, he died in a manner which caused his family to shroud the event in secrecy. Writing to Jerry Natterstad Stuart explained that 'the circumstances of his (Henry's) end were never mentioned to me as a child or youth', but that, as far as he understood, 'he suffered from prolonged and excessive drinking and possibly killed himself'.[27] Geoffrey Elborn's research, some twenty years later, turned up more facts about the death, and in his biography he asserts that Stuart's father suffered from an extreme persecution mania, and following several suicide attempts, finally succeeded in hanging himself with a rope made from a bed sheet.[28] The silence which surrounded the death allowed Stuart to fill the gaps in his knowledge with an imaginative portrayal of his father as an outcast, suffering the rejection and scorn of society, and to seek, through his writings, to project some meaning into his obscure and ignominious death.

As if to atone for the equivocal nature of his father's death, Stuart's early novels contain a recurring pattern in which the protagonist is led from a life of security to one of vulnerability and, from this point, he passes through isolation to a metaphorical crucifixion – a painful, humiliating experience which ultimately leads to the brink of illumination. The female character in *Glory* (1933) is typical of this since she goes through the whole process of isolation, rejection and insight and, at the height of her rejection by society, is told '… You have had the world shocked at you and jeer at you and be afraid of you, and you've learnt not to care… You've learnt to be an outcast'. (*G*, p.192) Later, in *Black List, Section H*, Stuart again gives significance to his father's experience by elevating the role of the outcast and aligning it to that of the writer: 'Dishonour is what becomes a poet, not titles or acclaim… A poet must be a countercurrent to the flow around him'. (*BLSH*, p.17) Stuart's conviction that the outcast's experience can be the source of creative insights again endows it with purpose: '… only to those who had passed through the depths of the night and come back again would the words be given'. (*TPOC*, p.231)

It is therefore possible to see that Stuart does appear to be acting out Professor Browne's theory in that he seems in his work to be attempting to achieve, through the workings of his imagination, a resolution of the subconscious anguish created by his father's mysterious death. However, while this may be partly true, it is certainly not the full story. For Stuart, the imagination is not merely a silent instrument capable of uncovering the writer's subconscious obsessions; instead he envisages a dialectical relationship between the imagination and the experiences of the writer.

> … the intensely activated consciousness of the artist is not only formed by the stuff of consciousness, but in turn reacts on it as molecules and their attendant particles react on each other, apparently jumping from one orbit to another and so on. (*TASS*, p.68)

For example, in *Memorial*, he suggests that Kafka, by writing about disease in *Der Prozess*, 'called down on himself the tuberculosis that killed him, while Mahler, by writing *Kindertotenlieder*, caused the death of his own child'. (*M*, p.159) This strange phenomenon is one which Jung attempted to explain in his work *Psychology and Literature*.

> Whenever the creative force predominates, human life is ruled and moulded by the unconscious as against the active will, and the conscious ego is swept along on a subterranean current, being nothing more than a helpless observer of events. The work in process becomes the poet's fate and determines his psychic development. It is not Goethe who creates *Faust*, but *Faust* which creates Goethe.[29]

This cause-and-effect movement between art and life is evident in Stuart's view that the creative process is not an abstract, intellectual pursuit, but one which involves the writer's whole being, preventing him from separating his art from his life.

> … for me no book, even the Gospels, even the greatest imaginative works of literature, wonderful and comforting as they've been to me, have been as important as experience and action. I'm not the sort of writer who could ever live a life of study or of intellectual pursuits. Far from it. And therefore, for good or bad, the best of my books have certainly come from experience and not from meditating on the Gospels or on any such works.[30]

While his novels have undoubtedly been influenced by his own experiences, so too have his experiences been shaped by his imagination, for whether consciously or unconsciously, Stuart found himself living through experiences that were present in embryo in his early work.

> I was inventing a great deal in my early novels. I had this very vague vision of events which might have a profound effect on the individual who went through them. But of course I had experienced very little actually, and led a comparatively sheltered life, except for the rather short period in the Civil War and my imprisonment after it. Therefore, to actually experience what I had envisaged was most valuable for the sort of writer I am.[31]

The progress which forms the basis of Stuart's early novels, from security to isolation and social rejection, is one which, either consciously or unconsciously, Stuart found himself experiencing. His decision in January 1940 to leave the relative security of life with his wife Iseult and his two children at Laragh Castle and accept the offer to lecture at Berlin University can certainly be seen as a pivotal point in his career. In *Black List, Section H* Stuart recalls the factors which were involved in this decision and undoubtedly financial considerations played a large part, as did the increasing difficulties within his marriage: 'What it would be like it wasn't clear to him, but anything was better than living in this state of constant nervous abrasion that he and Iseult inflicted on each other'. (*BLSH*, p.296)

However, Stuart's supposition that 'loneliness and pain'[32] provide an important stimulus for the imaginative writer, along with his obsessive interest in the experience of the outcast, must also have influenced his decision to lecture in war-time Berlin. Certainly he was well aware that his action would arouse hostility and place him in the position of social pariah, thereby granting him first-hand experience of that role which had for so long fascinated him.

> In agreeing, H was turning from the busy street to slink with thieves and petty criminals down dim alleys, leaving the lawful company to which he'd belonged to become in its eyes, a traitor. (*BLSH*, p.311)

By making the decision to go to Germany, Stuart was at last able to live up to the declaration he had made in *Things to Live For* some years earlier.

> I will remain with those on the coastline, on the frontiers. With the gamblers, wanderers, fighters, geniuses, martyrs and mystics. With the champions of wild loves and lost causes, the storm-troopers of life. With all who live dangerously, though not necessarily spectacularly, on the knife edge between triumph and defeat. (*TTLF*, p.137)

And, as if to ensure his complete rejection, he agreed in 1942 to broadcast to Ireland from Germany and once again Stuart retrospectively recognises that the main underlying reason for this decision was his need, as a writer, to experience life 'through the pure eye of the losers'.[33]

> ... somehow I felt the necessity to broadcast. I could never be a writer in the bosom of society... I had the opportunity of doing something that would cut me off from all the *bien pensants* in society. I did not regret it. I don't stand over what I did but I did not regret the consequences, though they were painful. Without them I could not have become the writer I am now.[34]

Stuart's ostracism was complete. He had achieved the role of outcast and, as he himself recognised, he was 'the kind of malefactor whose rejection was seldom rescinded because the crime was not merely against an individual but that society as a whole'. (*BLSH*, p.311) It was not until the end of the war that Stuart felt the full repercussions of this decision. In the autumn of 1944, with the Russians advancing from the east and Berlin under constant air attack, Stuart and Gertrud Meissner joined the stream of refugees leaving the city. During this time he diligently recorded their progress in a set of closely written notebooks which are now in the Francis Stuart Collection in the University of Ulster at Coleraine. These diaries record the hunger, discomfort and despair which the couple experienced during their flight which took them to Lake Constance, which formed the border with Switzerland. On 3 May 1945 they were still in Dornbirn, having been prevented from crossing into Switzerland, when French troops took the town. In his diary Stuart records not only the hunger and anxiety, but also an indication that his belief in the revelatory nature of suffering had been substantiated.

> What a month of horror April was! From Easter to the end: sleeplessness, three weeks without undressing, without a bed, cold and hungry. Cold, as the night in Lindau and others. Continual hunger. Sometimes our ration was five slices of bread and butter per day and seldom much more. The questioning, the anxiety of being taken – once being searched. And yet in spite of all that – what a month of miraculous revelations never to be forgotten.[35]

The notebooks, as well as being chronicles of the desolate conditions of the refugees particularly relating to the provisions of food or lack of them, also record the inner quest of the writer. Copious passages from the Gospels and the Roman missal are copied out as are numerous quotations from Rilke: the writing itself changes becoming smaller and tightly packed on the pages so that a great sense of intensity fills the pages along with those moments of inner peace.

> LINDAU 9.4.45. Yesterday the vision of death. The terror of coming to the point, but then a faint, faint glimmer of peace. This reached with S. [Stuart's pet-name for Gertrud at this time was Schumpel.] That final (or almost final) giving up of the Eigene Wille...

> What days of hunger and over-shadowing threat! What nights of hell and
> what inner beatitude![36]

Even in these conditions Stuart's concern is still with his writing and he
continually notes his resolution to write a novel which would reflect their
experiences.

> ... all suffering in its simplicity, in its primitiveness. Death by bombs...
> And hunger... The humiliation of the outcast, the thing of having literally
> nowhere to lay one's head... All this must be in the ground work so that
> the book has a new taste, a new slant.[37]

Stuart was at last experiencing the extremes of consciousness which he
believed were the source of creativity but before he could write out of these
experiences yet further degradation was to occur. On the morning of 21
November 1945, Stuart wrote in his diary 'Destiny leads us to more and
more life in strange unknown ways'.[38] Later that afternoon he was arrested
by the French occupation forces, interrogated, and subsequently detained
in Bregenz Oberstadt prison, near Dornbirn, until May 1964 when he and
Gertrude were moved to Freiburg in the French occupied zone of
Germany. In her published memoirs of this period Gertrud Meissner, or
Madeleine Stuart as she was later to become, gives her account of the
conditions in Bregenz.

> Life was specially bad in those chaotic times after the war. Once in prison
> you could rot there till doomsday, there were no lawyers, no friends,
> nobody to help you from the outside. Food was the worst we ever tasted –
> we got boils all over our bodies, lice and fleas had a bumper time.[39]

When Stuart was interviewed by Anthony Cronin in 1979 about his
experience in the prison he too remembered the hunger and the skin
diseases but the main thrust of his memory concerns his writing.

> ... in chaotic conditions... far too crowded, you know. I was with all these
> people, as well as having all sorts of nasty skin diseases. You know, you were
> starting. I thought I had reached the lowest ebb. And what struck me was
> as a writer I shall never get a book published. I would write one, you know,
> I had begun to understand certain things. But I thought, who's going to
> publish? I'm here in a cell of traitors...[40]

Stuart was probably right to worry about the effect his imprisonment might have on the reception of his work because, although it is impossible to measure the intricacies of public opinion, the negative perception of this period of his life was to remain with him throughout his life. While the rejection tended to be of a private nature, publishers refusing to take a book or readers refusing to buy them, Stuart certainly felt that he was being shunned. In a letter to the *Irish Times* he stated that he was

> ... well used to being on blacklists, public and private, such as, at various times, those of certain English publishers and literary agents, the British occupied zone of Germany (for a time after the last war), the Writers Union of East Germany, the Irish Censorship Board and the directorate of the Abbey Theatre.[41]

It would appear then that a complex intermeshing of influences led to the fulfilment of Stuart's desire for alienation and while his father's obscure death undoubtedly played a part, as did his interest in the mystical nature of suffering, there was also a strong motivating factor in the conviction formulated during his detention in the Curragh that 'literature was only to be experienced by those who dared to pluck it from the tree of life'. (*BLSH*, p.105) Like the writers to which he felt drawn Stuart was at some level driven to seek out 'certain extremes of isolation and exposure'.[42]

> Was there no contemporary writer of the kind of Baudelaire, Poe, Keats, Melville, Emily Brontë, Dostoevsky, Proust or Kafka... who because of alcoholism, sexual excess, tuberculosis, venereal disease, rejected love, condemnation, and banishment... had been driven beyond the place where the old assumptions are still acceptable? (*BLSH*, p.232)

What Stuart was really seeking then was not merely that form of self-exile endured by his fellow countrymen, Joyce and Beckett, but complete public degradation, so the imprisonment itself was unlikely to achieve complete isolation or condemnation since, as he discovered during his internment in the Civil War, imprisonment tends to create a common bond between inmates: '... what they shared were instincts and, perhaps, an outlook too subterranean to discuss except at rare moments'. (*BLSH*, p.73)

What made Stuart's ostracism so complete was the fact that it was self-sought, which served, he felt, to increase his isolation as it removed from him the protective mantle of the innocent victim.

> The message that reached his conscience from his deepest nature, suggested
> that he had to experience, in his own probably small degree, some of what
> they suffered, and on one level, even more, because he could not claim
> their innocence… thus ensuring that his condemnation would not, unlike
> theirs, arouse any sympathy. (*BLSH*, p.207)

There is yet again in this desire for self-sought mortification an illustration
of the continuing influence on Stuart of the writings of the mystics for
whom such practices were virtues in themselves.

The Judeo-Christian theory of penology from which this view derives
and which endows incarceration with the benefits of spiritual regeneration
and increased creativity has also entered the folklore of literary criticism. It
has been argued that Oscar Wilde and Jean Genet 'needed' prison in order
to write[43] and Joseph Skvorecky, in his work on the writer and human
rights, has even noted a tendency among Western writers to envy the
imprisoned writer.

> Sometimes one hears Western writers expressing envy for the writers who
> have come out of the cold or even for those who still pine away in the cold
> for they – say the Western writers – have a ready-made dramatic subject
> matter… Life in the cold certainly contributed greatly to the making of a
> Dostoevsky, a Solzhenitsyn, a Kundera, a Malparte, or a Günter Grass.[44]

So imprisonment was of importance to Stuart, not because it provided him
with subject matter, but because it gave him direct access to the kind of
experiences which he felt were necessary for him to gain the kind of
insights he was seeking.

As Ioan Davies found in his interesting study of prison writing, the
experience of being in prison forces the individual to confront the
dichotomy between the stereotype imposed on him by society and his own
self-image.

> The philosophy of the prison is a philosophy that contemplates at once
> finitude and infinity, it is a philosophy of the carnal and the spiritual, of
> the violence of space, of the subterranean and the galactic, of the self and
> of the many. Above all it is a debate between the imposition of human
> controls and man's involvement in making those controls.[45]

Isolated from a society which classifies him as criminal or deviant, the prisoner enters a culture of story-telling, a feature which Václav Havel noted about his own experiences in Czech prisons.

> Almost every prisoner had a life story that was unique and moving. As I listened to these different accounts, I suddenly found myself… simply in the world of literature.[46]

By telling a monologic, boasting story of surface achievements the prisoner attempts to re-establish a degree of control over his situation by reinstating a self-conception and social identity which mirrors his own desired image of himself. The limitations of this kind of project is well illustrated by Dostoevsky in *Notes from the Underground*, in which the character of the underground man attempts, through his storytelling, to show the world just how significant he is, an attempt which is doomed to failure: 'Not only couldn't I make myself malevolent, I couldn't make myself anything: neither good nor bad, neither a scoundrel nor an honest man, neither hero nor an insect'.[47]

The failure is due, for the most part, to the conflict which arises between the self-conscious discourse and the self-image of the prisoner for even if he tells one set of stories to others in order to be seen as a hero, to his inner self he conducts a different dialogue, one which sees himself in the act of storytelling, an image which necessarily exposes an inherent falseness and hollowness. In *Black List, Section H* the character of H encounters this distinction between external and internal dialogues.

> 'It's only when I'm with you,' H told him, 'that I'm not aware of guilty secrets that I'd better keep to myself. What most people here respect… I either despise, or if at first I do seem to share some of their beliefs, like about poetry or the Republican cause in the civil war, it soon turns out that it's for quite different reasons and that we're even further apart than had we disagreed from the start. (*BLSH*, p.10)

Prison therefore, forces the character to choose between acting out the role of criminal assigned to him by society or to rethink the whole process of imposition of a label on himself and attempt to be the author of his own story, a task which can only be achieved through a dialogue between inner and outer selves.

It is this struggle to distinguish between what is authentic and what is inauthentic which becomes the catalyst for artistic creativity for it is a struggle, as Bakhtin argues, which contains within it a sideward glance at the self.

> ... a vicious circle of self-consciousness with a sideward glance. The loophole creates a special type of fictive ultimate world about oneself with an undisclosed tone to it, obtrusively peering into the other's eyes and demanding from the other a sincere refutation.[48]

When he had finished writing *Black List, Section H* Stuart himself realised that such self-reflective writing was open to misinterpretation by its readers and suspected that he would have to 'expose it, and myself to their cold and probably hostile eyes...',[49] a suspicion which proved correct when the London publishers, McGibbon & Kee, returned the manuscript with a dismissive report.

> There's a flavour that isn't entirely convincing nor even very pleasant. The self-stated literary ideals and excerpts cut little ice and are... embarrassing... Have we here in H the description of the kind of mind that makes for the cold, sometimes sentimental-romantic fascist mentality?[50]

Since the attempt to elicit an authentic story of the self from the multiplicity of stories available from external and internal sources not only involves the writer in a high degree of self-awareness but also an awareness of the critical reaction of others, it inevitably throws the consciousness of the writer into a state of turbulence. This, combined with the impossibility of reaching an essentialist account of the self, leads to a state of total despondency which Stuart believes is essential for creativity.

> The darkest times were in the prison I've mentioned... In a cell meant for one or at most two, we were ten and twelve and we were starving. I remembered that I'd been a writer, but I felt I was no longer a writer, that I would never again be a writer. It was a despairing experience, but looking back, I see that the kind of writer I am probably had to reach that complete giving up of his vocation.[51]

The movement from despair to enlightenment is a common feature in accounts of the workings of the creative consciousness. French mathematician Henri Poincare, for example, notes such a phenomenon in his work on mathematical creation.

> ... sudden inspirations never happen except after some days of voluntary effort which has appeared absolutely fruitless and whence nothing good seems to have come where the way seems totally astray.[52]

Imprisonment forced Stuart into a state of self-reflectiveness and total despair about his writing career but, paradoxically, it also provided the ideal conditions in which to test the truth of his vision of reality and consequently, as he states in *The Abandoned Snail Shell*, 'to hit on the unlikely association that furthers his theme'. (*TASS*, p.68)

> ... man's inward turned reflective and responsive sensibilities, including the sub-conscious ones, require extreme experiences, often of pain and disaster of some kind, to condition them for registering signals from reality. (*TASS* p.68)

The suffering which lies at the core of Stuart's writing is therefore not simply that of the artist who chooses to suffer in order to create such as that contained in the image of the poet depicted by Pushkin.

> The Poet dwells absorbed in vanities
> And common worries and toils.
> Until Apollo calls him to holy sacrifice,
> His soul dreams in cold lassitude
> And his days are perhaps the most wretched
> Among the wretched sons of the earth.[53]

Nor is the suffering endured for the sole purpose of providing subject matter for his writing, a practice which the Polish poet, Tadeusz Rozewicz has noticed, and criticised, in other writers.

> The lives of poets are sometimes tragic, but suffering can be sold very lucratively. First you suffer, then you make money and achieve fame, and you spend the rest of your life in a golden halo of martyrdom.[54]

Rather, Stuart believes that suffering is instrumental in expanding the consciousness to its limits and thereby energising the imagination to the point that 'makes it possible to pass a hitherto uncrossable threshold, to think the unthinkable'. (*TASS*, p.67) In effect then, the experience of suffering drives the creative imagination towards a realisation of Stuart's model of reality with its interweaving of seemingly separate and distinct entities, in the merging relationship between the physical workings of the brain, the mental aspects of the consciousness, and the creativity of the artist.

> More decisive in the growth of the cerebrum with its twin hemispheres, is intense nervous stress. In responding the neurons create increasingly complex patterns... Life is sucked into the cerebellum at one open end and is ejected at the other as art. (*ACOL*, p.109)

The complexity of the interaction is such that it is at one and the same time a means of discovery and an aspect of that which is sought: 'Inward-turned consciousness, the attribute that makes us human, is both a means of discovering reality and an aspect of reality.' (*ACOL*, p.101)

It is this sense of infiltration between the physical functionings of the brain neurons and that which is imagined which lies behind the claim of the narrator of *A Compendium of Lovers*: '... the human mind, because its structure is an extension of the cosmic pattern, can, given the right conditions, add to or extend reality' (*ACOL*, p.97). In this novel, which has as its plot a plan to capitalise on a thoroughbred colt, bred under the influence of the aphrodisiac stardust borne on the tail of a comet, such a contention would seem to belong to the realms of science fiction. However, just as the seemingly outrageous proposition that

> ... comets from the stars... come rushing past the earth, bringing storms and whirlwinds and also tiny bits of life, smaller than a pin's head, from which we all come, plants, animals and humans. (*ACOL*, p.26)

is based on the Panspermia theory formulated by Sir Fred Hoyle and Professor N.C. Wickramsinghe in *Evolution from Space*,[55] Stuart's assertion that 'whatever is imagined intensely enough becomes reality' (*THC*, p.46) cannot be relegated to the realms of pure fantasy since the novel itself is in fact a practical demonstration of this theory.

For Stuart, as we have seen, the writer's imagination is energised by 'certain experiences, including pain' (*TASS*, p.11), in that the heightened awareness brought about by the extension of the consciousness gives a new perspective to familiar phenomena.

Thresholds open, glimpses are caught of creation at work on spirals, helices and eliptics in space, in gardens and in the intimate flesh where in the whorls at the entrance to the vagina there is a loosening in the overall seamless fabric. (*TASS*, p.71)

The sensation of glimpsing 'a tiny blueprint of reality' (*TASS*, p.71) in the midst of everyday experiences carries with it an intuition of its own truth. Recollecting an incident in which he had driven past a boy standing hugging a dog on a desolate bogland road, when both had seemed to hesitate 'on the verge of a hostile vastness', (*ACOL*, p.52) Stuart argues that the vividness of the memory endows it with a special significance.

Am I imagining more to the not very extraordinary scene than is justified? No. It was not so much imagining as familiar to me, so deeply present in my own consciousness, that… I remember those two mortal beings in a manner than makes a mockery of the tepidity of the word 'remember'. (*ACOL*, p.52)

In this way the consciousness grasps the underlying fusion of physical and metaphysical phenomena within the ordinary experiences of life.

… I thought I sometimes caught a glimpse at dusk, or very early on a still morning, of a treasure that all else should be bartered for. Then slowly and clumsily I began to grasp that if there was such a treasure it was quite a common one and certainly not buried but, if not exactly on offer at street corners, still part of the texture of everyday living. (*ACOL*, p.83)

The task which Stuart sets himself as a writer is to allow the reader to experience his model of reality and he does this through his themes of sex and religion, not only by casting a new light on these subjects, but by creating a form of fiction which proves the truth of his claim.

What is thought vividly enough takes form outside the imagining instrument, the brain, and becomes in a sense that I don't say I grasp, a small part of the truth. (*ACOL*, p.85)

3

An Analogy of Angels

If reality for Stuart is an intuitive insight into the unity of mind and cosmos and if it is imagination fired by pain and passion which brings consciousness into creative contact with reality, then it is the concept of woman which provides him with the means of articulating this vision. For Stuart, woman is the incarnation of his poetic vision – her presence is the source of sexual energy which intensifies the level of sensibility; her mediation ensures contact with the forces of natural life; while her body is inextricably linked with the principle of Creation. It is hardly surprising then that women play a major role in the works of Francis Stuart, not only providing the subject matter but also influencing the form of the novels.

In his first novel *Women and God*, Stuart draws his characters from the stock stereotypes of emotionless wife, passionate lover and celibate saint, and he defines each by means of familiar tropes – the wife as earth; the lover as fire; and the saint as water. The novel centres on the quest for meaning in a world that seems profoundly dark and empty. The character of Colin, the first of the many autobiographical personas which Stuart employs in his novels, is 'always lonely and unable to escape from the isolation of loneliness'. (*WG*, p.23) In the midst of an unsatisfactory marriage Colin turns to religion and to women.

> Trying to escape through religion, trying to escape through women, through a woman. Not merely by means of physical passion that didn't affect the inner void. Not any more deeply or any more permanently than drink for instance. It was only when a woman's body was like a doorway to come closer to her personality through, that the physical was an escape from his own isolation. Otherwise it was a blind alley leading nowhere. It was the physical for the sake of the physical. But he wanted more, always more. (*WG*, p.23)

This movement from the physicality of the woman's body to an imagined spiritual union is a typical manoeuvre of Stuart's, and at its roots lies the myth of woman as the High Priestess of metaphysical experience. In the Symposium,[1] for instance, Diotima, the great priestess of Mantineia, dictates to Plato the ideal, idealised concept of love as a unifying go-between, an agent of synthesis. This stands very much in contrast to the rather violent possession-love which Plato expounds in the *Phaedrus* which concludes that 'As wolves love lambs, so lovers love their loves'.[2] The vision of love which Diotima envisages is one which ensures harmony and survival.

> ... love, she said, may be described generally as the love of the everlasting possession of the good... The object which they have in view is birth in beauty, whether of body or soul... Because to the mortal creature, generation is a sort of eternity and immortality, she replied, and if, as has already been admitted, love is of the everlasting possession of the good, all men will necessarily desire immortality together with good.[3]

The assertion which Diotima makes, and it is one with which Stuart concurs in the above quote from *Women and God*, is that sexual passion in itself is a path that leads nowhere. It is rather passion combined with love which leads the lover on an ascent towards the supreme vision, which vision, according to Diotima, is a form of an intellectualisation of a pagan *jouissance*, the dazzlement of maternal fertility. As Keeper of the Womb, woman provides the key to procreation and immortality, but it is in the union of consciousness, of personalities, that the lover finds the power to give birth to beauty and harmony.[4] This is precisely the creative daemon which Stuart the writer seeks when he 'wanted more. Always more'. (*WG*, p.23) In *Women and God* this idealised communion between the sexual and the spiritual does not occur, primarily because the female characters Stuart creates in this novel are such narrow stereotypes, Anne, for instance, is a typical wife/mother figure.

> ... a strange, lovely thing. A part of her remained deep down; like a root thrust down into the dark clay. She was like a tree, like an evergreen oak, with roots deep down. And it was because she drew another life from what she called religion that she was such a lovely thing. She loved, not only her present physical life, but that dark charm to it too. It made love difficult.
> She was something secret, a lovely secret thing. (*WG*, p.134)

This image of woman as a silent, secretive being, deeply rooted in the earth is a strong, unapproachable one which leaves little room for the longed-for union. Anne's detached, passionless nature is a barrier to the warm, spiritual relationship Colin craves. All she can offer is '... a strong, but cold emotion, buried under an alert consciousness of so many other things'. (*WG*, p.144)

Laura, on the other hand, is all passion, 'for her there was the simplicity of following the strongest passion'. (*WG*, p.24) As the lover she is presented as warm, open and giving and, as befits such a passionate creature, she is portrayed as an irrational power who ignites the forces of creation in volcanic bursts.

> ... to Laura those 'moments', far apart, leaving behind them a trail of light like a comet, were, added together, the sum of life. And this night was one of those 'moments'; this night would shine and flare and pass in a trail of fire and leave behind it a scar on the mind. (*WG*, p.108)

In contrast to Anne's static earthbound image, the image of Laura is of a bright burst of fire, full of energy and always in motion, but both images, however, have the effect of limiting the characters to their stereotypes of passionless wife and passionate lover.

The third woman character in *Women and God* is Elizabeth who, having suffered a riding accident which has left her with open wounds, seeks a cure at Lourdes. The stigmata of her wounds, together with her quiet acceptance of suffering emphasises the spirituality of the character, as does her nunlike appearance. 'She had been reading under the large hood of the chair. Her face seemed very pale, almost white. A white stained with shadow.' (WG, p.43) Elizabeth's simplicity and faith is contrasted in the novel with her father's cold scientific manipulations, thereby highlighting her capability for loving.

> She was like the sea, the sea on a calm, wintry day. The slow, almost clumsy gestures of a large, deep thing… Everything must be risked, everything given. Like the sea that doesn't hoard its tides. Like the sea throwing itself on to the shores; sweeping up into bays; giving itself in little wavelets, in huge currents. (WG, p.105)

The scope and benevolence of this image attributes to Elizabeth a deep source of goodness, while her subsequent cure has the effect of linking her with a higher spiritual source. In keeping with her saintly stereotype, Stuart, unable to transcend the archetypal duality of spirituality/celibacy, denies the character any sexual dimension. As the epitome of sainthood, Elizabeth's love can only be accommodated within the confines of a convent so the novel reaches a rather orthodox religious conclusion. 'But I saw there was a discipline, a God one couldn't escape from. That human love wasn't the highest power on earth: that was it. (WG, p.249)

In this novel, therefore, Stuart draws his characters from the stock stereotypes of emotionless wife, passionate lover and celibate saint and he defines each of the types by means of familiar tropes – Anne, as the earth; Laura, as fire and Elizabeth as water, with the effect of linking each of them to the wider, cyclical forces of the cosmos. This strategy would seem to anticipate the work of recent feminist writers such as Mary Daly in Gyn/Ecology[5] and Margaret Atwood in Surfacing[6] who have attempted to re-establish the link between women and their elemental selves.

> This work… is a conjuring of the Elemental Spirits of women and all wild natures. Such conjuring of the Elemental spirits of women with our Selves and our Sisters, and with earth, air, fire and water. It connects us with the rhythms of the farthest stars and of our own sun and moon. It mends our broken ties with the Witch, with ourSelves who spins and weaves the tapestries of Elemental creation.[7]

But Stuart's main aim in relating women to the elements is not an exploration of the subliminal elementary nature of women, instead he uses the device to illustrate the main theme of the novel, the problem of reconciling spiritual and physical love.

The novel primarily sets out to highlight the increasingly materialistic nature of Irish society, which it does through the microcosm of male/female relationships. The quest, as in his earlier novels, is for a relationship which encompasses both sexuality and spirituality, at the heart of which search lies the embryo of the thesis which is a preoccupation of Stuart's later work, that in 'the intensely aroused lover... sensuality and metaphysics appear to overlap' (*TASS*, p.70). At this early stage though, the stereotypes of women which Stuart employs makes this synthesis more problematic. By aligning the wife with earth and the lover with fire, Stuart is locking the characters into a system of binary oppositions: passionless/passionate; cold/hot; static/transitory. While these polar extremities might help to emphasise the wife/lover dichotomy, they rule out the possibility of either character fulfilling a relationship which satisfies both the physical and the spiritual needs of the male character. The character who comes nearest to achieving that is Elizabeth, the saintly woman of the novel.

As the spiritual character, the element which should perhaps have been associated with Elizabeth is air, which traditionally[8] has been seen as a mediating force between the physical and metaphysical worlds, and would have illustrated well Colin's assertion that 'woman's body was like a doorway' (*WG*, p.23) since this image of the female gives the impression of a median space between two different realms of existence. However, Stuart avoids the obvious association, and by describing Elizabeth as the sea, he unconsciously creates an image which contemporary women writers and critics believe best captures the nature of woman. French feminist critics such as Helene Cixous in her description of *l'ecriture feminine* have attributed to woman a nature which is fluid and heterogeneous, and assert that feminine capacities are given their full expression in multiplicity, her libido being cosmic and her unconscious worldwide.[9]

> Heterogeneous, yes. For her joyous benefits she is erogenous; she is the erotogeneity of the heterogeneous: airborne swimmer, she does not cling to herself: she is dispersible.[10]

Luce Irigaray also locates feminine multiplicity in the body, stating that female sexuality is 'always at least double, is in fact plural'[11] so consequently the 'otherness' of woman resides in her inconstancy, her multiplicity and flux.[12] The sea, with its constant motion and varying shoreline, therefore, provides the perfect metaphor for female sexuality. The tidal movement of the sea, influenced as it is by the moon's cycle, also reflects the ebb and flow of the menstrual cycle, providing a link between a woman's body, and natural and cosmic forces. So by using the metaphor of the sea, Stuart is able to endow his character with sensuousness and mystery. The female characterisation here is rich with possible allusions, but at this stage Stuart seems to lack the nerve to develop it along the lines of Joyce's fluid women, Anna Livia Plurabelle or Molly Bloom,[13] and instead retreats to the safe stereotype of the saint, as Elizabeth turns her back on a loving sexual relationship and enters a convent.

Stuart's early novels repeat this same pattern, in that they tend to explore the dichotomy between religious and sexual impulses, and yearn for a means of accommodating both, particularly within the representation of a woman character, but so firmly fixed are the traditional constructs of women in his psyche, he is unable to conceptualise a character who is at one and the same time religious and sexual. Certainly, Stuart struggles, again and again in his pre-war novels, to find a way to describe his vision of the mystical experience. In *The Coloured Dome* , however, he finally veers away from the belief that this can be achieved through physical relationships.

> For him this bloody sap stinging his brain with a sweet anguish was the first thrusting forth of a human springtide that could not have for its culmination, its fruitful harvest, a woman. The fruit that must finally ripen in the shelter of its vernal depth must have a harsher taste. But a fruit that having eaten made one cease to hunger again. The fruit of a complete immolation that no woman could inspire or accept. (*TCD*, p.11)

To prove the point, Stuart creates in Tulloolagh McCoolagh a strong female character who combines sensuality and a mystical quality. Unlike the women characters in *Women and God* Tulloolagh is not limited by a single stereotypical nature. She is mother, wife, lover and, albeit in the disguise of a man, a leader of a revolutionary movement. Stuart also weaves a spell of mystery around the character. At different points in the novel she is described as 'a legendary figure in Ireland' (*TCD*, p.7), an 'anonymous being' (*TCD*, p.9), and 'aloof, hidden' (*TCD*, p.7). His delicate portrayal of her as she stands naked, watching the dusk spread over the fields and hills of Meath, has a mythical quality which synthesises the tangible and the intangible. Tulloolagh blends imperceptibly into the scenery, initially by being clothed 'with that pale butter colour of winter evening light' (*TCD*, p.25), which reflects the 'pools of liquid yellow sky' (*TCD*, p.24) and then by the dissipation of the image itself.

> She lingered at the window, getting cold, but gazing at the far woods and hills drowning to ghostliness in the deepening dusk. They seemed to tremble on the brink of materialisation and slowly to dissolve their bark and clay in a fringe of grey-blueness along the edges of that flood of fading primrose. And imperceptibly the fringe broadened and fields and woods nearer and nearer dissolved into its depths. (*TCD*, p.25)

The dreamlike quality of this image allows the solid diversity of the earth to assume an ethereal unity with the sky, while there is a complete blending of woman, earth and sky in the sexuality of the image.

> The pale yellow deepened to salmon, closed in between banks of dark grey, After a little while the glowing pool of sky had narrowed to a streak of red. (*TCD*, p.25)

The image of woman which Stuart creates here combines physical sexuality and spiritual intangibility, since she is strongly identified with natural reality while also maintaining a connection with the mythical spirit of Ireland. But Stuart creates this sensitive, composite image of woman merely to reject it as a means of attaining the mystical experience. The multicoloured nature of the image is in fact linked to the coloured dome of the title and the significance of this dome, as it is in Shelley's poem, is that it acts as a barrier to the true vision. 'Life like a dome of many coloured glass/Stains the white radiance of eternity'.[14] For Garry Delea, the protagonist of the novel, Tulloolagh provides just another distraction on the road to complete fulfilment, which he deems to be 'the white unstained snows of light beyond' (the coloured dome). (*TCD*, p.267)

Delea, an assistant in a Dublin betting office, is persuaded by Tulloolagh, as part of a deal she has made with the Irish government, that both should be executed in exchange for the lives of other IRA members. Within the confines of the prison cell, as both await the hour in which they will sacrifice themselves for Ireland, Tulloolagh takes on the mantle of Eve. In the intensity of the situation Garry's mind turns to the moment of his death, when 'consciousness would have escaped from his body', in contrast Tulloolagh's consciousness is enveloped by sexual desire.

> The seagull that had ridden on the surface of the storm had, as in some fairy tale, grown and grown, stilling the storm and diminishing the sea to a pool into which it dipped its white breast setting the water aglow. The little pool of consciousness in which she was imprisoned glowed with her body. She was immersed in it. (*TCD*, p.135)

The erotic fluidity of this image is violently at odds with Garry's rather bizarre mechanical perception of woman. 'He saw widely set breasts, curved and smooth like the polished heads of pistons.' (*TCD*, p.137) The moment of sexual consummation is marked by the blackness of the imagery used, a darkness which represents the shadow of woman blocking the white light of complete spiritual fulfilment.

> He was enveloped in darkness. Darkness fell across his closed eyes in showers. In black, sparkling showers. In scented showers falling from a fountain. A fountain sprung from an underground river. A swift hidden stream suddenly bursting through from the depths of consciousness. He seemed to stifle under the black, sparkling shower that was falling on him across his closed eyelids, stinging his flesh. (*TCD*, p.137)

Stuart's portrayal of women in *The Coloured Dome* is therefore heavily influenced 'by an acceptance of the myth of Eve's 'sin', as Tulloolagh is temptress and corrupter.

> She had turned him from that solitary quest into the broad path of human passion. The full chalice, for whose crystal-clear bitter-sweetness he had thirsted, had been made cloudy and poisoned by her body. (*TCD*, p.275)

This tainted vision of woman is in keeping with the tendency of the Western religious tradition to negatively evaluate women's biological experience and to build models of holiness and perfection around the rejection of women.[15] When the couple are unexpectedly pardoned and released the intensity of the relationship vanishes and they part. The final image of Tulloolagh shows her as a fallen angel. 'A dark seraph fallen out of the nightmares of Purgatory to the Earth, instead of to the heaven that she had expected.' (*TCD*, p.277) She can only 'follow from afar, peering down into dark, unaccustomed depths' (*TCD*, p.275) while Delea, rearrested for drunkenness returns to the isolation of the prison cell and, unburdened by 'the warm disturbance of passion' (*TCD*, p.285), finally achieves his 'cold, solitary peace'. (*TCD*, p.284) The sterile, deathlike quality of this final epiphany links into the female stereotype of the fallen angel, since the exclusion of women with their creative energy which is in harmony with nature, ultimately leads to a life-denying asceticism.[16] It is significant that Tulloolagh is cast earthwards, since it affirms her connection with nature and to a matriarchal principle which is at once biological and ecological. The interconnection between women and nature is viewed in Stuart's novel as a negative block to 'pure' spirituality, but more recent feminist studies of theology give a more positive interpretation to this connection. For instance, Ursula King in her exploration of women's spirituality, argues that this '... includes the full affirmation of the body, of the goodness and beauty of sexuality... we have to love with a radical love, with a love rooted in cosmos, nature and body'.[17] The dynamic life-affirming energy of this form of spirituality is in sharp contrast to the abstract, insular barrenness of the exclusively male spirituality depicted in *The Coloured Dome* , but in later novels Stuart increasingly moves away from this sterile position to seek the spiritual within the midst of life.

In *Things to Live For* (1934) published only two years later, there is the realisation that 'protecting oneself against life is not peace but death'. (*TTLF*, p.6) Instead Stuart maintains that spirituality emerges from the bowels of life itself.

> It is the falling in love with life, the dark deep flow below the surface. Subtle, crude, beautiful, terrible. A few have dared to open their arms to it, to plunge into it, and always they are wounded and humiliated; but they have been touched, have been caressed by those fiery fingers that curved the universe, and their remains about them a breadth, a spaciousness, a warmth of genius. (*TTLF*, p.3)

Such thinking continues to induce him into continually creating women characters who are wounded and humiliated but, in contrast to the earlier novels, in his later work he moves away from the fallen angel stereotype in order to create characters who are at once sexual and spiritual. In *Redemption*, one of two novels written at the end of the war, when Stuart was first a refugee and then imprisoned by the French, he challenges conventional morality and explores the possibility of creating a community in which a bond is created by the shared suffering and experience of the 'howling voices of the dark'. (*R*, p.224) The complacency of life in a small Irish town is interrupted by the return of Ezra Arrigho who is haunted by his experiences in war-time Germany. Through Ezra's accounts of the horror of the last days of the war, the breakdown of order and the waiting for 'the shapelessness of chaos'. (*R*, p.42) Stuart exposes the thin veneer of civilization and the close bond which is formed between those living on the edge of 'the unknown doom'. (*R*, p.42)

> There were no more differences between us except what could be seen or felt. Indeed there was only shape and sensation… .And when we prayed it was a different praying to most of the church praying; it was a turning of our dirty, pale faces to the face of darkness beyond the cellar darkness; it was the feeling in the trembling of the cellar and the falling of the plaster the passing of the angel of death and the angel of the end. And if a man took the hand of the girl huddled next to him it was another touch from the old touching, the old mechanical caressing. (*R*, p.43)

By embracing the full spectrum of life, the horror and corruption as well as the beauty and pleasure, Ezra acts as a catalyst, exploding 'the daylight smugness and security' (*R*, p.181) of Altamont (the fictional Irish town in which the novel is set) and in its place he was promoting the redemptive power of pain and suffering.

> After the days of vengeance there comes a new breadth. Here and there, among those who have survived, comes a new vision, further than the duck-pond vision. That's the only hope for us now: a new vision and a new god. (*R*, p.47)

Once again the typology of the women characters reinforces the main theme of the novel. Romilly Mellowes, sister of the priest, is representative of the sheltered, passionless existence of Altamont, with her 'carefully acquired culture and her piety and book-learning'. (*R*, p.51) As a virgin she would seem to epitomise the male ideal of female purity, but in *Redemption* Stuart uses the term to indicate a failing rather than a virtue. In keeping with its Latin root 'virga' meaning green branch, Romilly's virginity is a sign of her immaturity and the fact that she 'knew nothing, nothing, neither the terror, the weariness nor the rapture'. (*R*, p.26) She is 'untouched' until Ezra, in 'the sunless desolation' (*R*, p.25) of the cave, is momentarily transported back to the cellars in bomb-torn Berlin and reaches out for her.

> It was as it had been when the earth had rocked and split. His hand reached out and grasped an arm in the dark, he felt the fine material of Romilly's summer dress. He gripped it when she tried to pull it away, waiting for her to cry out. He did not know why he hated her. (*R*, p.26)

This show of pure emotion is enough to shake Romilly out of her prim world where 'all is small and delicate and closed in to itself and not writhing out at you in longing and torment'. (*R*, p.210) She turns her back on the safety of marriage to the Colonel which would keep her on 'the sure, broad road' (*R*, p.92) on which '... the very stones were gentle under her feet and there were no strange and agonised words spoken on it, no dark echoes from cellars or crosses'. (*R*, p.92) Instead she joins the humiliated and wounded by following her passion and offering herself to Ezra.

> ... because of the new feeling that had come to her in the last weeks in snatches, in touches like thorn-pricks... These were no more than hints and shadows ... but they made her reckless, and the passion that had had no gradual and easy unfolding was bursting out in darkness and distortion. (*R*, p.92)

In turning from innocence and security to look into 'the face of darkness', (*R*. p.44) Romilly abandons her virginity and is consequently cast into the role of whore.

> The moment came without tenderness or any softening of it by him. He had hardly touched her, nor spoken one word of endearment. With beating heart, she was stooping down and undoing her shoes. Like a street-girl, he thought. (*R*, p.125)

As with the virgin role, the conventional conception of the whore is reversed in the novel for, while retaining the full force of the violation, Stuart creates a scene in which the horror of rape and death are intermingled with religious ceremony.

> He would disarrange her neatness and spoil her niceness for her! Let her be a rose, but a rose in whose very centre was the worm! With this body I thee enclose… with this blood, with these tears… with this maidenhood I thee wed. He violated her, but she did not know it. Yet she was conscious of the horror too. She was Annie in the dark and the mud, and the knife going into her. And the light was the lights of the police torches shining on her, exposing her, illuminating her secret and bloody shame. She lay in his arms between living and dying. (*R*, p.127)

The effect is to place Romilly's experience within a wide range of natural and cosmic changes.

> … in that space of a quarter of an hour, in that little space of time and silence in which tides turn and cities are taken and the bright, virgin moon turns to blood. (*R*, p.127)

Stuart does not allow the reader to slip into a negative reaction to Romilly's experience, instead she is contrasted with the other women characters, in particular against Nancy, Ezra's wife. Nancy is depicted as being rather frigid, having '… remained looking out from (her) ivory tower, too proud or too fastidious to come down out of it' (*R*, p.137). Although she has been abandoned by Ezra little sympathy is engendered for the character who is shown to be 'aloof from and contemptuous of the circus' (*R*, p.139) with little passion.

> 'Sex', she said with that weary distaste. 'How nasty it is and how sick I am of it all around me.'
> 'Yes, I remember the scorn you always had for it', said Ezra, 'and how you used to speak with disgust of glands and membranes.' (*R*, p.138)

More damning from Ezra's viewpoint though is her inability to fully embrace life.

> She has lived so long in a tower of idealism that she cannot escape from it. She is trapped behind the wall of her own judgements. She has judged the world and most of its activity to be evil and foolish and has been proved

right, but what satisfaction is there finally in being right? To prove oneself morally right and to get no pleasure out of being so, is not that bitter? (*R*, p.141)

When compared to Nancy's cloistered intransigence, Romilly's wild abandonment to the flesh is seen as a more authentic mode of being.

The third female character in the novel, a local shopgirl called Annie, reinforces the positive aspect of sexuality since she is shown to have the capacity to enjoy both an active sex life and a childlike innocence.

> Annie had regarded the lithograph of St Francis with the rays from the crucified Seraph piercing his own hands and feet. The dead white rays, the crimson wounds and the blue-black, stormy sky were beautiful to her. Sin and repentance were not real to her. The lithograph was real, and the large stuffed fish in a glass case in the window of Kavanagh's shop. Each meant to her a certain atmosphere, a certain kind of life, the life of the flesh and the life of the spirit and she was quite ready to shift over from one to the other. (*R*, p.34)

Unlike Romilly and Nancy, she accepts all manner of experiences with an unthinking ease.

> She liked things to happen, even the sting of the needle: and she liked the thought of the bleeding picture. She liked the smell of drink on the breath of men. Heavy and passive in herself, she was like a sponge that soaked up sensation, excitement. (*R*, p.39)

Given this view of life, Annie could be read as a prime example of female subjugation since she is used sexually by Kavanagh, the local fishmonger, and by many others, and bears the brunt of Altamont's double standard of morality which condones sexual activity in men as a sign of 'masculinity' while condemning it in women.[18] She was, in Kavanagh's mind, one of his possessions.

> All the others had had her and had known her, had known the secret of her that was still a mystery to him. She was telling him casually of the repeated robbery of his one great treasure; he was listening to one long, agonising account of other men who, in passing as it were, had turned aside and taken what was his... (*R*, p.84)

Kavanagh's reaction to Annie's admission of her infidelity is to brutally rape and murder her and leave her body by the railway track. Kavanagh's justification for his act was one of righteous indignation that his possession, Annie's body, had been taken from him.

> 'How could I give it up to every fellow, every damned drover and shop-boy to take his passing pleasure out of?' said Kavanagh. 'How could I give up what was holy torment to me, miss, for others to have their fun with?' (R, p.105)

In this way Kavanagh's crime is shown to be justifiable in the light of Annie's promiscuity so Stuart is inviting the reader to judge Annie harshly thereby making her murder more acceptable. However, to interpret the character in this way is to fall into the trap of accepting a very traditional myth of female sexuality which, until quite recent times, deemed that women should be passive, and unwilling sexual partners.

> To have strong sexual passions is held to be rather a disgrace for a woman, and they are looked down upon as animal, sensual, coarse, and deserving reprobation.[19]

Such an interpretation is also at odds with the overall definition of female sexuality in the novel which has more in common with the celebratory approach to female sexuality of modern critics such as Kristeva, Cixous and Irigaray.

> Women's *jouissance* carries with it the notion of fluidity, diffusion, duration. It is a kind of potlatch in the world of orgasms, a giving, expending, dispensing of pleasure without concern about ends or closure.[20]

As we have seen, through Romilly, Stuart advocates the life-embracing quality of physical lust and when read from this perspective, Annie's death ceases to be a punishment for immorality. Instead her murder is linked to all the other senseless, meaningless deaths which took place in the war. Questioned by Romilly as to whether he feels he has committed a great sin, Kavanagh responds, 'A great sin? If so, then isn't the world full of great sins, miss? Has Ezra never told of all that went on in that foreign place he was in?' (R, p.140) This non-judgmental stance reflects Ezra's view of reality.

> There are two faces to reality, and I have seen them both. Therese was the

bloody face of the sister as I saw her a little later, one of all the faces of the raped, the dying, the horror-stricken and the other face, the face of 'Not a sparrow falls without the Father', and whoever has seen these two faces as one is finally delivered and at peace. (R, p.140)

The reader is led away from narrow moral judgements and made more receptive to the main theme of the novel; that facing up to 'the hunger, catastrophe, flight, death, loss' (R, p.140) of human existence creates a bond of compassion between fellow sufferers.

Stuart personifies this theme in the character of Margareta, Ezra's German mistress who arrives in Altamont crippled from the war and who, like her namesake in Goethe's *Faust*, understands her condition and submits herself it. 'Why must you carry on so? Isn't it time we bowed to what death has to say, and not go on with our foolish mocking of him...'. (R, p.219) Having come through the mental torment of the final days of the war with Ezra, and endured the physical suffering of her injuries, Margareta survives and displays an intuitive grasp of another way of being.

They felt the unexpected life of the little group encompass them. There was a dark and subtle field of power set up between those living in the house... There opened before him vast and strange vistas. He saw that, after all, there were other modes of communion beside the old and played-out ones. (R, p.191)

As they wait for Kavanagh's arrest she casts a glow over the small commune which she forms in the room above the fish-shop with Ezra, Romilly, Kavanagh, Nancy and Aunt Nuala. Within the framework of the group Romilly marries Kavanagh in order to support him in the hours leading to his execution while Margareta nurses the old aunt in her final days. Only Nancy rejects the offer of companionship; unable to 'come without prejudices and suspicions and the old angers' (R, p.183) she finds the whole idea 'muddy and common'. (R, p.184)

The female characters of *Redemption*, by reflecting a reality in which the binary oppositions are blurred, manage to break the normal stereotypical codes. Again Stuart is using a strategy which anticipates one used by feminist critics such as Julia Kristeva who detects, in writers such as Stephane Mallarme,[21] a subversive signifying process which ruptures the coherent logical discourse of phallocentric culture and reveals the cracks in

75

the social and cultural facade; a process 'which seems to be the prerogative of artists and women'.[22] For Kristeva the status of these two groups as outsiders makes them more open to traces of the semiotic which she sees as deriving from the pre-oedipal fusion of infant and mother. When this pre-linguistic erotic energy is channelled from the unconscious and set against the rationality of male discourse, then the iron grip of the symbolic is broken. Feminine discourse therefore, whether written by a woman or a man has, Kristeva believes, the effect of breaking down the symbolic order.

> ... if logical unity is paranoid and homosexual (directed by men to men), the feminine demand... will never find a proper symbolic, will at best be enacted as a moment inherent in rejection, in the process of ruptures, of rhythmic breaks. Insofar as she has a specificity of her own, a woman finds it in asociality, in the violation of communal conventions, in a sort of a-symbolic singularity.[23]

Insofar as *Redemption* ruptures the conventional images of woman, it is a feminine text, and it is this aspect of the novel which best illustrates its theme. This breaking down of social codes exposes the reader to the possibility of another way of being and it is this enactment which helps Stuart's text succeed. When he reverts to the old, rational descriptive narrative, his description of this other way of being ultimately collapses to the female ploy of the all-knowing silence of the enigmatic smile.

> Ezra and the two women waited for an answer. Even Margareta was waiting, knowing from the tone of Ezra's voice that he had asked a question. Ezra looked up. He saw Father Mellows' smile, the smile that he would never get quite used to, resting on them, and he know that that was the nearest to an answer that they would ever come. (R, p.226)

Once again Stuart's narrative strategies seem to pre-empt the work of feminist critics such as Tillie Olsen, on the centrality of silence in women's experience.[24] Adrienne Rich also suggests that it is in silence 'that we will find the true knowledge of women'.[25] As we have seen, Stuart in *Redemption* not only promotes silence as a source of knowledge, but as the critic Maurice Harmon points out, silence is also significant in his attempt to capture the core of reality.

> ... it is of the essence of Stuart's treatment that the reality is hidden: mere

words cannot express the hidden significance, the reverberations, of the event. By a quality of absence, of silence, by the refusal to even try to bring the experience into an imaginative reality through language Stuart affirms its importance.[26]

Moreover, just as women writers attempted to extend the patriarchal tradition which they felt had silenced and marginalised them because its forms did not easily express women's experience,[27] so too, in his later work, Stuart began to experiment with the form of the novel in order to fully express his instinctive vision of reality. The methodology undertaken by Stuart again foreshadows the recent tendency of women's writing to negotiate the silence by the inclusion of autobiography in the manner recommended by Adrienne Rich.

> ... in breaking those silences, naming our selves, uncovering the hidden, making ourselves present, we begin to define a reality which resonates to us, which affirms our being.[28]

Stuart has always 'made himself present' (*BLSH*, p.255) in his work with his tendency to merge real and imaginative events. In *Redemption* for example, the character of Nancy is obviously based on his first wife Iseult, Margareta on his second wife, Gertrud Meissner, and Aunt Nuala on his Aunt Janet but the fusion of fact and fiction in his work alters with *Black List, Section H* from autobiographical reportage to an in-depth analysis of the self and a consequential naming of himself in the fiction.

> ... in surviving perilous situations... he'd gain the insight he needed to reach whatever degree of psychic and imaginative depths he was capable of, and be able to communicate these in his fiction. (*BLSH*, p.255)

By exploring the obsessive, alogical nature of his imaginative consciousness Stuart goes through a process of self-discovery which is then transferred into his fiction by means of dislocating the narrative structure. The later novels have in common an unreliable narrator who has mental or emotional problems, being treated by drugs or addicted to alcohol, and unable to provide a logical, sequential account of events or distinguish between reality and hallucination, a situation which is compounded by a continual switching from fiction to fact with authorial interjections and autobiographical episodes.

> Howsobeit – a word interpolated here which, for those interested in such matters as literary technique, and who perhaps attend creative writing courses, serves to create space between or before more relevant phrases start jostling for room – howsobeit. (*ACOL*, p.57)

The result is a text which has the effect of plunging readers into confusion as they struggle to establish the relationship between the various levels of fantasy. This experience of flux and uncertainty not only creates a link between the reader and the narrator, but also to Stuart himself, since it mirrors his own process of delving into the fictions of his self. Faced with the deconstructive nature of the text, the reader grasps the autobiographical sections as secure ground and places a trust in Stuart and the hidden control of his creative consciousness. The interconnecting consciousness which forms the basis of the reality Stuart wishes to express is, therefore, experienced in this link between text, author and reader.

> We are all fragments of reflected reality, in the same molecular form as the cosmic structure. I had long had the illusion of being at the centre of reality which had been turning solitude into a very constricted state. Now I recognised companions, fellow-beings, whose cells contained the same basic quest for consciousness as mine, a consciousness that could merge to varying degrees with mine. (*ACOL*, p.29)

A Compendium of Lovers deals with this merging of consciousness in a way that brings into focus an important element of his women characters. It explores Stuart's belief that the sexual act can act as a catalyst for such a union through the relationship between the first-person narrator and Abby, an Arabian nurse.

> Now I was fully conscious again, and so was she, if she'd ever been anything else from the first move. We were both flooded with the consciousness of the other's sensation as well as our own – it's more than a guess in regard to her: we were exchanging communication at a mercurial rate. (*ACOL*, p.84)

In this novel Stuart moves beyond the romantic union of man and woman as the narrator slowly comes to the realisation that in his obsession with sex the identity of the woman concerned is of little importance. '... before my own orgasm, had another woman been substituted I'd have gone on unabashed and unabated'. (*ACOL*, p.84) By recognising this, the narrator sees clearly that his obsession negates woman and reduces her to an object of desire.

> I told Abby how, as a raw youth, I thought I sometimes caught a glimpse at dusk, or very early on a still morning, of a treasure that all else should be bartered for... For a time, quite a long time I thought it was women. At first romantically, even poetically, but gradually more precisely and crudely, it turned into the cunt. (*ACOL*, p.83)

Stuart primarily uses this image to illustrate the underlying fusion of physical and metaphysical phenomena in everyday experience, since it captures in a unity, the vulgarities of the flesh and the mystery of creation.

> All the sweetness and tenderness, magically, metaphysically, purged of the anguish, is hidden there in this grail of flesh that is also a very lowly receptacle situated between two drain-pipes. Think of the polarity, the deep counter-currents in which we drown or are carried off. (*ACOL*, p.169)

However, the image is also a voyeuristic one which strips women not only of any identity or personality but of body too. She becomes an absence, a space waiting to be filled, a nothing. Although denying a desire to 'define or subjugate the woman' (*ACOL*, p.170) Stuart would seem to have recognised a truth about himself during the process of writing this novel. The narrator is closely identified with Stuart, as the writer who 'recorded, in the third person, my own fictional relationship (with Emily Brontë), in a novel called *A Hole in the Head*'. (*ACOL*, p.90) It is therefore, the voice of Stuart himself which the reader hears owning up to his 'sex-obsession, crude, demeaning, unloosing'. (*ACOL*, p.210) By finally acknowledging this flaw in his nature, he realises that women themselves play no part in his imaginative constructs, they 'are blameless' (*ACOL*, p.210) because it is Stuart's consciousness which is reducing women to mere sex objects. Stuart's attention converges on the focal point of his interest and in doing so, all images of women disappear into a void and become self-evident projections of the writer's mind. The women characters in Stuart's novels are imaginative realisations of his fantasies and obsessions, not attempts to represent or define women in any realistic way.

Essentially what Stuart does is to make apparent the absence of women in his literary text and thereby effectively 'causes an upheaval of the carrier of masculine investment'[29] a manoeuvre which Helene Cixous surmises is a prerequisite to uncovering the feminine aspects of experience. Stuart's text therefore acts as a catalyst for the reader, forcing them to interrogate outmoded stereotypes and opening their minds to new ways of thinking about 'women'. This transformative act is very much in keeping with Stuart's proclaimed aesthetic which aims to 'change the expression on the faces of men and women' (*THC*, p.211), but it also concurs with the objectives of feminist criticism as outlined by Judith Fetterley.

> At its best, feminist criticism is a political act whose aim is not simply to interpret the world but to change it by changing the consciousness of those who read and their relation to what they read.[30]

Strange as it might seem then, by foregrounding the way in which his women characters are essentially aspects of his own fantasies and desires, Stuart is employing the kind of narrative manoeuvre recommended by contemporary feminist critics and to precisely the same end – to change narrow perceptions of reality. So, despite the weakness of his representations of women, they still perform many important roles in his work.

> The first person narrator in your novels would indeed be desolate, not to say desperate, without an intimate account with a woman. (*ACOL*, p.11)

One major role for the woman, which is shown in *A Compendium of Lovers*, is that of providing inspiration for the writer. This becomes clear in the novel when the narrator reveals how his consciousness moves from the reality of a written text to a flight of imagination which in turn finds a place in the reality of his own narrative.

> Some years ago, when I was reading the autobiography of St. Thérèse of Lisieux, (popularly known as 'The Little Flower', though only in English), and meditating on the final chapters – the earlier ones are mawkish – I imagine having been born forty or fifty years earlier – she died a few years before my conception – she might have taken up with me. (*ACOL*, p.85)

This allows the reader to see how Stuart creates his female characters since, given his contention that 'imagination, even the most self-supporting, must draw sustenance from facts' (*ACOL*, p.222), it is possible to observe how he derives inspiration from women he has met or read accounts of and then launches off into an imaginative relationship which he recounts in his novels.

> She – Eve, in this first and seminal confrontation – was there not to satisfy man's – Adam's – desires and in doing so propagate. She was, so to say, the source and fount of those desires, structured in a very cunning, if not actually miraculous, manner, to arouse, in quanta-like succession, ever more sensually. (*ACOL*, p.104)

Apart from acting as inspiration and providing the content of Stuart's novels, women have also influenced the form. As stated previously, since *Black List, Section H*, Stuart's writings have been explorations of his own consciousness which has produced a type of autobiographical fiction which is more precisely described as auto-graphical – a writing of the self. This again provides a further link between Stuart and woman writers, since, as Judith Kegan Gardiner claims, the woman writer uses her text '… as part of a continuing process involving her own self-definition'.[31]

> Women's novels are often called autobiographical, women's autobiographies, novelistic – like Mary McCarthy's *Memories of a Catholic Girlhood* or Maxine Hong Kingston's *Memoirs of a Woman Warrior*. Because of the continual crossing of self and other, women's writing may blur the public and private and defy completion. Thus we have writers like Dorothy Richardson and Anais Nin, whose lives journals, letters, and fiction become nearly coterminous.[32]

A further correspondence with feminine thinking is present in Stuart's view that transcendence occurs in the mundane ordinariness of life.

> … as a raw youth, I thought I sometimes caught a glimpse at dusk, or very early or a still morning, of a treasure that all else should be bartered for. Then slowly and clumsily I began to grasp that if there was such a treasure it was quite a common one and certainly not buried but, if not exactly on offer at street corners, still part of the texture of everyday living. (*ACOL*, p.83)

This view is remarkably similar to feminist accounts of spirituality, particularly those of Mary Daly or Charlene Spretnak.

81

In truth, there is nothing 'mystical' or 'other worldly' about spirituality. The life of the spirit, or soul, refers merely to functions of the mind. Hence spirituality is an intrinsic dimension of human consciousness and is not separate from the body. From one perspective, we realize we need food, shelter, and clothing,.from another that the subtle, suprarational reaches of mind can reveal the true nature of being.[33]

Finally, the view of reality as an encompassing network of correspondences which is explored throughout Stuart's work finds a companion in Ursula King's description of her 'matriarchal' world-view.

> ... a different kind of power, as a realm where female things are valued and where power is exerted in non-possessive, non-controlling, and organic ways that are harmonious with nature.a world-view that values feelings of connectedness and intuition.[34]

All in all, Stuart's writings contain numerous aspects which are deemed to be defining features of women's writing. The reason for this can, I believe, be traced back to Stuart's obsessive fascination with the writings of St Thérèse of Lisieux, who was, as he confesses in his last novel, 'guide and inspiration to me, beyond that of any great writer or philosopher'. (ACOL, p.163)

Certainly, the influence on Stuart of Thérèse Martin's autobiographical work, *The Story of the Soul*[35] is obvious from her inchoate narrative which dodges backwards and forwards in its chronology; her artless breathless haste in pouring out meaning on to the page and in her capacity to find in everyday objects, an illustration of chaos and order. The latter is noted by Vita Sackville-West in her biography of Thérèse.

> The kaleidoscope with which she played as a child affords her another illustration: investigating its works, she discovered that her pretty patterns came from nothing but irregular bits of paper and wool, but ah! there was a further discovery: a three-sided mirror down the centre, the Holy Trinity of course, turning the meaningless jumble into beauty.[36]

The belief that spirituality is hidden in the ordinary, small occurrences of life was the motivating factor behind Thérèse's decision to join the Carmelite Order, whose vows of poverty, chastity and obedience encourage inward contemplation and meditation as a means of gaining spiritual insight. For the religious life involved an overwhelming sense of love.

> My vocation is love! At last I have found it! I will be love itself! O luminous lighthouse of love, I know how to reach you… I have no means of proving my love save by throwing flowers, that is to say by neglecting no little sacrifice, no glance, no word, but to profit by the slightest actions and to perform than for love. I want to suffer through love and even to rejoice through love.[37]

But she also had the ability to shock, devising a coat-of-arms for herself and Jesus, and announcing her marriage to Jesus in a *lettre de faire part*.

> God Almighty, Creator of heaven and earth, sovereign Dominator of the world, and the Most Glorious Virgin Mary, Queen of the celestial court, are pleased to inform you of the spiritual marriage of their august Son, Jesus, King of Kings and Lord or Lords, to little Thérèse Martin, now Lady and Princess of the realms brought her as her dowry by her divine Spouse.[38]

However, it was the act of writing down her experiences, her visions and her dark nights of the soul, and her joy, that proved to be the greatest influence on Stuart. During her life Thérèse lived in complete obscurity within the walls of the convent and although her autobiography was not published until after her death on 30 September 1897, the effect of the book was phenomenal.

> The book, first read in the convents, was then lent to chosen friends; the circles widened rapidly, and before long the Carmel of Lisieux was inundated with orders for copies of the book from all parts of France. Not only orders arrived, but numbers of young women, all desirous of entering the convent of Lisieux and following in the footsteps of Thérèse de l'Enfant Jesus… The value of the written word had never been more clearly demonstrated than now, when it shot this searchlight beam into the recesses of Thérèse Martin's obscurity.[39]

This is not to suggest that her work received general acceptance, as Stuart himself points out. '(She was) debased and accounted a pathalogical, if harmless, fake. As in fact a large proportion of those who has heard of her took her to have been'. (*ACOL*, p.163) Thérèse Martin's influence on Stuart therefore stemmed not only from the example of a life lived in obscurity concerned with finding a spiritual path through small, everyday occurrences despite doubt and public ridicule, but also in her revelation of the power of the written word. In achieving sainthood, not merely by her actions, but primarily by expressing the intensity of her beliefs in her autobiography and in this way providing an inspiration far beyond the constraints of time and place, Thérèse proved an inviting paradigm for the writer.

Stuart's fiction, therefore, not only reflects Thérèse's beliefs, it also echoes her style, and like her autobiography, the novels pour intensely – felt experience into language with the result that the text becomes imbued with a potent energy capable of inspiring the reader. Consequently, Stuart's creativity becomes an act or process which links the reader with the characters, with Stuart, and with the source of his inspiration, in an ever-widening web thereby imitating his vision of reality. Like his image of woman, Stuart's books are at one and the same time, the 'source and fount' (*ACOL*, p.169), the storehouse and the origin of inspiration. In essence his novels are expectant parables waiting to give birth, a condition which consequently endows his work with its greatest strength – a profound religious sense.

4

From Metaphysics to Metafiction

Commenting on his later work (1971–1996) Stuart wrote that he saw it as 'religious, but not Catholic unless in a very wide sense'.[1] As we have already seen religion permeates all aspects of his writing, as a recurring theme and as the source of his obsession with suffering which so directs his reflections on the creative consciousness. Through his interest in the Gospel women[2] and in the writings of mystics such as St Thérèse, religion has provided a stylistic paradigm for his novels. But Stuart's later novels have been 'religious' in a profoundly different way from his earlier work in that they emulate the formal narrative strategies of the Gospels in order to achieve what he sees as 'the impact of reality'. (*F*, p.107)

Initially, the central religious concern for Stuart was the exploration of the dichotomy between spirituality and everyday experience in modern society. Critical of technological materialism, he tries in one of his earliest stories to find a credible way of expressing his belief in a mystical presence which underlies the physical world.

The future always glowed with a mysterious joy that withered as the

> present caught up on it. Like the thin, sweet clouds that disappear as they are about to pass across the moon. But occasionally a few moments survived into the present, a miraculous, unseasonal blossoming. (*TTLF*, p.137)

In keeping with Rudolf Otto's view of non-rational mystery[3] Stuart envisages this numinous experience as a mixture of beauty and dread and so combines the joyful vision of 'a higher, more human heaven in which love and tenderness were transfigured and shining' (*TTLF*, p.23) with an altogether more threatening sensation.

> I was brought to the edge of another abyss, different but equally dark, even harder to explain, I think. All the useless, inexplicable, lonely suffering in the world. How vague it sounds like that, but it was not vague in my heart, it was like a high, thin shriek coming from the underground. (*TTLF*, p.20)

Ultimately, the text collapses into a conventional expression of the ineffability of the mystical experience.

> A door had been opened to me, a secret revealed. I could not have said what that secret was, and I cannot say now. But I know that it was the first glimpse I had into life, beautiful in its terrible passivity, delicate and intricate with a savage strength. (*TTLF*, p.10)

In the early novels, then, Stuart strives to find a credible way to describe the mystical experience, an enterprise which was not entirely successful.

The miracle cure at the centre of *Women and God*, for instance, allows Stuart to present his view that metaphysical experience is a part of everyday existence by juxtaposing stock religious motifs and commonplace objects. Although the novel is initially set in Lourdes, Stuart resists the obvious and allows Elizabeth's pilgrimage to end in apparent failure, and it is only when the party returns to Paris and all hope of a cure is abandoned that the miracle occurs. Echoing the mystical accounts of St Thérèse[4] and recalling the Pentecostal, flame Stuart links the flame with pain thus succeeding in merging the flesh and the spirit.

> Pain licked, like a flame, about her flesh. A forked, invisible flame, swaying within her as in a slight breeze and making her tremble in agony at every touch of its searing tongue. Yet she felt that she was being consumed, burnt up, by a fire not of earth. (*WG*, p.96)

As the combination of physical pain and spiritual joy escalates to sexual ecstasy in a passionate outpouring which echoes many of the accounts of the women mystics, Stuart decisively undercuts any overt transcendentalism by drawing the reader firmly back to the modern, scientific world.

> By a fire that, at a certain moment, would sear her no longer, but would shine about her and in her and through her; the furnace of uncreated love, into which she would plunge; was even now feeling the first faint ripples of. Ripples of agony because of flesh that could not bear the encounter. An electric bulb blazed over her. (*WG*, p.97)

His attempt to endow everyday objects with a sense of mystery is intensified by the implication that things are never quite as they seem, that natural perceptions can be deceptive distortions of the truth.

> The light fell on to her face and hair and hands and was still with the stillness of speed, like a waterfall seen from afar. The hotel room, the furniture of walnut-wood smooth and veined, a greyish mauve, like water rippling under a bridge... The hot aluminium-painted radiator under the window, gleaming silvery and cold. All these seemed to Colin to have no solidity, to be but variations of the strong, white light. (*WG*, p.97)

Such manoeuvres serve to suggest that the miraculous is not limited to a metaphysical realm but is rather a part of everyday existence, a part which can be revealed simply by a shift in perspective.

> Like a sea that, because of some deep, unseen currents, takes on such different, unblending shades, sharp and distant; or like some polished surfaces or velvet that can be rubbed with a finger into patterns and pictures. Only the girl on the bed had a separate being; a blot of life in the expanse of coloured light. Something unexpected, disturbing, miraculous; human life. (*WG*, p.97)

This evocation of the metaphysical is a standard account of the mystical experience in both Eastern and Western[5] philosophy.

> So-called mystical consciousness, the moments when one has that sense of immense significances, when consciousness seems full of vibrations of meaning, is not different in kind from everyday consciousness; only, so to

speak, in pressure. The web is already there, stretching in all directions, but for the most part, it is in darkness. (*WG*, p.249)

But while this episode encourages the reader to contemplate the mystical experience as a potential of everyday consciousness, the novel as a whole fails to maintain a clear focus and ultimately reverts to the more orthodox view that spiritual experience can best occur in a state of isolation from the world.

> ... I saw there was a discipline, a God, one couldn't escape from. That human love wasn't the highest power on earth; that was it. I saw that human love wasn't omnipotent. There was something more powerful than that. (*WG*, p.249)

In this novel Stuart toys with, and then shies away from, reconciling spiritual love and physical passion as Elizabeth turns her back on her sexuality and embraces instead the celibacy of the nun. 'I love you. But I shall not see you any more on this earth. I am going to become a Carmelite nun. If you want to make sure of us being together again afterwards, become a Catholic.' (*WG*, p.244) This inconsistency in Stuart's perception of the spiritual experience in the novel is one of the main reasons that it fails to convince, a failure which Stuart himself later acknowledged.

> When I began to write and wrote *Women and God* there was a religious obsession, but it was and had been too mental and I was already escaping from it and turning to the world for adventure and inspiration.[6]

If Stuart's first novel, *Women and God*, is marked by its inability to reconcile spiritual and physical impulses and its insistence that spirituality must remain within the confines of the church, the novels which follow, *Pigeon Irish* and *The Coloured Dome*, opt for a more secular approach.

As we have already seen in *Pigeon Irish* Frank is torn between two women, his wife Brigid who represents an earthy physical passion, and Catherine Arigho, who like her namesake St Catherine of Sienna, symbolises the ascetic, world-denying religious spirit. Since the dualism of flesh and spirit is reflected in the structure of the novel, the symbolic allegory about carrier pigeons being juxtaposed with the realism of Frank's story, the background of which is the battle between the encroaching materialism of Western industrial society and the last stronghold of spirituality – a small sanctuary in Ireland, the romantic lyricism of the fable allows Stuart the freedom to explore the theme of martyrdom and to endow a sensuousness to the notion of mystical union in death.

> Not satisfied with the unmingling contact of flesh, but with wild longing for the undisentangible blending of blood in death. A mystical union. Very physical, very spiritual. Because she did not think that this shedding of their blood would be the only consummation. Beyond that, like the one shadow thrown by two embracing figures, was a vaguer, but vivid image. As though the archangels swooping down, remoulded the shed blood, the shining feathers into one vivid and immaterial bridge between earth and heaven. A rainbow over the receded flood. (*PI*, p.99)

Due to his wife's jealousy Frank is unable to establish an harmonious relationship with both women and therefore combine the spirituality and sensuality they represent. So the human story fails to parallel that of the pigeons. This failure to merge the sacred and the secular within the realist text is caused by an underlying belief that spirituality is ultimately corrupted by the physical.

> There was a painted wooden statue of St. Catherine of Sienna on the altar. There was a veil across her head and over the veil a crown of thorns… the dress fell down from her shoulders in straight wooden folds. It had been painted cream, but the paint remained only in the hollows of the folds. It had worn off the ridges, leaving the dark wood full of little punctures made by some parasite. (*PI*, p.30)

Here Stuart still equates spirituality with asceticism and self-denial and so ultimately his struggle to unite the metaphysical and the physical within his novels can only end in failure. His desire to espouse a pantheistic ideal is at odds with his attraction to the reclusive existence of the visionaries, and at this stage, as the title of his next novel *The Coloured Dome* reveals, the latter has the strongest hold. As is the case in Shelley's *Adonais*, from which the title is drawn, which shows that contact with life destroys the purity of the spiritual world. 'Life, like a dome of many-coloured glass/ Stains the white radiance of Eternity.'[7] The mystical moment is only achieved when the protagonist rejects all human comforts, turning away from a loving relationship and the pride that drives him towards political martyrdom, to languish in a cell filled with the sickening smell of damp bodies. 'A white radiance fell through his consciousness unstained by that coloured dome. As though life had become simple with the translucence of eternity.' (*TCD*, p.285) These novels contain the stirrings of Stuart's fascination with failure and martyrdom; the conclusion they reach is that the spiritual element can only survive in complete isolation and denial of the self. Yet again Stuart is drawing upon his study of the mystics about whom he wrote in his pamphlet for the Catholic Truth Society.

> And it is in this process of dying, of being crucified... that the suffering of saints and mystics consists; and it is only in proportion to the stage to which this death to self has been pushed that the new mystical life is given to the soul. (*MM*, p.23)

The spiritual moment has moved away from the prerogative of the church to a solitary redemptive process in which the denial of the self leads to a transcendent insight. However, in his next novel, *Try the Sky*, Stuart again grapples with the relationship between worldly and spiritual matters and comes to a different conclusion.

This novel divides the text into two distinct parts, the first 'The Abyss', deals with earthly aspects, and the second 'The Flight' with the search for transcendent experience. In the first part the worldly element is personified by a native American girl called Buttercup, who models plaster casts of an archetypal river. Like the pigeon of the same name in *Pigeon Irish*, Buttercup has a primitive, instinctual quality.

> It was as though the earth as a gesture in the face of our advancing civilization had become incarnate and articulate. A dark, mindless, brooding god, older than all the gods, and she was his prophetess to a world in revolt. (*TTS*, p.98)

By being linked with the earth, Buttercup is representative of the physical world with its natural cycle of life and death; of energy and decay.

> She had something of the secure permanency of the elements in her blood, of the water and skies... The dark laughter of the earth was on her side. She had risen out of it like a wave curling scornfully over a wreck, and she would sink, without a sigh, back into it again. (*TTS*, p.107)

In contrast to this mortality, religion is depicted as an eternal, sustaining force, especially for the male protagonist, Jose.

> In the end there is no reality on earth but that: I whispered to myself, looking at the cross! Only suffering and pity. Only defeat and humility. It was the only protection against the dark, impassive earth, with its ally, Time. (*TTS*, p.106)

Despite recognising this Jose believes the church is a barrier to the love he feels for Carlotta, since he already has a wife and child in Ireland.

> The Church doesn't understand lovers. It only bothers about 'marital fidelity' and 'ties of family'. With it everything becomes a duty and a means to an end. The white flame is stifled. The Church is no refuge for the passionate, lyrical thing that love is. (*TTS*, p.107)

Sweeping aside these objections the couple consummate their relationship and Stuart, by describing this in mystical terms, gives their union all the intensity of religious fervour thereby achieving that much sought after blend of the physical and the spiritual.

> Those days had been lit for me by that distant and desired shadow trembling, as it were, on the horizon. Then suddenly, in a moment, that far place had been reached, and at first neither the mystery nor the lyrical romance had suffered by possession. On the contrary, they had been fanned into a joyous flame in the heart. Mystery and possession and tenderness and secrecy had all blended into one joy. (*TTS*, p.133)

Despite achieving this intuitive insight Jose continues to yearn for an experience which he senses lies beyond the human realm.

> As when a wind rushes into the room and scatters the ashes and leaves uncovered a spark glowing, clean and naked. Oh, yes, yes, there was the hidden foundation of all the highest flights of man. A little beating heart that nurtured the greatest exaltation of the spirit. (*TTS*, p.168)

Jose's search, therefore, is to find a way of reconciling the romantic love which he experiences with Carlotta, with his belief in a purer religious love. '… the cross was a sort of defeat, a sort of negation of that lyrical beauty of human love. Through it one overcame the body, but then what was left of that romantic love?' (*TTS*, p.106)

The second part of the novel records Jose's attempt to resolve this paradox which is played out as a conflict between his idealism and Buttercup's contention that love is inextricably linked to the physical body. 'Love is a mood of the body, like the seasons are moods of the earth. No, No, you can't soar above the earth like you try to. If you try that, you will be broken by it in the end.' (*TTS*, p.143) Jose rejects such empiricism and continues to insist on the Platonic view that physical love is only a pale reflection of something greater.

> ... the body was powerless to create anything but a fleeting, illusory union and ecstasy. But out of that, as from a fiery, golden seed, a flower burst forth and blossomed, a sun-flower turning its rapt face slowly from east to south and from south to west in a wild aspiration. (*TTS*, p.275)

The group, Jose, Buttercup and Carlotta, agree to undertake a hazardous flight to Canada in an airplane named *The Spirit* in a symbolic enactment of Jose's desire to escape earthly confines. 'You see the culmination of the aspirations of our white civilization before you. The flight of love in the face of the earth.' (*TTS*, p.269) The flight of *The Spirit* becomes synonymous with Jose's spiritual journey as he abandons himself to an unknown, higher authority. 'We were trusting ourselves to something mysterious and powerful, of which we knew nothing.' (*TTS*, p.242) As the plane takes off from Munich it would appear that all of Jose's hopes and dreams are about to reach a climactic solution in a quasi-mystical experience. 'So this was the end of all that longing, of all that secret and almost holy aspiration, all those sweet promises! So this was 'the golden clime'. (*TTS*, p.281) All expectations are dashed though when the plane makes a rather undignified dive into an Irish bog and Jose is left convinced that he has 'been indulging in the most extravagant and preposterous of dreams'. (*TTS*, p.278)

> I might have know it if I had not been such a romantic fool. Ready to listen to every bit of high-flown nonsense I came across. There were only two ends to all that, the ludicrous or the tragic. Usually both. (*TTS*, p.286)

Despite this apparent failure Jose does go on to achieve what he was seeking, not as he had anticipated – soaring high above the earth, but as he lies on a wet road trying to fix the car which is taking them to Dublin.

> I lay very still under the car looking at her feet. Something was going on

inside me, deep and disturbing. As though the atmosphere of my country, austere and unearthly, behind its mask of gloom and dilapidation, was taking possession of me. Suddenly tears and oil mingled on my cheeks. (*TTS*, p.286)

The new beginning, which is indicated by the baptismal anointing with oil and water, is one in which Jose at last realises that the spiritual love he craves does not demand a rarefied atmosphere in which to reveal itself, since it is already present within himself and manifests itself in his love for Carlotta and for his country. 'O Ireland! Oh Carlotta! O Love! I thought passionately. What little, little faith I have. Oh yes, It is true, it is true, this is heaven. You are my heaven, you three together!' (*TTS*, p.286)

Although the means of expression here is overly melodramatic, the novel marks the beginning a turning point for Stuart, and one which *Glory*, written very shortly after *Try the Sky*, reinforces. Stuart's two aeroplane novels put an end his quest to define a pure, transcendental experience, in favour of uncovering the spirituality which underlies everyday existence. Writing in his diary in war-time Berlin Stuart firmly notes his conviction that the writer must remain rooted in the world.

> I have come by a long path. By many various ways, St. Thérèse, Lawrence, Blake, Keats, but it is all one way. The mystics reveal God in themselves and in Heaven, the poets in the world. The poet must remain in the world.[8]

This change of perspective also brought with it a change in style as Stuart moves from attempting to describe the mystery of religious experience in a realist narrative mode and instead he begins to use literary devices such as myth and metaphor to force his readers to go beyond literal interpretation. By employing this indirect approach he opens up new levels of understanding thereby drawing on the example of the scriptures.

> Jesus spoke in parables because the truth can only be indirectly revealed. They were the drama in which He showed it. For the truth is very difficult to receive. The chasm between knowledge of the world and the sensation of truth is deep. (*TASS*, p.33)

As theologians such as Rudolph Bultmann[9] and Paul Tillich[10] have recognised, symbols play a large part in religious and literary language.

Bultmann feels that the language of the New Testament is 'a mythological objectification of the experience of faith'[11] while Tillich is of the opinion that 'all arts create symbols for a level of reality which cannot be reached in any other way'.[12]

> A picture and a poem reveal elements of reality which cannot be approached scientifically… A great play gives us not only a new vision of the human scene, but it opens up hidden depths of our own being.[13]

Tillich considers that myths and symbols function by rising from the unconscious and participating in the reality they represent, at the same time remaining indeterminate since ultimate reality cannot be represented in finite terms. Myths cannot be replaced by scientific substitutes, but must be 'broken' or interpreted. The language of 'Being' in both Bultmann and Tillich has its source in the philosophy of Heidegger, as indeed does Stuart's contention that the poet reveals God in the world. Heidegger emphasises the role language plays in the process of interpreting reality and argues that the tired logical forms of Western thought separates 'Being' from thought and prevents what he calls, 'authentic existence'.

For Heidegger, everyday language is 'a forgotten and used-up poem from which there hardly resounds a call any longer'.[14] However, literature, especially poetry, in his opinion, can resurrect language and enable man to live authentically, since 'the poet names the holy'.[15] By using the poetic devices of myth and metaphor in his writing as a means of revealing the holy, Stuart is negotiating language in the way that Heidegger recommends, but more significantly, he is following the example of the Gospels, which recent theological studies such as that of Terence Wright claim, with a rather Anglophile bias, as 'the greatest literary achievement in the English language'.[16] Myths and metaphors demand a literary response from the reader and in this way reader, author, text and myth are drawn together in the act of interpretation.

> The Bible demands a response which alters our whole mode of being in the world. It provides an answer to the meaning of history but one which is couched in the form of myths, stories, chronicle, poetry, sermon and prophecy, a variety of literary forms which require literary interpretation.[17]

In the years following the publication of *Glory*, Stuart published two further novels; *In Search for Love*, a hastily written satire of the film industry, and *The Angel of Pity*, a philosophical exploration of the aftermath of a future war. However, his use of mythic symbol as a means of indirectly revealing the truth is most successfully achieved in *The White Hare*.

The mythic symbol adopted in the novel, that of the white hare of the title, is linked to the main character, Dominic de Lacey, a young boy who lives with his brother, Patrick, in a run-down estate, Rosaril, on the west coast of Ireland. 'The White Hare! To him it was "the" not "a" because it had become for him an almost mythical animal. A symbol in his imagination of his own destiny.' (*TWH*, p.149) Less obviously, the hare is also linked with Hylla, the young girl who comes to the house and whose mannerisms reveal distinctly leporine characteristics. 'The quieter you are, when you sit with your back straight and your hands like they are now and say almost nothing you are startling.' (*TWH*, p.89)

The strange and unconventional 'wildness' of the main characters of the novel is emphasised by the fact that although Hylla agrees to marry his older brother Patrick, her relationship with Dominic has an underlying brooding passion which at times bursts through. 'You're my bride too. You're more my bride than anyone else's, Hylla.' (*TWH*, p.129) As the marriage is envisaged as the encapsulation of an untamed spirit, the white hare also stands as a symbol for all that is wild, instinctive and spiritual. It is hardly surprising, therefore, that on Hylla's wedding day the hare is hunted down and killed by Dominic's dog.

> … the white hare sped on through the gap with the speed of the little bright shadow of reflected light that he had sometimes drawn swiftly across a wall or ceiling with a small mirror. Just through the gap the hare turned again, but this time the Princess was only a yard or two behind, and came round so quickly that the yard or two was covered and the jaws snapped on the white shadow, and it was still. (*TWH*, p.129)

The destruction of the hare heralds the fate of the major characters as they move to Dublin in search of work. Dulled by the routine of mundane employment, and deprived of the spiritual strength gained from living at Rosaril, Patrick becomes little more than an empty shell.

> He never consciously delighted in the life there as Dominic did, but he moved in it and drew it in as a fish water, and, no more than the fish, ever

> dreamed about becoming lyrical over it. And here all the time he was drawing on those reserves that he had found there... He drew on them to keep himself at the office, working away at tasks which he did not like, without any ambition... beyond making himself stick to it. (*TWH*, p.245)

And as Dominic grows older, the bond which exists between the three characters is increasingly frowned upon. Eventually Dominic tears himself away from Dublin and returns to the wildness of Rosaril before embarking on a life at sea. While at Rosaril he unearths the whitened skull of the hare and when later he drowns as his boat sinks during a violent storm, there is the suggestion of a final spiritual union with Hylla. 'He had gathered his treasure. And when he whispered her name over and over it was not in anguish or despair, but with an inflection of surprise at the miracle that had made her his bride.' (*TWH*, p.312) By the end of the novel, Hylla, all life and spirit drawn from her, comes to resemble the dry white bones of the hare's skeleton.

> Her pale, thin face had now more than ever the stark beauty of a thing that has been stripped of all inessentials and is left bare. Her grey eyes appeared to grow a shade darker as though the wild light that had shone in them... had receded farther into her like a lamp that is carried into an adjoining room. (*TWH*, p.313)

The symbolic use of 'the white hare' therefore introduces the Christian sub-text of redemption through sacrifice on several levels. Symbols, as Paul Ricoeur maintains, take root in physical objects but are 'firmly bound to the cosmos'.[18] The 'white hare' moves beyond the depiction of the physical animal and the link with Dominic and Hylla to suggest something beyond expression, and in doing so, enacts what Terence Wright sees as the prime function of the symbol.

> There is always an element of mystery surrounding a symbol, an opacity, a surplus of meaning, an enigma which no interpretation should attempt to eradicate. The deeper meaning to which the symbol points remains inexhaustible and ultimately inexpressible.[19]

The symbol works, he suggests, by compelling the reader to move beyond the literal to unlock elements at the deepest level of the subconscious.[20] In order to achieve this effect the symbol must take root in the psyche, whether as a Jungian archetype[21] or the psychic residue of a culture which, Wright suggests, 'continues to swarm with half-forgotten myths, decaying hierophanies and secularised symbols'.[22] The tendency of the symbol to compel the reader to move beyond the literal to the 'self-realization of an essential truth', in effect echoes the outcome of the novel which extends beyond earthly loss, with Dominic's death and Hylla's drained persona, to the redemption of their spiritual union. This final union is reinforced by the intertextual connotations of the hare symbol which also unites both characters.

Unlike the more traditional symbols of the cross or the fish, the hare has no obvious Christian connotations, and indeed in the novel Stuart seems to suggest that he is at a loss to explain its frequent recurrence in his work or why it was part of his own private mythology. However, intertextual references give a clue as to the way in which it works. In a diary written between June 1943 and May 1944 Stuart has sketched a hare inside the cover and later acknowledges his admiration of Blake, writing about him in his diary as a poet who writes 'great, mystical poetry' which 'peoples the void with... prophets and visionaries with a wider grasp of reality than mankind'.[23] It is not difficult to see how the hare in Blake's 'Auguries of Innocence'[24] with its link between the suffering of the hare and human suffering, gives an added dimension to the hare symbol in Stuart's work as it increases the sense of inevitability of suffering and death which permeates *The White Hare*. 'Each outcry of the haunted hare/A fibre from the brain doth tear.'[25] Inevitably too, the hare symbol provides a link with Yeats who used it to symbolise Stuart's wife, Iseult, in his poem 'The Death of the Hare'.

> Then suddenly my heart is wrung
> By her distracted air
> And I remember wildness lost
> And after, swept from there,
> Am set down standing in the wood
> At the death of the hare.[26]

More relevantly, for an understanding of the development of the religious theme in *The White Hare*, is the image of the skeleton of the hare which brings to mind a similar image in a poem by Yeats.

> I would find by the edge of that water
> The collar-bone of a hare
> Worn thin by the lapping of water,
> And pierce it through with a gimlet, and stare
> At the old bitter world where they marry in churches,
> And laugh over the untroubled water.[27]

Read in the light of this poem, 'the smooth white collar-bone' of the hare which Dominic finds, becomes symbolic of a natural religious sense which stands in opposition to the repressed morality of the orthodox church and it is this opposition which forms the basis of Stuart's post-war fiction.

In *Black List, Section H*, Stuart, through the character of H, retraces his religious development from his obsession with the mystical experience to a realisation that his interest did not lie in any orthodox forms of religion which seemed corrupt and constricting.

> Not that these reflections reconciled H to what he saw and heard of the functionings of the local church, and of the average priest with his stomachful of indigestible dogmatics and a half-starved mind, self-poisoned by the complementary toxins of love of authority and fear of its loss. (*BLSH*, p.140)

To H, this unthinking form of religion breeds a complacency in its followers which runs counter to a more natural and powerful force.

> It struck him that their central pulses, whose vibrancy determines the depth of men's responses, had a mechanical tick. Set to a parochial clock, they went tick-tock, piously recording the do's and don'ts for each day of the week, while around the cosmos the lingering echo of the original upheaval was merging with the first rumbling of the final bang. (*BLSH*, p.146)

The religious experience for H, is far removed from righteous moralising, instead it involves an intensity of consciousness brought about by extreme conditions, the prime example of which he feels were those endured by Christ at the crucifixion.

> The psychology of the hours on the cross he recognised as belonging to the deepest experience. This was a familiar nightmare, the longing of exposed tormented beings, stripped of their protective aura, for the coming of

darkness. How often, for no conscious reason, had he experienced the shadow of terror in the part of him – the neurones and chromosomes? – he shares with the brute creation? He grasped instinctively the trapped beast's hope for some slight respite when darkness falls. (*BLSH*, p.139)

Stuart links this image of Christ as an abandoned victim whose suffering is inexplicable with a disruptive power which throws into question the fixed certainties of civilisation. As we have already noted, in the early works the disturbance caused by suffering leads inevitably to a condition of openness to the Holy; however, in the post-war novels there is no guarantee of any redemptive vision.

> Although he was still far from coming to understand the necessity for what had happened to them, he did begin to see the silence that he had entered as the deep divide between the past and what was still to come. Whatever it was that was at the other end there was no way of telling. It might be a howl of final despair or the profound silence might be broken by certain words that he didn't yet know how to listen for. (*BLSH*, p.139)

In the three novels written in the immediate aftermath of the war, *The Pillar of Cloud*, *Redemption* and *The Flowering Cross*, Stuart explores the dynamics which occur among small groups of people who have been bonded together by shared suffering and the experience of hearing the 'howling voices of the dark.' (*R*, p.224) In *The Pillar of Cloud*, for instance, Dominic Malone is an Irishman who, like Stuart, ends up in the French-occupied zone of Germany immediately after the war. Malone finds life meaningless until he befriends Polish refugee sisters Halka and Lisette who have just been released from a concentration camp but it is only after he has been imprisoned himself and released that he can understand their capacity to forgive those who had tortured them.

> While I was in the cellar... I saw how good life could be if only we understood the secret of real communion – not just physical contact or even friendship, but fraternity, and especially fraternity with a woman... (*TPOC*, p.76)

Bound together in this way the relationship between Malone and the sisters deepens and, although he loves Halka, he marries Lisette so that he can take her to Ireland to seek a cure for her severe tuberculosis. Their attempt to leave Germany fails and Lisette dies, but because of this Malone, re-united with Halka, begins to see the world in a different light.

> They had come through fire and were tempered… They had not sought to save themselves in the world, to save their lives, and life was being given to them. They felt it poured into them… from a measure full and running over. It was something that they could not speak about. They each, in their own way, felt this fullness of life in them… (*TPOC*, p.231)

Redemption in *The Pillar of Cloud*, and in the other post-war novels, comes from the sense of fraternity which arises from suffering, a view very much in keeping with the Christian message; but Stuart moves from the conventional interpretation by pointing out that such redemption would not dispel 'the power of darkness', nor would it promise 'peace on earth'. Instead redemption is the acceptance of desolation and suffering.

> … that would be the ultimate horror – if Christ had not suffered these things and foreseen them, then it would be the end. But He was the one prophet who did not promise peace on earth, but destruction and desolation… He did not preach revolution or any counter measures. He said… above all "Love one another as I have loved you". That is, through all these things, even through passion and death. And that is our fraternity, and the only true fraternity. (*TPOC*, p.131)

In Stuart's most recent works, however, redemption becomes a matter of chance, a case of mishearing, drug-induced hallucinations, psychoses, or hangovers, through which a glimpse of a possible order may occur. It becomes a state of consciousness, a disturbance of normal thought patterns which reflect the chaotic nature of existence. In setting out to recreate this disruption in his fiction, Stuart's work reveals a complex appropriation of the methodology of biblical myth, which in turn has the effect of bringing into his work many of the suppositions of contemporary literary theory.

Biblical scholarship has, in recent years, made use of literary criticism. Prior to this, the accepted position was that expressed by C.S. Lewis: the Bible could only be read as literature by 'a tour de force'[28] or as T.S. Eliot argued, by parasites who had long ceased to believe it to be true.[29] However, using the insights of New Criticism initially, biblical scholars began to submit the text to close criticism and to pay attention to its formal devices. In *Mimesis,* Erich Auerbach draws a comparison between biblical and classical narratives, arguing that the account of Peter's denial of Christ in Mark's Gospel could not have been written by a classical author since it offends the convention of separating comic and tragic styles. The Bible is, in his view, a revolutionary piece of writing which makes certain demands on the reader.

> Far from seeking, like Homer, merely to make us forget our reality for a few hours, it seeks to overcome our reality; we are to fit our life into its world, feel ourselves to be elements in its structure of universal history. [30]

Biblical narrative has also proved enticing to structuralist critics since, as Roland Barthes has pointed out, it provides so many examples of multiple meanings developed from an initial germ of narrative.[31]'Used as a sieve, a receptacle for catching codes, the biblical verse has an excellent size.'[32] In *The Great Code*[33] Northope Frye sees the Bible as a self-enclosed system in which language, myth, metaphor and typology work to form a meaningful whole, while, in *The Genesis of Secrecy*,[34] Frank Kermode argues that the writers of the Gospels turned to the Old Testament to augment and corroborate their narratives. 'So Matthew [writing about Judas] finds the thirty pieces of silver in Zechariah while Achitophel, hanging himself out of remorse, provides the model for that grim episode.'[35]

This process of subsuming earlier narratives is also present is Stuart's work, where the repetition of the myth of loss and redemption echoes the biblical narratives of Noah's ark; the Prodigal son; the death of Lazarus; and above all the death and resurrection of Christ. It is the ability of literature to secularise the biblical myths in this way which Kermode feels provides proof that 'myths are the agents of stability' in that they satisfy a need for unanimity. 'We achieve our secular concords of past and present and future without falsifying our own moment of crisis. We need, and provide, fictions of concord.'[36] Structural critics would therefore see Stuart's reworking of biblical myths as an example of intertextual continuity, a redemption of the myth of redemption, in which the open nature of myth itself provides its own authenticity. 'A myth is designed not to describe a specific situation but to contain it in a way that does not restrict its significance to that one situation. Its truth is inside its structure, not outside.'[37]

However, Stuart's use of biblical myth is not merely a continuum of myth since, for him, such myths deteriorate and lose their powerful significance when they enter the public realm. For this reason, in his later novels, he attempts to revitalise the myth by emulating the capacity of the biblical narrative to disrupt and reformulate the reader's expectations.

> The priest was commemorating a calamity. The obscurity in which it had taken place was part of its pain. The victim had been defenceless and almost friendless. Now, through centuries of over-exposure, the tragedy had been formalised and diluted. And I saw that it could only haunt me again, as it had once, by association with the utterly obscure and unpublishable, one known to nobody but you and me. (*M*, p.20)

Such an endeavour inevitably leads Stuart firmly down the postmodernist path, away from many of the assumptions of structuralism which insists that reading is a rule-governed process in which a message encoded by the sender is decoded by the receiver. In the literary text, then, the words are signifiers for which the reader supplies the signified.[38] Stuart's work in this period has more in common with the deconstructionist who sees the 'message' as full of potential accidents, contradictions and inconsistencies, and the pleasure of the reading being derived from the play of signifiers. Yet again recent biblical scholarship highlights the way in which Stuart is keying into the example set by the Bible itself.

Herbert Schnedau claims that biblical narrative deliberately undermines those comforting mediating myths which transform our fears and desires into 'mental patterns that can be dealt with'.[39] John Dominic Crossan, in his exploration of parables, sees them as fundamentally disorientating. The premise that a Samaritan could be a good neighbour was, for example, a reversal of the reader's expectations. 'Parables give God room by shattering the deep structure of our accepted world, removing our defences and so opening us to the transcendent.'[40] Crossan emphasises the subversive nature of the Gospels and presents a portrait of a Derridean Jesus puzzling those around him with self-reflective parables and shocking them out of their habitual modes of thought.[41] It is this strategy which Stuart utilises to the full in novels such as *Memorial*. Returning to the myth of the hare in *Memorial*, Stuart links the suffering of the hare and the suffering of Christ in such a direct manner that, in certain quarters, it could be deemed to be blasphemous.

It started with the tender nativity. It was the leveret sucking from the dropper and covering its muzzle with its paws when – as you explained it – I had had enough. As the priest held wide his arms with the palms inward and slightly apart it was a frail new creature that he was displaying to my rapt gaze. A small, nose-twitching, speckled Babe needing sleep and warmth. (*M*, p.21)

The identification of the hare with Christ is also apparent through the character of Herra whose wrists swell and redden like stigmata when she becomes preoccupied with the suffering of the creature. However, this saintly characteristic is quickly undermined by the character's uninhibited sexuality.

The dark, secret, semi-shameful sexuality of my youth for you didn't exist. You saw it partly as a game of skill you wanted to shine at, as a respite from the fears that beset you at most other times... but not as sacred to two people, not as a marriage bond which was the old shutting out and shutting in in another form. You, who were born so serious, didn't take sex very seriously... (*M*, p.95)

Such seemingly irreconcilable traits work in the same way as Crossan's biblical parables, in that they disrupt the reader's normal mode of perception and conventional expectations, and open the way for a wider range of experience. By making the character of Herra combine the innocence of youth, the intuition of the visionary, the compassion of the saint, the provocativeness of the coquette and the wantonness of the whore, Stuart demands that the reader questions the assumptions of everyday morality. 'It was a universe away from the world of the pornographers. Your fantasies, neurotic ones by general (that's to say, corrupt) standards, created their own ethic.' (*M*, p.63) Within such an open framework even the rape of Herra by the narrator, Fintan Sugrue, becomes an instrument of spiritual redemption and ultimately a natural act.

I won't say I dropped on my knees before you... I got awkwardly down on them, touched the hem of the garment that my misery had made holy and said; 'Please, please, for the true love of Christ, forgive me!'. You bent and touched the top of my bowed head with your mouth and... a warm tear percolated to my scalp... I made you feel like a small, harassed, hunted

103

animal.' 'Oh,no,no! Just a little bitch that scratches and bites when she doesn't happen to feel like it. (*M*, p.136)

As stated previously, this combination of religious sacrament and abandoned sexuality is a manoeuvre which Stuart continually employs in his later novels, time and time again lulling the reader into accepting situations and experiences which lie outside the boundaries of conventional morality. In *The High Consistory*, for example, his writing skill endows the relationship between the female character and an ocelot, not only with an air of normality, but with an enviable passion. Stuart achieves this by contrasting the impotency of the sexual relationship of the human characters which is described in a faltering, hesitant tone, with a powerfully potent image of the animal.

> Not that there weren't other times when I just shivered and waited for him to spring. One night I was sitting in bed reading a book about Amazonian wild life and he was prowling round the room in a figure of eight. The bed was at the junction of the two circles, and suddenly, instead of swaying round it as he'd been doing, he tilted over like a speedway bike and suddenly sprang. (*THC*, p.77)

Almost imperceptibly Stuart entices the reader beyond the limits of restrictive ethical codes to a more open form of morality by ensuring that the reader agrees with the charge levelled against the male character.

> You're just a miserable Irish Catholic with a veneer of the great, imaginative artist! One of those who remake the untamed world into the image of the mediocrity in their hearts, diminishing the wild wonder to a mean morality! Incapable of true, self-forgetting passion, there's no compassion possible. (*THC*, p.163)

This deconstructive strategy is further reinforced by the many other metanarrative devices such as self-reflectivity, disruption of chronology, and authorial intrusion laying bare the narrative process,[42] all of which Stuart uses in his later works. The result is that these novels are writerly texts whose plurality and openness demand an active reading and it is this hermeneutic act which gives a significance to their religious dimension.

In his tribute to Francis Stuart on the occasion of his ninetieth birthday,[43] Fintan O'Toole highlighted the bitter honesty of his work. 'In spite of his mysticism, he refuses a mystique. And in spite of his attachment to a heroic spiritual quest, he refuses in his novels to pretend that he has found anything tangible.'[44] Certainly an initial reading would tend to confirm this judgement since the theme of failure runs through many of his novels, with high expectations being constantly dashed, and hoped-for revelations failing to materialise. Even the New Testament story is re-worked in this light.

> Read the account as related by the evangelists and you'll see that failure dogged Jesus in his journeys through Palestine, ending in the fiasco of the final period when his disciples came back from the mission he had sent them on to report nothing but rejection or indifference. (*F*, p.80)

In *Faillandia*, the attempt to enlighten a society corrupted by politics and the church through the publication of a radical magazine seems to end in total failure, without the comfort of any final redemption.

> Gideon remembered Frere Emanuel's comments on the passage in the Dutch theologian's treatise in which he argued that apparent failure was a part of all great endeavours if they were ultimately to bear fruit. He found it difficult to accept such a metaphysical attitude. It was all very well for Pieta to say: 'It isn't our lives.' But, faced with its loss, he saw how much of his life it had been. (*F*, p.80)

This failure could be taken as a metaphor for Stuart's own work which has also failed to gain wide public acclaim. However such a reading does not take into account Stuart's use of the parable form. *Faillandia* ends with Luke's account of Jesus's appearance at Emmaus in which his followers fail to recognise him.

> And they said to Him, 'Concerning Jesus of Nazareth, who was a prophet mighty in deed and word before God and all the people, and how our chief priests and rulers delivered him up to be condemned to death, and crucified him. But we had hoped that he was the one to redeem Israel.'[45]

This prime example of high expectation and ultimate failure is not overtly corrected in *Faillandia*, Stuart foreshortening Luke's text and opting instead for a more enigmatic ending. 'He appeared to be going further, but they constrained him, saying, "Stay with us, for it is toward evening and the day is now far spent." ' (*F*, p.352)

Stuart's narrative, therefore, forces the reader to work harder than Luke's account which goes on to describe the way in which Jesus 'opened He their understanding',[46] by interpreting the events for them. The reader of Luke's Gospel is left in little doubt about the ultimate success of the endeavour, as it goes on to describe the Ascension and claims that the disciples were 'continually in the temple, praising and blessing God'.[47] Stuart's refusal to entertain such an obvious, self-explanatory conclusion is not, as might at first seem, merely an attempt to reinforce his theme of failure, but is, rather, an example of the strategy which lifts his work from being 'about' religion, to being a form of narrative theology in itself.

This aspect of the work is best understood through a comparison with Mark's Gospel which also struggles with two opposing discourses, a realistic presentation of Jesus as a revolutionary human being who associates with outcasts in order to subvert the dominant class structures of his time; and a 'mythological code' which is responsible for such miraculous scenes as the transfiguration. It is the ending, however, which presents the greatest difficulty for readers since, like *Faillandia*, it comes to an anticlimactic close.' And they went out and fled from the tomb; for trembling and astonishment had come upon them; and they said nothing to any one, for they were afraid.'[48] This as Kermode argues, is either 'intolerably clumsy or incredibly subtle'[49] far too subtle for the second-century Church which added an appendix enumerating further resurrection appearances and took the story up to the ascension. In *Theology and Literature*, T.R. Wright claims that to give full weight to the final verse as it stands, to accept that the women failed to pass on the message and that the disciples' misconceptions were never corrected, is unthinkable since it upsets all the reader's expectations.

> It would make the narrator 'a very nasty ironist' who has allowed all Jesus's predictions to be fulfilled but to no purpose, everything being put in jeopardy by the final verse. Even Hardy would hesitate before torturing his readers so cruelly.[50]

What happens of course, is that the ending is supplied by the reader who is therefore forced by Mark's text into the same role as the disciples, that of struggling to make sense of the indeterminacy of the ending.

So Mark's Gospel can be called a self-consuming artefact, a story which encourages its readers, especially at the abrupt ending, to break out of the story world, to return themselves to Galilee, the place where the kingdom was first preached and where the *parousia* is expected, to follow for themselves the difficult road of discipleship.[51]

In other words, the reader's experience is an integral part of the meaning of the text, since the fact that the reader is reading about the events at the tomb is itself evidence that the story was retold. This link between past and present can therefore be read as the proof of the truth of Jesus's prediction that 'my words will not pass away',[52] yet again drawing the reader into a direct confrontation with the Gospel narrative. It is this 'awakening' to the significance of the part played by the individual reader in the wider Gospel narrative which is a component element of narrative theology.

> Revelation becomes redemptive when it is appropriated at the level of personal identity and existence, when the story of God's action in history intersects with the stories which comprise the identities of individuals and communities.[53]

This interlocking of stories is also present in Stuart's work and gives it its ultimate significance. Taking, first of all, the passage from Luke's Gospel which Pieta reads to the disillusioned Gideon, Stuart's distortion of the traditional narrative of resolution forces the reader to seek a more satisfying conclusion. Since *Faillandia* repeatedly questions the way in which the established church has interpreted the Gospel story, the reader cannot easily slip into overruling the negativity of the passage by superimposing the image of Jesus as 'the Universal Saviour proclaimed by the Churches'.[54] Instead the novel itself provides the key to a more optimistic interpretation. 'Failure, fiasco, deteriorations of the brightest hopes, erosion of the deepest faith: these are the signs that we are truly within the shadow of the Kingdom of God.' (*F*, p.80) An article on the 'Underground Jesus' published in the magazine which forms the subject matter of the novel gives a clear indication of the way in which this can be achieved.

> There is no place in our Church for the outcast figure of the Gospels, often weary and dispirited, growing more aware of his failure. What he was seeking was a sign, the simplest one of all, the sign of pure, disinterested

love from another being. A drink of water was enough, a place where he
could lay his head. (*F*, p.195)

Read in this light the simple act of compassion which ends *Faillandia*
becomes a sign of the success of the mission, a sign that, although
unrecognised and hidden, the spirit of Jesus remained with his followers.
This commonplace, demystified evocation of the Doctrine of Incarnation
is central to the view of Jesus advocated in the novel.

> Meanwhile this Person dwells among us, as He promised he would, still
> seeking the disinterested, spontaneous response of love without which he
> cannot establish the Kingdom of God… If sometimes He seems to perform
> miracles on behalf of those who believe in Him, He admonishes them, just
> as long ago, not to spread the news abroad, thus making it more difficult
> for Him to find men and women attracted to Him, not by his magical
> powers, but by words and sayings that were the very opposite of the ones
> that were beamed at them from every organ of authority. (*F*, p.195)

By providing an illustration of the novel's vision of Christ as a private and
personal divine phantom, indwelling and hidden, the conclusion is proof
of the possibility of a hidden truth.

The next step for the reader is to transpose this revelation on to the novel
as a whole and find a means of overcoming the sense of failure which
permeates the concluding chapters. The difficulty of providing a true
counter-current to popular opinion is shown by the fate of the magazine
whose popularity is manipulated and then suppressed by the various
political groups and the attempt to continue publication on an off-shore
island is finally revealed to be possible only by compromising the
magazine's independence.

> … we don't live, you and I, in the kind of place that can be protected by
> treaties and charters or by us finding sympathetic allies to have them
> observed. (*F*, p.196)

This fate is a demonstration of the pitfalls which face writers like Stuart
who wish to question and disturb the common assumptions of their
readers. In an article in *Irish Times* in 1972 Stuart described himself as 'a
writer of dissent', a claim which he later clarified in an interview with J.H.
Natterstad.

... the dissident writer, from the very nature of his own attitude, will go counter to the assumptions of many of his readers... He will be very far from being a spokesman for his society in any sense... he will not be honoured by them. He will not receive any wide acclaim from society as such.[55]

In *Faillandia* the sense of failure stems from the fact that the magazine fails to produce a dramatic change in public opinion. Like the disciples who, having expected an all-conquering Saviour, cannot recognise the quiet revolution that was taking place within them;[56] Gideon, the Editor, equates success with public recognition. However, the 'message' the reader gains from the final passage is that redemption is a matter of personal transformation rather than an acknowledged revolution in public opinion.

> The religion offered by Jesus in the Gospels is evidently one for individuals and not for collective or institutional man. His more intimate sayings, loving and prophetic, are either addressed to a single person or his dozen disciples. (*TASS*, p.60)

So although the magazine fails to produce any radical social change, it does, as Pieta recognises, inspire some readers, 'though not nearly all those who were reading it at its peak of popularity'. (*F*, p.351) The measure of its success therefore does not lie in its continued wide distribution, but in its ability to 'awaken' the consciousness of the reader. The articles with their mixture of 'love, sex, death, books and even your horses' have an enlightening effect on the reader: '... they are transported in spite of themselves, into another way of thinking, or rather feeling, about the situation. They catch gleams of light in the darkness that they thought was impenetrable.' (*F*, p.351)

Despite the fact that the magazine fails to achieve any tangible change in society, it has brought about a more subtle, hidden revolution. In an article on the relationship between the writer and society, Stuart argues that 'a handful of poets and novelists is not going to bring down a whole complex edifice'[57] however he feels that a certain type of passionate writing can have a slower, more insidious effect. '... passion, particularly imaginative passion, is a slow, underground, eroding process, and it spreads from mind to mind and heart to heart, until one day... unforeseen events are suddenly inevitable.' The significance of a certain text may not be immediately apparent but Stuart believes that it enters the consciousness of the reader, like a seed which may, or may not,take root. 'A consciousness into which even a tiny seed has fallen leads, as in the parables, to intensification of awareness, one not just seeking reality, but which strays over many aspects of creation.' (*TASS*, p.47)

The suggestion is, therefore, that the experience of reading the magazine could at some stage reveal a truth that is already present, unrecognised and dormant, in its audience's consciousness, but since the text of the novel provides no evidence to substantiate this, the reader of *Faillandia*, like the reader of Mark's Gospel, must look inward to validate the claim.

By struggling to make sense of the ambiguous ending of the novel, the reader experiences a tension which can only be resolved by imaginatively merging the religious and political themes. While the themes of the novel seem to be entirely unconnected, there are underlying similarities in that it is thought that the solution to the corruption in both systems is to find 'another way of thinking' and that this could be achieved through experiencing the pain of failure.

> What you will come to understand – you've already been given inklings which you've tried to dismiss – is that in your case loss and failure is part of the story… They are the vital part of many of the world's greatest stories, from the Gospels, through fiction, to obscure and squalid personal ones. (*F*, p.299)

Also in both themes, change is brought about in an unexpected way, through inner transformation rather than public acclaim, and so, despite appearances, there is a careful structure to the novel. This network of correspondences within the narrative gives the reader an insight into Stuart's model of reality which he sees as an interconnecting web. In binding together these ideas in the consciousness, the reader's experience becomes an integral part of the interpretation, a further link in the network of correspondences which binds past, present and future. But if the text provides an incarnation of its own thesis, its very obscurity makes it difficult to recognise. Instead, the reader merely intuits what T.S. Eliot called, 'the hint half guessed, the gift half understood'.[58]

Faillandia, like all of Stuart's later work, deconstructively leads the reader beyond a myopic concern to a wider network of relationships. His novels, like Mark's Gospel, frustrate the normal reading process and refuse the comfort of a final solution, and so force the reader to experience at first hand the same sense of confusion and disorientation experienced by the disciples as they struggled to make sense of the events of the crucifixion. Stuart frustrates the normal reading process with his refusal to pander to the convention of creating the comforting consolation of an ultimate solution, and in doing so, as Fintan O'Toole rightly points out, he leaves himself open to misinterpretation.

> ... he refuses in his novels to pretend that he has found anything tangible. Were he prepared to fake it, to announce that all his mistakes and casual callousness had led to some great insight or reconciliation, he would have been loved and forgiven. A prodigal son.[59]

Although the contents of Stuart's novels certainly do not proclaim any resolution to his quest, as we have already seen, the combination of content and form provides a tangible example of his philosophy, and therefore it can be argued that the insight is shown rather than stated. However, the ability to share this vision depends solely on the receptiveness of the reader's consciousness since Stuart does not set out to actively indoctrinate his readers, and in this, the New Testament yet again provides a precedent.

> The way the New Testament goes about it is original and significant. There is no attempt to prove anything, but a seed is dropped into the consciousness that either quickly dries up or energises it. Not that the fertilisation is not accompanied by doubt, ambiguity and confusion. (*TASS*, p.52)

Stuart's work, in effect, recreates the Gospel narrative in a new and startling way, revitalising the story and forcing the reader to reflect on its significance. In this way a link is formed between the text of *Faillandia*, the New Testament and the reader, reinforcing the synthesis between the metaphysical and phenomenal worlds within consciousness, and providing continuing proof of the promises contained in the Gospels. *Faillandia* itself is a manifestation of the type of literature which the magazine sets out to encourage, and the response it engenders is therefore an emotional rather than a rational one.

> The roots of this literature are in the past and its shoots in the future. 'I am

111

> the Vine and you are the branches'. Here is one of those sentences that
> reverberates inside the nerve cells, by-passing the rational and intellectual
> filters. It is the language that the writer giving expression to new concepts
> has to use. (*F*, p.105)

The reader who responds to Stuart's work is not swayed by logical
argument or clever rhetoric; instead, as with the New Testament, the key
to understanding is intuitive and personal, an awareness within the
consciousness; and, as we have already seen, it is this ability to reach the
consciousness of another, rather than wide public acclaim, which is, for
Stuart, the measure of the success of his novels.

Stuart's later work is then 'religious' in the sense that it re-interprets the
story of Jesus using the style of the Gospel narratives which force the reader
to search for a resolution of the ambiguity of the text; so that, as with the
New Testament, 'meaning' comes from the reader's interaction with the
text. Religion permeates Stuart's novels as subject, form and consequence,
but primarily it acts as a paradigm for his fiction with the Gospels
providing a blueprint for his novels.

> Reasoning can't distinguish true from false except on fairly extraneous
> levels. Do you never feel inside you... a series of nerve cells, some sort of
> fine chain, linking you with reality? I think, if we haven't broken it, we're
> aware of something like consciousness, transforming the vibrations into
> what can just, at the last link, enter the mind as thought. What I'm getting
> at is that the Gospels, transmitted to us by this route, do have the impact
> of reality. (*F*, p.105)

Stuart's works, with their ever-widening intertextual links and extra-textual
connections between writer and reader, have an equally powerful effect, the
energy of which lies in their involvement of the personal.

5

The Significance of the Self

In a statement on the role of modern literature Francis Stuart sets out clearly the central motivation of his own work.

> I think fiction is now forced to do the one thing it can do supremely well, better than science and better than any of the other art forms: to delve deeper into the self, into the human system, and also to develop that outwardly. There are these two prongs of exploration, one is science – astrophysics – which is recording extraordinarily exciting discoveries of cosmic reality, and fiction, which is burrowing deeper to find what are also exciting phenomena.[1]

A literature which delves deeply into the self must, by its very nature, be autobiographical and, as we have already seen, from the outset Stuart's work has drawn on the facts of his own life. However, his work is not autobiographical in the narrow sense of mere self-portraiture; rather there is a dual orientation, inwards and outwards. Just as Yeats hoped to reveal 'all life weighed in the scales of my own life'[2] so, too, Stuart's concern with the self is not narcissistic but an attempt to highlight the complex patterning which he perceives to lie at the heart of all existence, and it is the honesty with which this task is undertaken which gives its work its unique integrity.

In the pre-war work the autobiographical influence is clearly evident, in that, for the most part, the novels are an articulation of Stuart's philosophy and a reflection of his interests. *Women and God* draws on Stuart's experience as a stretcher-bearer in Lourdes and his obsession at the time with mystical experience.[3] The novel is set on a farm just like the one in which Stuart and Iseult lived and the unsatisfactory relationship it explores is a thinly disguised reflection of the state of their own marriage. As Yeats's commentary on shows, it too is a vehicle for Stuart's personal interests and opinions.[4]

> ... what a lot this fanatical student of St. John of the Cross knows about chicken farms, carrier pigeons, parabellums, aeroplanes, Irish military, the Curragh races, and where did a man with a style so literary learn the points of a horse? (*TCD,* cover)

However, although these early novels draw freely an aspects of Stuart's life, more importantly, they are an attempt to explore his intuitive longing for a certain type of experience.

> I always, I suppose, subconsciously had a feeling that all I could do at that time was to make certain sketches, to imagine what I didn't know much about, to relate experiences that I hadn't yet been through... therefore, those early novels could be called sketches for what became more realistic or more complex later novels. And in another way they were, although I equally didn't know it at the time, a kind of aspiration for, almost longing towards, experiences that I hadn't yet had.[5]

By being a conscious articulation of Stuart's subconscious drives the early novels played an active part in the way his life developed, since they brought to the fore and reinforced the need for a certain type of experience. From the start of his writing career then, Stuart's fiction reveals a concern with the inner self of the author, and in this he is following the example of the type of writing which so obsessed him at the time, that of mystics.

As we have previously noted, in the latter part of the 1920s Stuart spent a great deal of time emulating the reclusive existence of the early mystics in the solitary confinement of a hut in the garden at Glencree, meditating on the accounts of the lives of saints such as St Catherine of Sienna and St Thérèse, and painstakingly copying and illuminating their manuscripts. It is hardly surprising, therefore, that the influence of such texts is evident in Stuart's work in its stress on subjectivity and personal experience. In her study of the writings of female mystics Ursula King notes that:

> ... unlike their male counterparts who tended to portray the mystical quest as the ascent of a mountain or a path towards a summit or goal, women were more likely to use images of inwardness such as the cave, the rooms of a mansion or a castle, to describe the mystical experience.[6]

Like the texts of the religious women he was studying, Stuart's writing reveals an underlying belief that spirituality is intrinsically a potential of human consciousness and that inner contemplation is the best means of achieving a fuller life. This dialectical relationship between inward transformation of self and outward change is also evident in the way in which the exploration of the psyche involved in the writing of the early novels preconditioned Stuart to seek out alienating experiences.

> ... I was inventing a great deal in my early novels. I had this very vague vision of events which might have a profound effect on the individual who went through them. Therefore, to actually experience what I had only envisaged was most valuable for the sort of writer I am.[7]

The writing which emerged out of Stuart's war experiences, *The Pillar of Cloud*, *Redemption* and *The Flowering Cross*, is autobiographical in a different way to the pre-war novels in that, rather than primarily reflecting his subconscious drives and desires, the facts of his life in Germany and his imprisonment are assimilated into the fictional storyline. The effect is to create a literary text in which the main characters gain an authenticity by being a thinly disguised portrayal of the author and those close to him, and in which the narrative is enriched by being set in the backdrop of his lived experience. This intermingling of fact and fiction gives the texts an intensity which Olivia Manning, in her review of *The Pillar of Cloud*, felt was due to its being 'written with a poetic force that comes out of the very core of suffering'.[8]

> Mr. Stuart writes with convincing certainty of the reactions of a starving man from whom a promised food parcel is withheld by the incompetence

of officials, the simple acceptance of a-morality, the spiritual triumph of these people who somehow surmount the desolation of their physical condition, the evolution of the Irishman who voluntarily chooses that condition.[9]

Certainly the poignancy and power is clearly evident in those passages which deal directly with painful events endured by Stuart, such as the depiction of the ordeal of those living in constant fear of bombing in *Redemption.*

> Shells are different from bombs. Shells are the first touch of the others, the sign of their presence; shells begin to strip away the familiar air and bring the first breath of the unknown darkness with them. (*R*, p.41)

In *The Pillar of Cloud* the description of life in the ruins of war-torn Berlin has all the force and familiarity of a lived experience.

> Because they had passed through the night of dungeons and prisons, of prison-cells in which time stagnated and air-raid shelters which trembled and filled with smoke and glowed with reflected fire, they could be together in this room, happy in a singular fraternity. (*TPOC*, p.231)

The Flowering Cross begins with an account of prison life in post-war France which draws heavily on incidents from Stuart's own imprisonment. Louis Clancy, wrongly accused of being a communist agitator, is imprisoned when, through the bars of his cell, he sees a young blind girl, Alyse, at exercise. This is an incident which Stuart relates again in his autobiographical novel, *Black List, Section, H.*

> For nights H was haunted by the apparition at the window. As he lay awake on the floor, everything seemed to indicate that it was Halka; one night he interpreted unaccustomed sounds overhead, where he thought the punishment cells were situated, as the result of her having been found by the warder on his nocturnal rounds, hanging from a window bar. In the mornings he was less sure that it had been her; no one had appeared at the window during exercise again. (*BLSH*, p.422)

In these post-war novels the autobiographical detail provides a starting block for an imaginative narrative which reflects Stuart's belief that through such anguish the writer attains a new perspective and significant spiritual growth. The problem with using his war experiences to illustrate his philosophy in this way is that it leads to a certain amount of repetitiveness, a failing which was noted by the reader employed by the prospective publisher Victor Gollancz.

> Stuart is not really a novelist at all, but a poet philosopher. He is incapable of approaching a novel as a piece of craftsmanship, to be undertaken for the pleasure of the craft (or to pay the rent): he must be conveying his vision.[10]

It is hardly surprising, therefore, that Stuart's continued use of this method of producing a fiction with an autobiographical base was to lead to a deterioration in his work, as Olivia Manning, in her review of *The Pillar of Cloud*, recognised, when she stated, 'I doubt if even Mr. Stuart could write another novel about these experiences... he has beggared them of emotion'.[11]

Despite this warning, Stuart's novels continued to be a variation on this theme, for although *Good Friday's Daughter*, *The Chariot* and *The Pilgrimage* are not specifically about the war, they convey the vision of his earlier post-war works. The main female character in *Good Friday's Daughter*, like Halka and Alyse in the earlier novels, has lived through the 'eternal Good Friday of captivity' (*GFD*, p.126) and gained strength from the experience. *The Chariot* too, has an autobiographical link since the main character is an unsuccessful writer who struggles through social rejection and poverty to find that love and comfort arises from shared suffering. *The Pilgrimage* is again concerned with the quiet intensities of an unremarkable existence, which reflected the lifestyle of Stuart at the time, living in London working at various mundane jobs. Just as the drama of Stuart's wartime experiences was responsible for the dramatic intensity of novels such as *The Pillar of Cloud*, the mediocrity of his existence in London can be seen to be responsible for the lack of significance of these novels.

> He did not accept that his particular method of writing fiction which used incidents from his own life had its hazards. He had done nothing of the slightest interest in London, and without the framework of something significant to report, novels like *The Chariot* reflected this.[12]

Given this fact, it is understandable that Stuart should go back to his war experiences for inspiration.

Victors and Vanquished, though it returns to the war, is more directly autobiographical than any of its predecessors. Although the characters have fictional names they are easily identifiable as Stuart, Iseult, and Madeleine, but more importantly, rather than acting as a catalyst for the imagination, Stuart's own experiences and memories are closely followed in the narrative. The poet Luke Cassidy, following the break-up of his marriage, decides to leave Ireland where 'it seemed we were in for a long reign of mediocrity, banality, and dire cowardliness'(*VV*, p.43). He travels to Germany where he has spent some time as an English assistant and had met a young nurse, Myra Kaminski. In a world which seemed to be disintegrating around them, the Irishman and the young Jew lead a fugitive life. Even when the war comes to a close, the suspicion, fear and hunger do not cease and the couple wander among the ruins as displaced persons until Luke joins a refugee convoy and finally reaches Paris. Once there, his wife joins him and Luke tries to persuade her to shelter Myra in Ireland. When she refuses Luke goes back to Myra with whom he begins the kind of lifestyle first glimpsed amid countless sufferings and persecutions. The novel, therefore, retells Stuart's own story, and this concentration on the small personal story, rather than the wider political situation, is justified in the novel.

> It's not much to make a fuss about, the protection of one family, but do you know, I'm beginning to see that the supreme importance given to numbers is one of the fallacies that the war breeds like bacilli. For it's only out of love for one single, tangible person or family that there can come any genuine concern for the fate of millions. (*VV*, p.43)

As already explored in Chapter 1, the basis of Stuart's view of reality is a network of correspondences between the individual and the cosmos. Since the literary convention of endowing the personal story with a universal significance effectively illustrates this thesis, it is hardly surprising that Stuart's later work continues to use autobiography, but in a markedly different way.

With *Black List, Section H*, Stuart enters a new phase in his career by ceasing to use autobiographical facts as a starting point for his fiction, and instead turns to an exploration of the self, a movement which has the effect of highlighting the fictionality of autobiography. The nature of autobiography has come under the scrutiny of literary theorists in recent times, with an emphasis on the problems of differentiation between fact and fiction. Roy Pascal, for example, argues that the process of selection and interpretation involved in autobiography leads to a conflict between historical truth and narrative design which includes 'the unconscious polemics of memory'.[13] More recent studies informed by poststructural thinking find more difficulty in differentiating between fact and fiction, and end up claiming that autobiographical work is 'viable only when one recognises that it creates truth as much as expresses it'.[14] James Olney, too, makes the point that to construct a coherent narrative out of the scattered events of one's life, is to interpret those events as part of a significant plot with an overall meaning.

> It involves discovering not only a metaphor of the self, a focal point on which to build a sense of the subject's identity, but also a mythic statement of the world, the creation of a symbolic universe which enables the individual to understand and interpret, to articulate and organise to synthesise and universalise his human experience.[15]

Autobiography, therefore, becomes a good place to find literary constructs of the self since, as most critics now tend to agree, the 'subject' of an autobiography, the character created in the world of the narrative, is a literary fiction; an 'autograph', a written version or interpretation of the self constructed by gathering together or 'recollecting the disparate elements of experience'.[16] It is this reading of the genre of autobiography which forms the basis of Stuart's recent work.

Right from the opening paragraphs, *Black List, Section H* reminds the reader that autobiography is always a transformational or metaphorical act in which a version of the self, rather than the self per se, is being attempted. The narrative commences with a precise topographical description.

> His window looked onto a derelict mill half-hidden by a small wood above the three ponds, each on a slightly lower level. A last patch of vivid sunshine, coming in intense, isolated gleams in this northern country, caught the slope of grass close to where dusk was already gathering under the ruined wall, the wet ivy glinted against the black stone, and short, intense intervals of silence formed between the cawing of the rooks.
> (*BLSH*, p.1)

Stuart immediately undermines the realism of the piece by laying bare the creative process.

> He started scribbling, scrawling through the lines and substituting others, his nerves vibrating to a kind of rhythm. It was not another shy love note to one of his girl cousins that he was feverishly writing, but his first poem. (*BLSH*, p.1)

The fictitious nature of the text is further reinforced by transforming the opening scene into the self-evident literariness of the lyrical poem.

> The sun is dropped and shadows grow
> As swords for the world's overthrow
> And through the depths the lightning crawl
> Each like a wounded nightingale. (*BLSH*, p.1)

This foregrounding of the narrative process encourages the reader to adopt an interpretative approach, so that the topography of the opening paragraph is more likely to be seen as a metaphor for the creative consciousness. 'The window' looking on to a 'half-hidden' scene illuminated intermittently by 'intense, isolated gleams' of sunlight, brings to mind the way in which Stuart envisages the creative process being activated by sharp bursts of intense experience. The self-reflective nature of the text reinforces its fictionality and allows the reader to question the representation of the self offered by Stuart.

Since *Black List, Section H* begins with the character H (Stuart's full name is Henry Montgomery Francis Stuart) writing his first poem it places him firmly in the role of writer. As a writer, the character's imagination is sparked by events and experiences which seem to be endowed with a special significance, the first of such incidents effectively setting the central character apart from his family and society as a unique, sensitive consciousness.

> What was behind it was an instinct, far from conscious, to cut himself off from the world of his cousins once and for all. And the resolution to act on this impulse came indirectly, from a kind of faith in himself and his confused instincts that the news of the Russian Revolution that he'd heard during his last term at an English public school, had given him. (*BLSH*, p.2)

It is significant that in the novel the 'facts' of Stuart's childhood are glossed over with a few references to his 'English public school', his 'family name' and 'his uncle's estate'. As we have already seen, there was a conspiracy of silence in the family circle over Stuart's father's death and this incident is presented with due vagueness in *Black List, Section H*. Apart from this unhappy event, there is no shortage of available information about Stuart's family since his parents, Henry Irwin Stuart and Elizabeth Montgomery both came from well-known Ulster families, whose genealogy can be easily traced in Burke's Irish Family Records.[17] The lack of family background in the narrative can therefore be seen as an enactment of Stuart's instinct to 'cut himself off from the world of his cousins'. The selection between Pascal's 'historical fact' and 'narrative design' is clearly evident in this instance, once again ensuring that the reader recognises the fictionality of the portrait offered.

Black List, Section H is, then, a self-consciously imaginative enterprise which clearly demonstrates the relativity of autobiography. As David Wright acknowledges, in Yeats's *Myth of Self*, complete objectivity is impossible in autobiography since, given the limitations of memory, knowing retrospection radically alters past experience.

> Autobiographical writing seeks pattern. Where no structure spontaneously appears in a recalled life, structure may need to be imposed artificially. Thus the events of the past will be in turn heightened and reduced, juxtaposed for comparison, and reshaped turning points and moments of revelation often achieve in retrospect an intensity which they lacked while being experienced.[18]

Repeatedly in the novel, incidents from Stuart's life are heightened by the interpretative emphasis of the text. For example, continual interpolations give explanations of previous intuitive experiences.

> Long ago... he'd told Iseult that what the poet needed to keep him unspotted from the world was dishonour. It hadn't been a phrase he'd thought up. It had come out instinctively without premeditation. Now it was time to catch up and to come to a conscious grasp of his attitude. (*BLSH*, p.44)

This attempt to delve into the subconscious and draw out previously unrecognised conclusions gives the impression of self-analysis on Stuart's part but the self-conscious repetition of the underlying pattern of hope, dejection, despair and insight, which, as we have already seen, is the hallmark of Stuart's vision of reality, forces the reader to question whether or not this pattern is created in order to justify his actions. The novel continually reinforces Stuart's intuition that the writer must experience the despair of complete social rejection.

> He believed that nothing short of the near despair of being utterly cast off from society and its principles could create the inner condition conducive to the new insights that it was the task of the poet to reveal... If he survived the ordeal there would flow from the depths of his isolation fresh imaginative streams to melt the surrounding freeze-up. (*BLSH*, p.44)

Far from seeking approval in his novels, Stuart encourages the reader to adopt a judgmental stance as far as his actions are concerned, his apparent indifference to the death of his daughter being a case in point: 'While he'd been daydreaming of entering the isolation of truly imaginative spirits, more or less ignored by him in the room next door a fragile life was being destroyed.' (*BLSH*, p.45)

Any attempt to justify his actions would be seen by Stuart as a desire to seek the approval of a society from which he wishes to be isolated, since, like his characters, he is critical of 'any gathering mass or consensus of thought'.

> It's all the same whether it happens to be liberal or authoritarian, because they sense that even a liberal doctrine held in common tends to produce that sort of assured moral attitude which is fatal to them. (*BLSH*, p.45)

So rather than seeking forgiveness for his actions, Stuart emphasises the awareness with which he made certain decisions in his life, particularly his decision to remain in Germany during the war.

> This was a kind of malefactor whose rejection was seldom rescinded because the crime was not merely against an individual but that society as a whole. The deed was done. H's first reaction: relief at in the end it being so easy to take this step outside the moral Pale. (*BLSH*, p.45)

More controversially perhaps, Stuart links his own wartime suffering to that of the Jews, but even here he is knowingly offering the reader a clear invitation to judge him unsympathetically.

> ... he had to experience, in his own probably small degree, some of what they suffered, and, on one level, even more, because he could not claim their innocence. He also realized that he would go to certain lengths in association with their persecutors, in violent reaction against the mores of home, thus ensuring that his condemnation would not, unlike theirs, arouse any sympathy. (*BLSH*, p.45)

Quite firmly and deliberately then, Stuart places a question-mark over his head but it is a question-mark which many critics have been unable to see beyond.

In an article written for *A Festschrift for Francis Stuart on his Seventieth Birthday*, Tom MacIntyre captures well Stuart's need to seek disapproval: 'He lives, moves, and has his artistic being with his back to the wall; moreover, whenever he feels that condition slipping, he will instantly move to recreate it'.[19] Twenty years later, Fintan O'Toole, writing on the occasion of Stuart's ninetieth birthday, notes the same refusal to compromise, the same need to shock.

> It would be redundant and ill-judged to celebrate the survival to the age of 90 of a man whose life and work has been a long and largely successful courtship of ignominy, neglect and even disgrace. Whereas, 10 years ago, the sense that he would soon be a famous dead writer produced a rush of recognition... his persistence with life, and indeed with work, now holds sentimental tribute at bay. Only with the dead or almost dead do we forgive and forget. By remaining unforgivable, Francis Stuart remains very much alive.[20]

Up to his death Stuart continued to make himself 'unforgivable' in the eyes of 'conventional' society. The decision of the Arts Council of Ireland to elect Stuart to the position of saoi of Aosdána, the highest literary honour available in Ireland, was the subject of much controversy in the press. In the *Irish Times* Kevin Myers voiced, what was for many, the main objection to the honour, namely Stuart's wartime broadcasts in Berlin.

> To have volunteered to serve that enemy of civilisation and of art is not just a mistake on a par with life's other little blunders. It is a cosmic error from which no full escape is possible. That is the inevitable consequence of

aligning oneself with the greatest enemies humanity, and humanity's arts, have ever known, though the resulting experiences provided wonderful material for a writer as indisputably fine as Francis Stuart is.

He has told us that he went to Germany because he sought life on the fringe, on the very margins, in a land inhabited by martyrs and mystics. Fine. And untrue. He went to Germany not in the hour of Germany's defeat, but at the moment of victory, as Poland lay in ruins. More conquest, more subjugation followed, all of it commanded from Berlin, where he had made his home and from where he broadcast. He was at the centre of things.[21]

Writers such as Fintan O'Toole, Dermot Bolger and Eileen Battersby came to Stuart's defence, Battersby noting that 'Francis Stuart has often fulfilled the public role of icon of hatred; he makes his critics feel righteous'.[22] However, another furore erupted in October 1997 over a statement made by Stuart in a Channel 4 documentary, *A Great Hatred*, presented by Simon Sebag Montefiore. The programme dealt with anti-Semitism in Ireland, and during an interview Stuart stated 'The Jew is like the worm in the rose'. He was also quoted as stating, when asked about working for the Nazis, 'I regret nothing, nothing at all'. Predictably, Kevin Myers saw the programme as proof of Stuart's anti-Semitism.

> Why has this State honoured a man who served such a dark and bestial state? Is it some kind of perverse neutralism, a badge of pious separateness, that we can single out someone whom we know beyond any shadow of a doubt was a collaborator of the Nazis and turn that act into an artistic deed?[23]

Anthony Cronin protested that the editing of the programme was such that Stuart's line about the Jews was quoted out of context as his attitude towards the Jews in Germany, whereas the line is a misquotation from *Black List, Section H*, where H is contrasting Iseult's anti-Semitism with his own more tolerant and liberal views. 'If there was a Jewish idea, which was surely a contradiction, it was a hidden, unheroic and critical one, a worm that could get into a lot of fine-looking fruit.' (*BLSH*, p.64) Anyone familiar with Stuart's work would know that, for him, these were words of praise, not contempt. Despite Stuart publicly apologising for the impression which the programme gave, the poet Máire Mhac an tSaoi attempted to arraign him at an open session of Aosdána in Dublin Castle on the 26 November 1997, the motion reading – 'That Aosdána unequivocally reprobates the sentiments and opinions expressed by Mr Francis Stuart concerning the Holocaust in a recent television interview broadcast by Channel 4'. Following a long and at times bitter debate, only one person voted for the motion, Mhac an tSaoi herself, while about thirty members voted against, and as a result Mhac an tSaoi resigned from Aosdána.

At the age of ninety-five, then, Stuart could still cause a controversy, but that is hardly surprising for someone who has stated that the role of the imaginative writer is someone who is a 'traitor to the inculcated virtues' who should seek, like Dostoevsky, 'to shock the community out of its complacency by something quite extraordinary'.[24] Stuart's work is not driven by a desire to seek self-justification but is rather motivated by a wish to expose the inner workings of his consciousness, no matter how unacceptable.

> Where a lesser man or a more gifted stylist might have found tasteful evasions or rhetorical conclusions to avoid or compensate for his guilt, Stuart has refused to do so. He does not try to remake his life through fine writing, does not try to hide his face behind a Yeatsian mask. His descriptive prose... is marked more by precision and painstaking clarity than by any striving after effect.[25]

The self-scrutiny of his work reveals the basic human need to make sense of one's own experience, and it is the uncompromising honesty with which Stuart does this, which eventually strikes a chord in the minds of many readers.

As we have already seen, Stuart invites a negative reading by emphasising the question mark placed over his activities. He also resists the temptation to glorify his self-martyrdom textually with a firm assertion of illumination gained as a result of his suffering, concentrating instead on the waiting and hoping, with only the slightest suggestion of ever having achieved any great insight.

> I'd had a glimpse of sanctity that day on Holy Island. I'd had it before in fragmentary flashes and gleams. The Headmaster knew only its name. I knew a lot more about it, but was further from its radiance than any of them. (*THC*, p.291)

This leaves the way open for the sceptical reader to cast doubts on Stuart's whole philosophical enterprise and to see his dogged refusal to admit to the error of his ways and seek reconciliation, as proof of his culpability. The question mark which Stuart places over his own head is therefore a double-edged sword since, though initially it arouses interest and draws the reader to his work, it also shapes the reading, causing the reader to seek out evidence to confirm the view of Stuart as a fascist collaborator.

As far as his wartime activities were concerned Stuart never seeks to hide his initial attraction to the Nazi cause, casting Hitler in an heroic mode. I saw him (Hitler) and other dictators like Stalin, however much I disagreed with them on other matters, as blind Samsons pulling down the pillars of society – war lords. The system had to be destroyed by someone and after it was destroyed, I hoped, a whole new society would emerge.[26] Although quite quickly Stuart changed his opinion of Hitler, seeing him as 'a little bourgeois man... making hysterical speeches and screeching'[27] it was not that he questioned the whole destructive enterprise, only Hitler's ability to carry it out.

> I went to Germany under a misapprehension of course... I thought Hitler would have been some sort of international revolutionary destroying the whole system, which I soon found he was far from.[28]

Instead he turned his allegiance to Stalin, whom he saw as 'a figure of comparative dignity'[29] and thought seriously of leaving Berlin for Moscow until Hitler's invasion of Russia in June 1941.

As David O'Donoghue notes in his book, Hitler's *Irish Voices: the Story of German Radio's Wartime Irish Service*, Stuart's involvement with Irland-Redaktion, German radio's Irish service, began following his introduction to Ernst von Weizäcker, State Secretary at the Foreign Ministry, who requested that he write some talks for William Joyce who broadcast under the name of Lord Haw Haw. Stuart noted in his diary on 18 February 1940:

> Was asked by Dr Haferkorn of the Foreign Office if I would write some talks for William Joyce... I agreed and wrote three, the first of which Joyce will broadcast tonight and, as I have no radio, have arranged with William Warnock to spend the evening with him at our legation and listen to it there. The theme of my contributions, which I know is not exactly what

either the Germans nor Joyce want, is a recollection of some historic acts of aggression on the part of the United Kingdom, similar to those which British propaganda is denouncing the Nazis for.[30]

One such act was the execution in Birmingham on the 8 February 1940 of IRA men Peter Barnes and Frank McCormick for their part in the Coventry bombings of August 1939 in which five people died, a reference to which Joyce was unlikely to have approved since he did not share Stuart's republican views.

> Something about Joyce I didn't like was his deeply anti-Irish background, as indeed all these Mosleyites had. He was very anti-Irish in his early days in Galway and had collaborated with the Black and Tans.[31]

Stuart's time as scriptwriter for William Joyce was therefore short-lived.

> As it turned out, the talks I wrote were not what Joyce wanted. Above all they were not what the German propaganda people wanted – there was naturally nothing anti-Semitic and nothing in great praise of Hitler – because they had no interest in British atrocities throughout the ages.[32]

However he continued to work as interpreter for Irland-Redaktion but it was not until St Patrick's Day 1942 that he made his first broadcast at the request of Hans Hartmann, the head of the station and a doctoral student at Berlin University where Stuart was lecturing. He agreed to broadcast only if he had a free rein as far as the content was concerned, but despite this his talk, which was entitled 'Ireland's place in the new Europe', reflected the station's ethos of the time in its support for Irish neutrality and opposition to the arrival of US troops in Northern Ireland.

> I am not trying to make propaganda. You have had plenty of it and I only hope that you have now a good idea of what is true and what is false… I only want to put forward my idea of Ireland's place in the world and her future, which I am perhaps able to view with greater clarity from a distance. What a blessing it is that we are celebrating this day at peace, not having escaped war by dishonourable and cowardly means, but by refusing – as far as lay within our power – to waver from a strict and fearless neutrality. As an Ulsterman it is galling to me that a large number of foreign troops are today occupying that corner of our country. But though we have escaped the war, and I hope may be able to do so until the end without sacrificing

127

anything of our national integrity, we cannot nor do we desire to escape taking our share in building the new Europe... Ireland belongs to Europe and England does not belong to it. Our future must lie with the future of Europe and no other.[33]

Stuart returned to the question of Irish neutrality in his third talk which was entitled 'Easter 1916: Ireland's Safety in 1942' which was broadcast on 5 April.

As this evening I walked about the Berlin streets as a neutral, I remember the country (Ireland) has nothing to do with the war being forced by Britain. I know that had those few men not barricaded themselves into a few buildings in Dublin that day 26 years ago our position now would be a very different one. The spirit of Easter Week is the one thing which will bring us safely through this crisis. Please God, we shall be able to remain neutral to the end... I hope and believe that the end of this war will give us back our national unity, and that the struggle which began in its latter phase on that Easter morning in Dublin will then be, at last, at an end.[34]

By the middle of 1942 Stuart agreed to Hartmann's request that he should contribute a series of weekly talks to Ireland under the title 'Through Irish Eyes', and again he insisted on some control of the content.

Wrote the first of weekly talks to broadcast to Ireland. Had lunch with Frank Ryan and discussed these with him. He agreed that they must not be propaganda in the sense that the flood of war journalism from all sides has become, and that of course they must support our neutrality. He suggested, and I fully agreed, that there must be no anti-Russian bias.[35]

In this talk Stuart told his listeners that he had no 'desire to join the ranks of the propagandists' and went on to spell out why he had chosen to work in Berlin.

I am heartily sick and disgusted with the old order under which we've been existing and which had come to be from the great financial powers in whose shadows we lived. If there had to be a war, then I wanted to be among these people who had also had enough of the old system and who, moreover, claimed that they had a new and better one... I had begun to see that no internal policy for Ireland could ever be completely successful unless joined to an external one that would not shed our ancient links with

Europe and European culture... I not only want to bring something of Germany and German ideas to you but I also try, in Berlin University and elsewhere, to make people here, and especially young Germans, conscious of Ireland and interested in her problems and outlook.[36]

O'Donoghue's study of Stuart's broadcasts between 1942 and 1944 show that he stuck to his pledge that there would be no anti-Russian bias and also that they 'generally seem to have been remarkably free of anti-Semitism'.[37] By 1944 more pressure was being put on Stuart and he was finally sacked in January 1944.

> I was pressurised. What I did say on one broadcast, perhaps more than one, was that if I suddenly stop broadcasting it would be because I refused to say certain things, and that's why up to the present I'd never been asked to say things which I wouldn't agree to. But they began to suggest to me that the Bolsheviks, as they called them, must be extremely unpopular in Catholic Ireland, and wouldn't it be good if I cashed in on this and began talking about the Russian atrocities and the atheistic world view. I immediately refused because of all countries waging war... the only one which was waging what one might call a really honourable war were the Russians. They had been attacked in an extremely vicious and underhand way. They were protecting their country. They weren't carrying out devastating bombing on civilians such as the Germans and the Allies were. Whether, if they'd had the bombers, they would have, that's another matter. But they weren't doing it and, therefore, I refused to make anti-Russian or anti-Bolshevik propaganda. Then my broadcasts were terminated. I didn't get into a camp but I was threatened with all sorts of things, and certain facilities I'd had were withdrawn from me. That was the end of my broadcasts.[38]

From the extracts of the broadcasts published in O'Donoghue's book it is apparent that Stuart's political interest was not with Nazism, as J.J. Lee points out in his foreword.

> How much Stuart believed of the gloss he put on the reality of life in the Germany of his time remains an open question. But his politics seem to have had little to do with Nazism in itself, and much more with a type of tormented personality searching for some unattainable ideal of a humankind purged of the contaminating influence of materialistic liberalism through purification by suffering. Whatever demon of

destruction lured him on, it was not apparently a particularly racist demon. Bourgeois society was the enemy that had to be destroyed before his version of redemption could be realised.[39]

Whatever his involvement, Stuart himself never felt as if he was taking sides, seeing both regimes as equally corrupt, a point which becomes clear in his interview with O'Donoghue when questioned if he ever felt that he had been taking the side of evil against good in wartime Berlin.

> No, I didn't. I felt I was too closely involved with a brutal and barbarian regime for my own good or for my own liking. That I was opposed to good, I never felt for a moment, because I never felt that the Allied nations were anything but probably equally evil. Although, equally or not, it's a very fine point, but at least probably even more corrupt and more hypocritical. [40]

No matter how one views Stuart's activities during the war, as far as their depiction in his work is concerned, it is not difficult for the reader to adopt a high moral stance, particularly as they are presented as a self-indulgent exercise in improving his skill as a writer.

> I begin to see that the new difficulties that have arisen out of my attitude during the war have gone to help in my development as a writer. Not only were the war years in Germany necessary to me as a writer. I can never recall too often that in those quiet years at home I did not as a writer progress.[41]

Such self-reflective honesty makes it all too easy for the reader to point an accusing finger at Stuart and to see him at best as naive and misguided, and at worst as a fascist sympathiser. Stuart, I feel, deliberately sets himself up in his post-war novels as a scapegoat and goads the reader into taking a high moral stance. For a writer who asserts that the true writer must provide a counter-current to 'the platitudinous complacencies' of popular opinion, there must be some reassurance in evoking a sense of moral outrage in the reader since this firmly places the reader in the anonymous mass of the moral majority. The reader, therefore, becomes instrumental in the ostracism of the writer, pointing the finger and demanding an act of contrition. That many of his readers fail to see beyond the question-mark, confirms Stuart's opinion that the vast majority of humanity accepts, unthinkingly, the consensus views of society. 'Jung found from a wide experience that most people live unconscious of their psyche, distracted and outward turned and smoothly blended into a consortium of inertia.' (*TASS*, p.18)

Just as redemption, within the novels, comes when his characters find a small company of like-minded individuals, so Stuart envisages a small readership whose outlook is similar to his own: 'I mean a writer whose readers he hopes will be those like himself, either outside society or unable to adapt to society, criticised and perhaps even ostracised by society'.[42]

It would seem, therefore, that Stuart envisages his readership re-enacting the philosophy of the novels in which a small band of outcasts find common ground in the face of a larger, unthinking society. But Stuart is not content merely to preach to the converted; on a subtler level he sees fiction as a subversive means of initiating change in society.

> ... as long as a piece of fiction remains on the fringes of their thought, haunting them, they listen for answers... All this questing, questioning, doubting, builds gradually up to inner disorder, just what the institutions of State are there to combat. And the deeper this sense of chaos the more compelling is the artist's impulse to construct a new order out of it.[43]

In keeping with the recurring motif in his work of the seed entering the consciousness to lie dormant until suddenly, unexpectedly, taking root and sending shoots out into the visible world, Stuart sees the ideas and questions raised in his work entering the mind of the reader, energising it and causing a positive response.

> ... I realise that the dreaming of a handful of poets and novelists is not going to bring down a whole complex edifice. But passion, particularly imaginative passion, is a slow, underground, eroding process, and it spreads from mind to mind and heart to heart, until one day... unforeseen events are suddenly inevitable.[44]

In his novels Stuart sets out to encourage a direct interaction between reader and text and in this it follows many of the tenets of contemporary reader-response criticism in which the meaning of the text is created by the subjective involvement of the reader.

We can see how this works if we consider the various stances the reader takes to the text. As already stated, Stuart forces the reader into an accusatory role, and encourages a negative approach as the text is scoured for damning evidence. The open way in which Stuart not only describes his wartime activities, but admits to an awareness of the consequences of his actions, immediately disrupts the reader's expectations of having to search out proof of culpability. The pleasure of discovering hidden guilt is therefore denied the reader and this disruption of the hermeneutic code adds a disguised tension to the reading process. Denied any satisfying resolution or disclosure, the reader must turn elsewhere to give the text meaning. Earlier chapters of this book have revealed Stuart's method of using deconstructive strategies, the chief of which is the blurring between fact and fiction, to disorientate the reader and leave the way clear for the introduction of new ways of thinking about morality and religion. The reader is placed in the position of trying to reconcile the conventional moral position assumed in order to take on the role of accuser, within the new open morality which Stuart entices the reader to share. Of course, for those entrenched in the 'mean morality' of the mediocre society, Stuart's novels provide proof, not only of his treason, but of his blasphemy and depravity too.

> Some of my pre-war books were banned. My post-war books were mostly banned. My last novel, a novel called *Memorial*, was seized by the customs and given to the censors to examine. Now, about a year and a half later, they're still examining it. They haven't yet banned it and certainly won't ban it. But in a provincial bookshop, I've heard the bookshop owner-manager has been told by pressure groups to take it out of his window, even out of his shop.[45]

In many consciousnesses, therefore, the 'seed' simply falls on barren ground and 'quickly dries up'. For some readers though, the discrepancy between conventional morality and that portrayed by Stuart in his novels, the gap between accepted biblical interpretation and the 'deconstructive' Jesus offered by Stuart, and the blurring between fact and fiction in the text, all serve to activate the consciousness, raising doubts and producing questions to be answered. In short, the act of reading Stuart's novels can, in some cases, create a catalyst which initiates a process of self-scrutiny similar to that which Stuart undergoes in the process of writing. Readers, having been forced to question and reassess the whole system of values which forms the basis of their self-identity, must re-create their own autobiographical myth of self. The reading process becomes a transformative act.

The interaction of literary text and the human consciousness has long been established. Freud believed that the writer aimed at awakening in the reader the same 'mental constellation' that produced in him the impetus to create'.[46] Recent literary criticism has also highlighted the active role of the reader: 'The reader of fiction is always an actively mediating presence; the text's reality is established by his response and reconstituted by his active participation'.[47] All texts are to some extent 'scriptible', to use Roland Barthes's term, that is, produced rather than consumed by the reader. Stuart's recent novels, combining as they do, autobiographical fiction and metafiction, are a double challenge to the reader. In blurring the distinction between his art and his life Stuart is continually disturbing the reader's expectations. Stuart's particular kind of self-consciousness, with its explicit recognition of the fictiveness of self-portraiture, draws the reader's attention to Stuart's struggle to make sense of his life, through the structure of his literature, and the way that this in turn imposes a shape on his life. This is a feature which David G. Wright also notes in his study of autobiographical prose.

> In constructing a self to mould the attitudes of others, autobiographers also mould their own attitudes. Seeking truth they create it by their manner of approaching. To know that one will write of an event later may give that event a literary shape even as it occurs. Thus life may be consciously directed in the service of art, and so create the 'facts' on which that art can build.[48]

The pattern of loss and redemption which is central to Stuart's work cannot, therefore, be verified merely by reference to events in Stuart's life, and with the normal expectations of autobiography frustrated, the reader is further assaulted by the metafictional elements of the text.

Although all of Stuart's recent novels call attention to their linguistic and fictional nature, *The High Consistory* makes a feature of this self-reflectiveness by evolving a structure around the arbitrariness of autobiography. The work begins with an introductory note explaining that the manuscript had been misplaced as a result of being in a plane crash.

> The copybooks, notebooks, loose leaves and lesser fragments, anything
> with writing on it that the salvage squad had collected from the four
> corners of the airfield… The record of a lifetime had been lightly shuffled
> by chance, as is the past, more thoroughly and repeatedly, by memory. In
> neither case can the imposition of a strict chronological design improve the
> general picture. (*THC*, p.7)

True to its imaginary conception the narrative proceeds at random with
extracts from diaries Stuart kept in Berlin in 1942 and Paris in 1950
intermingled with the story of the relationship between an artist, Simeon
Grimes and Claire de Brusy, as well as news clippings, scraps of memory
and even a section which anticipates the funeral of the main character, 'A
Forward Look to the Day of the Funeral of Simeon Grimes'. (*THC*, p.117)
The opening section of the novel lulls the reader into a false sense of
confidence with its obvious literariness allowing full scope for
interpretation.

> High above the snowy wastes of Labrador, I watched a long grey cloudbank
> wedged between the shadowy, rumpled whiteness and the blue clarity of
> sky… By leaning closer to the thick glass and peering directly downwards,
> I could see the cruciform shadow keeping pace… (*THC*, p.9)

Almost immediately though, the reader's immersion into the literary
landscape is sharply interrupted by being made aware of the text's
production: 'This, as must already have been surmised, isn't anything in
the nature of a travelogue. Not being a writer by vocation, I sometimes find
it hard to resist what they call scene-setting.' (*THC*, p.9) The outcome of
such narrative self-reflectiveness is that the reader becomes aware of the text
as an acknowledged fictional universe and of his or her own role as reader:
'By reminding the reader of the book's identity as artifice, the text parodies
his expectations, his desire for verisimilitude, and forces him to an
awareness of his own role in creating the universe of fiction'.[49] Faced with
the disorder of the text with all its unconnected snippets of information,
the reader struggles to create order and meaning, and attempts to enact a
coherence from the disparate fragments.

Through the process of reading in this way the reader acts out the pattern
of loss and redemption so prominent in Stuart's work and life, and in doing
so gains an insight into Stuart's consciousness. Faced with bridging what

Wolfgang Iser termed 'gaps of indeterminacy'[50] and coping with what Frank Kermode called 'hermeneutic confusion and problematic closure',[51] the reader can experience a great sense of loss. With the 'certainties' of normal novelistic expectations shattered, the reader is forced to re-examine and re-evaluate his relationship to the text, and indeed his relationship to reality. Left trying to give significance to both the literary work and to a sense of identity battered by doubts and questions, the reader begins to recognise in Stuart someone involved in a similar project, and racked with the same self-doubts and uncertainty.

> Is there not a monotony in that, and does it not show in this last phrase of mine? Possibly, but I can't be sure, nor have I had any expert critical assessment of what I am doing. If so, it does not greatly matter as long as there is also the other quality that I hope, and at times have enough faith to believe, has crept in, as by chance, to the canvasses. (*THC*, p.214)

This common bond makes the reader more receptive to Stuart's vision of reality, especially since the reader is consciously aware of an intangible link with Stuart's own consciousness. Stuart's texts therefore are like those described by Murray Krieger in his work on modern poetics: '... an enclosed set of endlessly faceted mirrors, closed in on itself, which becomes, 'magically,' a window to the world. The reader is both trapped in the looking glass and led through it'.[52] Stuart does indeed lead the reader through the confusion by offering a tangible example of the way in which the imagination can draw together, in a coherent whole, heterogeneous incidents and influences, in the picture of the 'Holy Sisterhood' painted by Simeon Grimes.

> Thérèse Martin from nineteenth-century France in her white woollen choir habit, Katusha from nineteenth-century Russia in padded jacket and long, red-leather boots, a gift from Tolstoy, Libertus Schultze-Boysen in the blue ski-pants and high-necked jersey I'd last seen her in, the ocelot in his spotted ochre coat, the girl-patient from the asylum in Dublin, and Claire. (*THC*, p.228)

This imaginary painting is an expression of Stuart's whole philosophy since it blends together the spiritual and sexual; past and present; fact and fantasy; sanity and insanity; and life and art so the reader is shown, albeit obliquely, the way in which the creative consciousness can reconcile the seemingly irreconcilable. As well as disturbing the reader's consciousness, causing a re-evaluation of expectations and beliefs, the text also gives a glimpse of a way out of such confusion with this all-embracing image. So, rather than merely articulating his beliefs, Stuart causes the reader to directly experience them, and in this way it becomes impossible for the reader to separate the work of art from his own interaction with it. In effect the reader no longer glimpses himself in the mirror of the work: he becomes the mirror itself. During the process of reading, the reader recognises the parallel patterning which links Stuart's consciousness and his own and so it is the reader's own consciousness which gives 'significance' to the text, by recognising within it the common bond of humanity.

> About how the nerve cells of body and brain were once like bunches of grapes ripening with the others on the common vine stock in a sun that was a star in a great star-cluster. We all belonged together, not yet blighted by isolation. (*THC*, p.57)

When read from this perspective, Stuart's work becomes an honest record of the frailties and aspirations of human nature.

Re-reading Stuart's work from a human perspective rather than that of Prosecuting Counsel, one is struck by the self-mocking humour of the later work.

> She leaned over and with a touch of her finger caused the door, almost as wide as the side of the car, to swing smoothly open over the snowy sidewalk
> – Do you mind going in from the back?
> Why was I giving the simplest remarks and circumstances far-fetched erotic interpretations? Just because, according to what I've read, of my declining powers when it comes to the act. (thc, p.14)

There is also a recognition, by Stuart, of his own psychological make-up and failings.

> I was often lagging in the rear... my responses too retarded... and perhaps, but for my being born some years too late, my father could have been saved. Had I been there to accompany him to that long, narrow room in the discreet looking, terrible house in Townsville, Australia, I might have persuaded him that currents from the deep store of imaginative compassion... were turning his hopeless isolation into an integral part of the human drama.

> Because he had ended in utter despair, I myself had come into this world with a fatal flaw, which, as I now see it, inhibited my responses when they were most crucial. (*THC*, p.278)

This passage not only reveals Stuart's awareness of his own fallibility, it also shows the very real, underlying sense of guilt he feels about his father's death. Although, as we have already seen, this guilt forms the basis of Stuart's desire to speak for the victims of suffering, the desire which drove him to experience, in his own way, the suffering of the victim, he refuses to use this as an excuse for his war-time behaviour. Instead he maintains that this does not require any excuse.

> It's high time I came to my own conclusion about what I've tended to ignore. Not, of course, to answer critics but for my own enlightenment and better self-appraisal.
>
> According to all the evidence, Hitler was a monster. But it wasn't from him I caught my evil tendencies. (*THC*, p.67)

Although he refuses to pander to public outrage, it is with more honesty and a greater conviction, that Stuart confesses to the private hurt he has caused.

> On my own, and in association with nobody, I have been the cause of torment suffered by other beings. The circumstances were obscure and known fully only to myself, and no-one shall ever be charged in this connection. And no German or other monster has much to do with it. (*THC*, p.57)

For the reader still intent on finding a scapegoat for all the suffering which occurred during the war, such an admission of guilt on a small, personal scale can only seem inadequate. However, for the reader involved in a process of self-scrutiny, such an admission finds echoes in his or her own experience, since it is easier for the human mind to recognise and understand hurts inflicted on a personal basis. In *The High Consistory* the guilt which Stuart feels about the Holocaust is related in human terms, as a haunting by the one case in which he had an indirect involvement, that of the Schultze-Boysens.

> One night I was ushered into Libertas Schultze-Boysen's cell in the Alexanderplatz on an evening before Christmas 1942. Without hope, even

of a tolerable death, abandoned to the ravages of her jailers, she was crouched in a corner, her bruised eyes staring. (*THC*, p.67)

By presenting suffering in this personalised way Stuart ensures that his readers relate more immediately to the drama involved, by forcing them to step into the victim's shoes and feel the pain.

> 'Each outcry of the hunted hare
> A fibre from the brain doth tear,'
> wrote Blake. It is imagination that leads to compassion and makes every act of cruelty to man or beast intolerable. (*THC*, p.67)

The reader whose imagination is activated by Stuart's works is made aware that suffering, whether human or animal, is an everyday occurrence. More importantly though, the reader also comes to understand his or her own ability to turn a blind eye to this. Viewed from this perspective Stuart's 'guilt' becomes an altogether more human failing: the ability to block out another's suffering. In his work and in his life Stuart has always owned up to, and been aware of his own 'guilt'; what he does in his writing, both by the content, but more particularly by the form, is to encourage others to come face to face with themselves.

6

Self Reflections

Unlike John Banville who asserted that 'art is a cold fish, not interested at all in the artist's personal affairs',[1] Francis Stuart has created his art from his life and his life from his art. To read his work comprehensively is to gain an insight into the workings of another mind. Incidents are related time and time again but always from a slightly different perspective mirroring the way memory, randomly and imprecisely, recollects incidents from the past. Relationships are examined and re-examined by Stuart in an ongoing assessment that attempts to make sense of those that have failed, and to wonder at the mystery of those that succeed. Stuart not only writes about his personal affairs, he works through them and analyses them as he writes. So reading Stuart's work provides a unique opportunity to eavesdrop on another's life but, as we have already seen, Stuart encourages his readers to be more than just voyeurs; he entices them to be participants, judges, arbitrators, confidants and co-conspirators.

The active participation of the reader is an integral element of the web of correspondences which forms Stuart's conception of reality, but it is also the proof of the truth of his reflections. When Stuart inveigles his readers to sit in judgement over him, he is essentially starting them off on a path of self-discovery. The nature of the journey can best be defined by a diary entry, written by Stuart in the harsh conditions of Freiburg in 1948, which essentially takes the form of a meditation on the act of judging.

> But how weary all this 'disapproval' this tacit abrogation of the right to 'judge' makes me! By what laws and concepts can we judge? For me only by the pure movement of the heart, or soul, only through that, through the inner passion, will one become integral and honest enough to be able to judge, and then one won't want to 'judge' anymore... if I say: 'My inner spirit', and feel it when I say it, then I do not think I dare act or judge falsely in its name. I know very well when I act against it, and I can never invoke it to excuse cowardice or compromise or indifference.[2]

Here Stuart is advocating a form of judgement that comes from a strong inner conviction, rather than publicly proclaimed morals or laws. The ability to listen to this 'inner spirit' only becomes possible, he believes, when 'one is freed from the mediocrity and falsity of petty moralities and made to submit to the deep uncompromising Moral'.[3]

> Without great courage truth will never be gained. Humility alone is not enough, there must be humility and daring. Humility to discard one's own 'life' and concepts, and daring to go out towards what seems at first darkness and chaos.[4]

We can clearly see then the direction in which Stuart hopes to lead his readers as he first of all makes them question his past and his beliefs and then, having firmly located them within the moral majority, he exposes the suspect nature of such complacent moralising. In order to reinforce the difficulties inherent in the act of judging, Stuart integrates autobiographical details into his fiction, and thereby self-reflectively blurs the distinctions between fact and fiction. Stuart's fictional accounts of his life are as 'real' as his factual accounts since he makes it clear that both go through the mediating processes of the imagination. It is irrelevant whether the character of the novel is called Sugrue, Grimes, H or Ezra, they are all easily recognisable images of Stuart and of his attempt to create a coherent account of his own psyche. The reader, trying to differentiate between art and life in the narrative, is ultimately overpowered by this integration of fact and fiction and, finding it impossible to judge, is left in a state of uncertainty. But the process goes much deeper than mere narrative discomfort, it goes right into the psyche of the reader.

Again, in his diary, Stuart provides us with the key to understanding what lies behind this manoeuvre when he offers an insight into his thinking on the whole process of writing.

> The upper level on which life is lived and events take place cannot be the ground of art. Neither in painting nor literature that is concerned with surface life and surface appearances, no matter how dramatic or sensuously beautiful, have I any more interest. Because on this ground no important revelation can be made. I cannot write on this upper level – all that I write (no matter how clumsy) will be about the 'subterranean' life, what is and moves below the sensual surface. But read as though it were a surface account it will of course never be grasped. There has always been this misunderstanding even in regard to the greatest works.[5]

This confirms what we have already discovered through a reading of the works, that Stuart is drawn to delving below the surface. But we have also seen that his answer to the Modernist dilemma of equating inner and outer lives, is not, as in Beckett, to collapse into solipsism, but instead to create an articulation of the way in which what we perceive to be the 'outer' factual life is shaped and moved by the 'inner' imaginative life. Read as factual accounts Stuart's novels are, as he predicted, open to misinterpretation, but read as an honest account of human nature, the reader comes to recognise his or her own experience. By continually reinforcing how fact and fantasy impinge on each other Stuart reminds his readers that they, too, undergo the same process to create myths about their own identity. The purpose of this is, as set out in his diary,[6] to make his readers discard their own preconceived ideologies and to take a step into the darkness and chaos of uncertainty in the hope that in this state they will be able to make a more honest appraisal of human culpability.

Given this aesthetic it is hardly surprising that Stuart measures the success of his work, not by public acclaim, but by an altogether more private and unnoticed goal – that of the inner transformation of the individual reader: '... the artist at his most ambitious does not seek to change maps but, minutely and over generations, the expression on some of the faces of men and women'. (*THC*, p.41) By openly acknowledging that the consciousness of his reader plays an integral part in his artistic process, Stuart in effect draws him or her into the fictional world of his later novels, with the consequence that, as the readers read into their own involvement in the process they experience the same merging of art and life as that which forms the content of the novels. The result is to highlight the fictionality of all constructs of the self and to demonstrate the interweaving of consciousness that constitutes Stuart's conception of reality. Terry Eagleton takes Stuart to task for this aesthetic manifesto declaring that

> ... to change the expression on the faces of a few men and women leaves the Romantic radical with nothing to pit against political barbarism but a change of heart. It is a politics so utterly uncompromising and absolute that it disappears from the light of common-or-garden society and leaves everything exactly as it was.[7]

Such a condemnation, understandable as it is from a Marxist perspective, overlooks a very important, but until quite recently, under-researched aspect of the literary process – the relationship between the reader, the text and the writer. It is here that the revolutionary aspect of Stuart's writing becomes apparent.

In his essay, 'From Work to Text', Roland Barthes maintained that the literary text is the result of an interaction '... it exists only as discourse... In other words, the text is experienced only in an activity, a production'.[8] The text therefore becomes a dialogue or process of exchange between the writer and the reader concerning the signification provided by the linguistic medium, and the textual reading process does not privilege the creator or the decoder of the message since both the writer's and the reader's subjectivity are being inscribed simultaneously. The significance of Stuart's texts, therefore, does not lie solely in their representation of his experience, but also in the reader's experience of the texts. For this reason a self-reflective examination of the way in which the reading of Stuart's work has both been influenced by and had an influence on the reader, has an important part to play in any interpretation of Stuart's work.

My own interest in Stuart's work began in 1987 and arose out of a remark overheard on the bus from Maynooth to Dublin, about the 'question-mark over Stuart' and the chance discovery the same day in

Greene's Bookshop in Dublin, of a battered copy of the first Penguin edition of *Black List, Section H*. My initial reading therefore grew out of a curiosity about the controversy which surrounded him and I remember reacting quite negatively to the novel, feeling something of the same misgivings as those expressed by Terry Eagleton in his assessment of Stuart.

> ... there is something morally offensive about a man offering his own experience of imprisonment as a source of wisdom, when that brief interlude happened in the aftermath of his quiescence in a regime which butchered and incarcerated so many more.[9]

And yet I was driven on to read more, partly because I was intrigued by Stuart's view of the creative process and partly because I was interested in his obsession with victimage and the insights which he believed came to those who experience disgrace, humiliation and social ostracism. But mostly, I think, I was driven by a need to expose what I saw then as the suspect morality of Stuart's thinking. This was the standpoint from which I embarked on my research. Like Stuart, I was on a quest for knowledge – his search was to find a way of expressing his view of reality; mine to find out the 'truth' about Stuart. The force that lies behind both projects is one of domination, for, just as Stuart wished to 'master' reality by defining it and articulating it in his work, so too, my desire to reach beyond the literary text to the 'real' Stuart stemmed from a need to 'master' a text that was in some way disturbing.

The desire for dominance is a major element of the male critical debate and so it is clear that my initial reading of Stuart was undertaken from a male perspective, which the feminist critic, Judith Fetterley, would see as a consequence of the education system in which I was immersed: 'As readers and teachers and scholars, women are taught to think as men, to identify with a male point of view, and to accept as normal and legitimate, a male system of values'. [10] Feminist critics have long recognised the effect that the study of literature, with its focus on predominantly male texts, has upon the female psyche.

> Women are estranged from their own experience and unable to perceive its shape and authenticity. They are expected to identify as readers with a masculine experience and perspective, which is presented as the human one... they have no faith in the validity of their own perceptions and

143

experiences, rarely seeing them confirmed in literature, or accepted in criticism.[11]

Literature, to a great extent, still tends to operate within a male system of values so that women readers and critics continue to find themselves experiencing a sense of alienation, of difference, of not fully belonging to literary society. Certainly my initial research was undertaken at a time before I had fully succumbed to feminist critical methods and so I found myself torn between trying to judge the merits of the literature and responding to the challenge within the work to question the grounds of such judgements. Increasingly I felt unable to keep my reading of Stuart's texts within the accepted approaches of literary criticism because the texts themselves demanded such a personal involvement. In this way I was, in a sense, becoming isolated from the literary community in which I was meant to be operating, and finding myself in uncharted territory, at a loss to find a way of expressing the personal within the restricting genre of the academic thesis.

Given this subconscious sense of estrangement it is hardly surprising that my reading of Stuart's novels changed from an essentialist quest for truth to an interest in the experience of the marginalised. By ascribing a value to the experience of the outcast throughout his work, Stuart encourages a reassessment of all isolated groupings. This, combined with the narrative strategies that Stuart employs to initiate the process of self-discovery in his readers, certainly compelled me to reassess and re-evaluate my own experience. I began at last to read as a woman reader and as a feminist critic. From this perspective it became increasingly apparent to me that the journey Stuart advocates in his work is one that parallels many of the strategies of contemporary feminist criticism; a fact which perhaps is most clearly demonstrated in the way he depicts women.

Terry Eagleton also accuses Stuart of continually perpetrating 'a sexist idealisation of women as suffering spiritual redeemers'.[12] On one level this is true, but it is only part of the story. As we have seen, the first step on Stuart's journey involves stripping away conventional patterns of thought. This move is also the first step for feminist critics. Virginia Woolf, for example, in *Orlando*, uses a clothing analogy to describe this need to step beyond the comfort of conventional conditioning.

Vain trifles as they seem, clothes have, they say, more important offices than merely to keep us warm. They change our view of the world and the world's view of us… Thus, there is much to support the view that it is clothes that wear us and not we them; we may make them take the mould of arm or breast; but they would mould our hearts, our brains, our tongues to their liking.[13]

More recently, feminist critics such as Monique Wittig have argued that breaking free of the mould involves a rejection of the stereotypical images of 'woman' because these are merely social constructs. This move is not as straightforward as it might at first seem because this challenge to accepted stereotypes involves women, not only in a recognition of the way in which others frame the concept, but in an examination of the way she herself has absorbed and perpetuated the myth.

Our first task is to dissociate 'woman' (the class within which we fight) and 'woman', the myth. For 'woman' is only an imaginary formation. Furthermore, we have to destroy the myth inside and outside ourselves.[14]

Stuart's attempts to create a representation of a woman who encompasses both sexuality and spirituality reveal many of the problems associated with the enterprise of rejecting stereotypes.

His first efforts to change the stereotypes concentrated on emphasising positive rather than negative attributes and resulted in various formations which tended to magnify the mystical aspect of woman's nature and highlight the direct link he believed woman had to creativity and intuitive knowledge. The women in Stuart's pre-war novels, Elizabeth, Buttercup or Hylla, would not be out of place as representations of the image of woman espoused by many feminist critics of the late 1970s, having much in common with, say, Mary Daly's 'elemental women'[15] or Clarissa Estés' 'wild women',[16] but while this image of woman has succeeded in bringing to the fore and celebrating a previously under-valued aspect of woman's experience, it does so at the cost of putting into the shadow all the more worldly aspects of woman's experience. We can see this in the difficulty Stuart initially has in ascribing to these characters a sexual dimension, which of course in part arises from the way in which sexuality was negatively perceived at the time, but also because it undercuts the other-worldly pinnacle he was then striving to achieve. As Stuart moves from a transcendental goal to one in which an inner spirituality becomes part of a corporeal chain so too does his handling of the sexuality of his women characters change.

In *The Angel of Pity*, as well as giving an imaginative foretaste of the impending war, he begins to shape a woman character who is to reappear time and time again in his post-war novels. In the novel the main female character, Sonia (an obvious reference to Dostoevsky's character in *Crime and Punishment*) is repeatedly raped by soldiers but, rather than falling into the stock representation of woman as victim, Stuart turns the violence of rape into a redemptive possibility; a move that is both shocking and profound. Sonia forgives her attackers which has the effect of showing the full, almost incomprehensible, force of the true Christian message; but also in a strange way, shows her to be strengthened and empowered by the attack.

In *Redemption*, written immediately after the war, but the notes for which are contained in Stuart's wartime diaries, Annie's rape culminates in her murder, but as we have previously seen, this does not necessarily cast her in the role of victim, rather as one who has lived life to the full. Herra, in *Memorial,* asks Sugrue for forgiveness for withholding sex following her rape by him. There is much to disturb the reader in these depictions of woman and certainly a surface-level reading would give plenty of ammunition to feminist critics who wished to argue that Stuart is glorifying rape. I would agree that in the novels rape is portrayed through a provocatively male perspective which fails to show the full implications for women, but the underlying reading is one which moves the women characters beyond victim status to one which shows women in control.

As Stuart begins to delve into the self in order to find his material, he becomes less interested in creating well-wrought characters, particularly women characters. As his novels become reflections of his being, of his imaginative life, so too do the women characters become more obviously constructs of a male mind, of a male fantasy. On reading *A Hole in the Head*, John McGahern wrote to Stuart saying that 'Emily Brontë was never real for me in the work, other than as a good or daring idea.'[17] The same could be said of Stuart's depiction of St Eighty-fifth, or of Pieta, or Abby or any number of his later woman characters and this is precisely because he is making it evident that they are not women but formulations of his own mind. Stuart in his later work has taken a step beyond creating new stereotypes of woman; he owns up to the fictionality of all such constructs.

This is a fact, as we have already seen in Chapter 3, that he openly admits to in *A Compendium of Lovers*. Here, in his last full-length novel, the Stuart persona comes to realise that what he had formerly seen as an obsession with woman, in reality had little or nothing to do with them. At last he focuses in on the centre of his fascination with women. Stuart describes this as the gateway and source of creativity but also, in keeping with his vision of reality that links the spiritual and the material, as 'a very lowly receptacle situated between two drain-pipes... At first romantically, even poetically, but gradually more precisely and crudely, it turned into the cunt' (*ACOL*, p.169). The cunt provides him with an image that links the most basic of human endeavours, urination and defecation, with sexuality and with the mystery of creation itself. It is an image which again promotes the male gaze, as it is one which is not excessively familiar to most women and it is a disturbing image because the remaining aspect of the woman, body, emotions, and spirit, are not only irrelevant but non-existent, even imaginatively. What we are presented with is an opening, a space, an absence. With this, all pretence of producing an image of woman has dissolved and what Stuart presents to his readers is a blank space. For the woman reader this provides both a shock to the system as she finds herself negated; and an opportunity, as it forces her to explore her own image as 'woman'.

In postmodernist terms what Stuart has succeeded in doing is to break down the binary oppositions inherent in the text thereby promoting intuitive as well as rational knowledge. This has the effect of overturning conventional readings of 'victimage' and foregrounding the fictional nature of all constructs of the concept of woman. By overtly flaunting the male perspective Stuart upsets the hierarchical order of the phallocentric value system and thereby leaves the way open for the woman reader to turn to her own experience and begin to read as a woman.

By encouraging readers to question the patterns of conventional thinking, and more importantly their own participation in it, Stuart challenges the woman reader to examine how her own concept of 'woman' has been shaped by others and by herself. That is not to say that she achieves a pure state of womanhood, rather she becomes more aware of, and is able to negotiate with, patriarchal concepts which she would previously have blindly accepted as fact. After discarding 'one's own "life" and concepts'[18] the next step on Stuart's journey is 'to go out towards what seems at first darkness and chaos'[19] and here is where the real difficulty arises. The woman reader who is in the process of discarding patriarchal assumptions must, of necessity, take a step towards the unknown as she begins to read as a woman since this is, to all intents and purposes, an unknown territory. Few guidelines are offered by feminist critics, but most acknowledge the need to introduce the personal into criticism: 'The immediate connection between the critic's personal vision and the text characterises much feminist criticism and is one of the main sources of its energy and creative power.'[20] If, for example, she looks into her own experience, the woman reader should recognise the truth of Stuart's contention that there is a form of knowledge other than conventional rationality; one which, he claims, lies in those experiences normally thought of as irrational, illogical and ineffable. What Stuart describes here is very similar to Luce Irigaray's idea of what constitutes the 'feminine'.

> 'She' is indefinitely other in herself. That is undoubtedly the reason she is called temperamental, incomprehensible, perturbed, capricious – not to mention her language in which 'she' goes off in all directions and in which 'he' is unable to discern the coherence of any meaning. Contradictory words seem a little crazy to our logic of reason, and inaudible for him who listens with ready-made grids, a code prepared in advance.[21]

Helene Cixous has also suggested that women have a pre-conceptual, non-appropriative openness to the other within and without themselves. In addition, just as Stuart suggests that the consciousness can become aware of the 'seamless garment of existence', (*TASS*, p.65) Cixous writes of becoming aware of a universal voice.

> A woman's voice came to me from far away, like a voice from a birth-town, it brought me insights that I once had, intimate insightful, naïve and knowing, ancient and fresh like the yellow and violet colour of freesias rediscovered. This voice was not searching for me, it was writing to no one, to all women, to writing… in a foreign tongue, I do not speak it but my heart understands it, and its silent words in all the veins of my life have translated themselves into mad blood, into joy-blood.[22]

For the woman reader this glimpse of being linked to an essential network of 'the feminine' is as intangible and fleeting as Stuart's glimpse of a universal reality that links all existence, but once the suggestion is authenticated through communion with others, it becomes less possible to accept male concepts of woman.

So through Stuart's work, the woman reader is not only encouraged to undertake a feminist exposé of patriarchal assumptions in others and in herself, she also finds a reflection of her own reality and an expression of her own experience. One reason why this is the case is the strong influence of St Thérèse's autobiography on Stuart's work. Another reason is that Stuart's role as an outcast gives him an insight into the 'feminine' mind. Such a supposition is in accord with Cixous's assertion that a feminine practice of writing can 'be conceived only by subjects who are breakers of automatisms, by peripheral figures that no authority can ever subjugate'.[23] Whatever the reason, it is obvious that Stuart's texts parallel many aspects of feminine writing, not least in his desire to transform the consciousness of a few like-minded individuals which is similar to the feminist reader's urge to share her experience with others. In fact, the power of the personal is intensified when the vision is shared. The integrity of that vision reveals its commonality, for, as Doris Lessing has remarked, 'nothing is personal, in the sense that it is uniquely one's own'.[24] Those involved in feminist criticism know that a sense of authenticity is gained by the realisation that others have gone through the same doubts and self-scrutiny in an attempt to break free from conditioning and ground oneself in one's own experience. The process of introspection only gains a power when it is shared and understood by others.

Stuart, while at pains throughout his work to share his vision with his readers, was always aware that 'if read as though it were a surface account it will of course never be grasped'.[25] What is important then is the way in which the texts are read as 'subterranean'. To read below the surface level requires a personal involvement at the deepest level, one that has a profound effect on the reader. Again Stuart's diary clarifies this in his description of his own reading of the New Testament.

> The Gospels may be read as if they dealt with an event in the upper, three-dimensional life. I have often read them myself in this way and been left cold by them. But I am inclined to think they are one of the very deepest

> goings down into the great sub-life, which Christ calls 'abundant life'. (I am come that ye may have life and have it more abundantly.)[26]

Given that Stuart's texts mirror the narrative techniques of the Gospels, it is hardly surprising that they too have the ability to engage readers in the same way, making them delve deep into their own inner resources. It must be obvious by now to the reader that in my own case, reading Stuart's work had a transformative effect on my own work, that I moved from taking a male critical stance, being concerned to uncover the 'truth' about the author and his ideas, to a feminist approach where my concern lay, not only with showing how Stuart's writings worked, but also the effect of his work on the reader. More honestly perhaps I should state that my concern lay with the effect of his work on me, because the process of getting from A to B, from male critic to feminist critic, not only involved a professional engagement with Stuart's texts and literary theory, but also a very deeply personal soul-searching and transformation. One could not have been achieved without the other, and so my experience of reading Stuart in effect became an integral part of the research. Once I realised this, it became clear to me that the only proof I had of the validity of many of Stuart's ideas came from my own experience.

As we have seen, Stuart's work demonstrates a merging of his life and his art, a fact that he explains by a quasi-scientific theory that at first seems somewhat implausible.

> … the intensely activated consciousness of the artist is not only formed by the stuff of consciousness, but in turn reacts on it as molecules and their attendant particles react on each other, apparently jumping from one orbit to another and so on. (*TASS*, p.68)

Such a seemingly improbable assertion is however grounded in the theories of astrophysicans such as Eddington, on whose work Stuart comments in his diary.

> I think there is much in Eddington's contention that all that science reveals about the cosmos is what we have already put into the cosmos. When science finds a footprint in the void, we may be sure that it is our own. [27]

That the imagination has the power to make things happen in the real world is established by the entangled patterning of Stuart's art and life, but such a claim can only be proved if it is shared by the reader. Those who undertake prolonged study of an individual writer often undergo an increasing sense of identification with their subject, and this certainly was true of my experience of reading Stuart, despite the seemingly insurmountable differences in gender, age and class. However, it is only in retrospect that the full extent of the influence and parallelism becomes evident, though even yet I find it difficult to ascertain which events were pure coincidence and which emanated from a subconscious desire to live out the material in which I was immersed, in much the same way as it is impossible to determine whether Stuart's decision to go to Germany was driven by a subconscious desire to experience the conditions about which he had been writing for so long.

How to explain, for example, on one of my trips to the British Library, finding myself staying in the small room, off Tottenham Court Road, shared by Stuart and Iseult when they eloped to London? The accommodation had been arranged by a friend, one who knew nothing of Stuart or his work and so it had all the hallmarks of pure coincidence. But time and time again I was surprised to find myself in places connected with Stuart, or finding pieces of information about him when I was not looking, or coming across passages in books I would half recognise, only to discover later that Stuart had read these and been influenced by them. All this is indicative of the intuitive aspect of research, which is not always recognised, but which draws the researcher to sources of which they seem to have no conscious knowledge. However, one incident does stand out powerfully in my mind as being somewhat more inexplicable.

At the stage when I came to understand the very real influence that Thérèse Martin had on Stuart's thinking and his work, I was very keen to read her autobiography, which had been translated as *The Story of a Soul* I searched for weeks in local libraries and had requested it on inter-library loan but without success. I felt unable to progress until I had read it and so was somewhat obsessed by it. While driving to Donegal to walk away my frustration at not being able to obtain this book, I felt compelled to turn off the road and down a rather overgrown track. I had realised as I approached the turning that this was probably the site of a house called Sharon Glebe, which was where a magistrate, Rev William Hamilton, had been killed by his tenants in 1797. I had come across the story that

151

morning in an old newspaper picked up in the library where I had been looking for *The Story of a Soul*. The house was still there but empty, derelict, and darkened by huge bushes of musk roses that were in full bloom. The front door was open and, rather uncharacteristically but curiously, I entered. To my right, the kitchen seemed remarkably fashionable with stone flagstones on the floor and a blackened range holding court over rustic wooden cupboards. To my left, were the remains of a library, and a huge desk covered in dust was the only piece of furniture in the shelf-lined room. The panes of the bay window had been broken and the rose bushes had made their way into the room at one end, along the empty shelves. The room smelled of decay and damp, but overpowering that was the smell of the roses. I went over, intent on picking a rose and saw lying on the shelf a copy of Thérèse Martin's *The Story of a Soul* almost hidden under the previous years' leaves. I still have the book on my shelf, an American edition sent to the last owner of the property, the parish priest of the area.

The question that this event raised in my mind was, did my 'intensely activated consciousness' somehow lead me to this book, or as my more rational side would counter, did my over-active imagination encourage me to make connections where there were none. This question, of course, is very relevant to any reading of Stuart's work because one is constantly wavering between these two positions when trying to assess the truth of many of his assertions. Often the rational approach would find little of substance in many of Stuart's ideas, but somehow, someway – perhaps in what Stuart's terms the 'inner spirit' – I knew them to be true, but it took time and insight into the experiences Stuart was writing about, before I learned to listen.

So how did these 'insights' come about? Well, one thing I did feel I had some understanding of was Stuart's relationship with Iseult. When I embarked on my research I was part of a conventional unhappy marriage, respectable and idyllic on the surface, but harbouring hurt and resentment. Like the Stuarts, we had married young and grown up into two incompatible people whose only common bond was their children. Since neither of us wished to leave, we took lovers, but none so important that they broke the status quo. This was the type of marriage Stuart needed to get away from when he agreed to go to Germany. This I can understand since I, too, put an end to the status quo, but not by going away.

When Stuart and Madeleine were trying to leave Freiburg following their imprisonment in 1946, he wrote to Iseult asking if they could come to live with her at Laragh. Both *The Pillar of Fire* (which was published under the title of *Victors and Vanquished*) and *Redemption* tell the story of an Irishman's struggle to get the woman that he loves back to Ireland following the war, and of the wife back in Ireland who fails to understand her husband and his hope that she and the German woman might live amicably together under one roof. In the latter novel Stuart writes of Iseult's reaction, thinly disguising her as Nancy, the wife who will not join Ezra's little community. She 'remained looking out from her ivory tower, too proud or too fastidious to come down out of it'. (*R*, p.137) Stuart's disappointment at Iseult's refusal to allow Madeleine and him to come back is written into his condemnation of Nancy's inability to move beyond the conventional and to embrace life. Certainly, within the novel, the idea of a community bound together by need and by love, seems an admirable idea, and Nancy's refusal to accept the shared love, seems cold and forbidding.

I still find it difficult to ascertain whether or not this idea of Stuart's had an influence on me when I moved my lover into my home. The reasons I gave to myself and to the others involved were purely practical. We all knew what was going on, I argued, and the time had come to be more honest about it. Looking back, I can hardly remember the young woman who made such a decision but I know that what mattered to me then was that those I loved most in the world at that time were together. And I know that, for the two years or so that it lasted I was, and still am, convinced that the small community worked. It worked until I allowed doubts to creep in, and with that, the whole thing collapsed.

The collapse gave me an insight into another of Stuart's experiences, that of the sufferer who is to blame for their own suffering. I am not equating my own situation with Stuart's who found himself in real danger, homeless, stateless, hungry and ostracised, but I too faced homelessness, poverty, humiliation and uncertainty, but more importantly, like Stuart, I did not have the comfort of knowing others were to blame, for like Stuart, I was the instigator of my own downfall. Stuart makes great claims for the condition of living on the edge. What I did find to be true was his assertion that you come, very quickly, to recognise hypocrisy in others, and at the same time you also intuitively know when someone has experienced suffering in some way. I did find, as Stuart writes, that there is a bond of shared compassion, more often than not just silently recognised, between those who have listened to the 'howling voices of the dark'. But did this experience bring with it the revelation of Stuart's seamless reality? In a way it did not have to because I already knew that to be true, but it made me realise how I knew it was true, and this had nothing to do with Stuart or his works, so I put it to the back of my mind again.

Having read my thesis, Brendan Kennelly cross-examined me. 'How', he asked, 'do you know?' I gave him the academic answer – the way in which the work itself provides a link between Stuart's mind and the reader's, the network of correspondences he sets up and the use of postmodernist disruption, etc. He asked the question again, this time more slowly. 'How' (with the emphasis on the How) 'How, do you know?' I tried the feminist response – the way in which the work exposes the patriarchal conventions and keys into the 'feminine'. Silence. He leaned forward, looked me straight in the eye, and said seriously, or as seriously as a man whose eyes twinkle can, 'How do you know?' So I told him. I told him of a morning, just before dawn when I was all alone, giving birth to my daughter. I slipped the chains of convention and went back into a knowledge that was always there. I came face to face with the animal in me. I knew to crouch in the corner, my back supported by the walls; I knew to pant and moan and loosen every tissue of my being. It was not pain I felt as she slipped from me but something more akin to an orgasm, every nerve in my body aware that it was connected to something greater. I licked her clean, eagerly devouring the placenta, and as I sat there, covered in blood with my child at my breast – I knew. And he knew I knew.

But knowing is not enough. There is another task to perform and that is the job of the critic. To do justice to Stuart's work I have found that I have had to write myself into the story. I know that some will see this as personal and irrelevant, but I know that I am being true to the kind of criticism I now wish to write, and more importantly, I am being true to Stuart himself, for after all it was he who wrote himself into his works. Also he was aware that conventional criticism would fail to get to the heart of his work.

> The very fact that a 'critic' goes into the story of my books shows that he fails from the first to grasp what I am doing… I am only journeying safely toward my goal when I walk in the shelter of comparative obscurity. [28]

Publisher's readers and critics have long found fault with Stuart's plots, his characters and his writing style – finding the plots improbable; the characters unconvincing; and the writing uneven and clumsy. What they fail to understand is how these novelistic 'failings' operate to give a sense of immediacy; the integrity of intensely felt experience. The power of Stuart's writing lies, not in the well-polished phrase, or the well-rounded character, but in his vision, the way in which he refuses to shrink from the full horror of the world, but yet can embrace, what one critic called 'the sad poetry of life'.[29]

So what then can be said about Stuart's writing? The unique quality of the work, apart from the prose style honed to a careless awkwardness to suggest the intensity of the moment, and the careful haphazardness of the form, is the underlying voice of a profoundly honest and courageous writer who has looked into himself and revealed the essential truths of human nature. His work, when read properly, is powerfully transformative. He is an innovative and a revolutionary writer who will someday be awarded a place along with Joyce and Beckett as one of the leading Irish novelists of the twentieth century.

Those of you who distrust the personal response will be relieved to know that this is not just my opinion but that of a growing number of enthusiasts, mostly it must be said, other writers. That writers should appreciate Stuart's work is hardly surprising, since they, of all people, know the commitment and effort needed to produce any novel, never mind novels so personal or so soul-searching as Stuart's. Nor is the appreciation due merely to his longevity, the case of the young paying homage to the elder statesman or the irascible old man. Instead, what we now have is a whole generation of younger writers whose work has been influenced by Stuart and his ideas.

The originality and quality of Stuart's work has always been recognised by other writers. It was a young F.R. Higgins, a poet himself, but better remembered as director of the Abbey Theatre, who arranged to have Stuart's first little book of poems, *We Have Kept the Faith,* published privately in 1923, while Stuart was still detained in Maryborough. Yeats, though personally scathing about Stuart's behaviour to Iseult, famously wrote of *The Coloured Dome*, that it was 'more personally and beautifully written than any book of our generation. If luck comes to his aid, he will be our great writer'.[30] Liam O'Flaherty encouraged him in his writing and introduced him to Edward Garnett of Jonathan Cape, who agreed to publish Stuart's first novel, and when O'Flaherty moved to Victor Gollancz, so too did Stuart, a move that was to prove important in the post-war period. Compton MacKenzie was so impressed by *Women and God* he wrote to Stuart praising it [31] and began a friendship that lasted until his death. His review of *The Coloured Dome* is interesting in that it shows that he too, was struck by the personal effect of reading Stuart, so much so, that he reverted to silence.

> No young writer's work has impressed me so deeply as these last two books of Francis Stuart, and it was encouraging to find on the dust-jacket of "The Coloured Dome" that the literary critic for whose judgement I have most respect was as much convinced as myself of Mr Francis Stuart's genius. I am really at a loss for words. The effect of reading "The Coloured Dome" is too intimate an experience to be communicated. I am not in the habit of narrating my dreams.[32]

The writer, Ethel Mannin, now almost forgotten, but a prolific and successful novelist in the 1930s and 1940s, remained in touch with Stuart throughout his stay in Germany, and warned him that 'he was killing Francis Stuart the writer'.[33] But whatever misgivings she had, it was she who travelled to Freiburg[34] and brought back the manuscript of *The Pillar of Fire* and *Redemption* and trailed them around publishers and agents, almost giving up hope of it being accepted, when Victor Gollancz took a risk and agreed to publish *Redemption*.[35] This began a relationship that only ended in 1960 when Gollancz refused to publish 'A Trip Down the River', a novel which remains unpublished today.[36] The letter he wrote to Stuart at that time reveals his own personal commitment to the writer.

17 February 1960

My dear Francis,

Having published you so long, and in good times and bad, so to speak, I feel horrible about turning down a novel by you.

The fact that book after book of yours has not been in any way 'a commercial proposition' has never worried me: I have published them because I have enormously liked them, and I haven't worried a bit about the financial results. But here is a book that I cannot bring myself to like; and that does change things. Behind it all, there is of course your old vision: but this time I can't help feeling that it doesn't "come through".

I really am awfully sorry.
    Yours ever,
    VG[37]

This generation of writers had one thing in common – they all thought that Stuart's writing had a special quality, a quality that did not depend on public acclamation or blockbuster sales. For the next generation though, Stuart became something more – he became a mentor.

One of the unfortunate side-effects of the continued focus of interest on Stuart's wartime activities is that attention has not been given to the very real influence Stuart has had on the Irish writing scene. He has supported and sustained writers such as John McGahern who also fell foul of the moral majority in Ireland.[38] He inspired and influenced Hayden Murphy in his avant-garde newsletter. His influence on Anthony Cronin's work and thinking is worth a study in itself. Cronin's novel, *Identity Papers* (1979),[39] dedicated to Stuart, owes much to the innovative writing style that he forged in his postmodern novels. And surely Stuart was foremost in Cronin's mind when he persuaded Charles Haughey to set up Aosdána, the organisation which provides a much-needed financial lifeline to Irish writers, including Stuart.

Black List, Section H, so impressed the young Dermot Bolger, he persuaded Stuart to allow him to republish *We Have Kept the Faith,* in 1982, adding to it a selection of new poems. This was one of the first imprints of what was essentially a one-man publishing outfit, Raven Arts Press. Bolger went on to publish a selection of Stuart's prose, his novels, *Faillandia* and *The Compendium of Lovers,* two more poetry collections and the short philosophical piece, *The Abandoned Snail Shell,* written for his eighty-fifth birthday in 1987. Raven Arts expanded into New Island Books and under this imprint, Stuart's two war novels, *The Pillar of Cloud* and *Redemption* were republished. In recent years, Bolger also published

Arrows of Anguish (1996), a poetry collection, and yet another short novel, *King David Dances* (1998). In this way, Stuart has played his part in the revitalisation of the Irish publishing industry which occurred in the 1980s because of enterprising small presses, such as Raven Arts Press.

Another writer who was closely associated with the beginnings of Raven Arts Press and who has written many poems dedicated to Stuart, and indeed is his literary executor, is the poet Paul Durcan. Stuart's influence is apparent in Durcan's poetry in the social criticism, the distrust of the church, the incorporation of the personal and the painfully honest delving into the self. However, in contrast to Stuart, Durcan will often take on the role of judge while Stuart, significantly, has never been interested in apportioning blame, or taking sides, and this difference is the key to Stuart's unique stance as a writer.

Two years after the war, Stuart wrote 'I came under suspicion not because I was a Nazi, which God knows I never was, but because I was not on any side'.[40] There are those who have argued, and no doubt will continue to argue, that being in Berlin and broadcasting on Irland-Redaktion are proof enough of culpability. The facts, they say, speak for themselves. Stuart in his diary goes on to explain:

> Perhaps I was wrong to speak, perhaps it was identifying myself too much with the horrors of Nazism and it was a later revelation of this that made me refuse to speak further, but had I not done so, had I not suffered I would not have come to my present knowledge. I had to experience the whole horror first hand, a horror that was not merely the Nazi horror, but this horror of a world of which the Nazi was but a part... No I am glad that I suffered... and I know what I suffered for, because in my blind way I was not on the side of the victors, because I know there was no real victory.[41]

Given the horror of the Holocaust, we all want to be on the side of the victors; the side that could not countenance such inhumanity towards fellow human beings. We have a basic need to cling to a sense of our own moral superiority; to know that we would not have allowed ourselves to get into Stuart's position; to know that we would have spoken out against such evil; to know that we would have been one of the righteous. We need Stuart to confirm that he was wrong, so that we can feel justified in our moral indignation, but Stuart always refuses to go the whole way. He will say he was guilty, but he will add that he was not the only one. He will say that he was mistaken in his initial attraction to the regime in Germany, but he will also point out that the Allies, too, were responsible for morally suspect acts with the bombing of Dresden, Hiroshima or Nagasaki. In doing this, he is not trying to score points, or suggest that two wrongs cancel each other out. His refusal to take sides stems from his belief that all ideologies are suspect, a belief which leaves him open to the charge of political naiveté.

Stuart's concern, like many other writers in the post-Holocaust period, is with the collective guilt of humanity in the face of such overwhelming suffering. But unlike Beckett, for instance, whose tragic awareness overpowers his work, or Sartre for whom the Nazi atrocities were not merely a cause for moral indignation, but a stimulus for the imagination,[42] Stuart does not indulge in total despair or in graphic details of mutilation and death. Instead, for Stuart, the suffering of others is never directly recounted, it occurs only in glimpsed intimations in his imagination.

In *Black List, Section H*, for instance, H recalls a visit to Vienna when the torture of others broke through his own self absorption.

> On the return journey he sat in his corner – the compartment was that of a train rather than a tram – and with the summer evening fading from what he thought was beyond the Danube, which remained out of sight, he had an intimation of horrors taking place not so far away, in, roughly, the direction that, till now, the intensity of his own private life had kept him largely insulated from. Later, he thought of this afternoon and evening as the, up to then, most wretched evening he had ever spent. He had lately read of the encirclement of whole Red Army units without its registering except as another piece of war news at a time when sensation after sensation of that sort had produced in him a certain degree of indifference. The situation of these hundreds of thousands of Russians marched off to prisoner-of-war camps where they would slowly starve to death or be ravaged by epidemics was one of the signs that conditions on a vast scale were being created in which not only were the victims deprived of any kind of compassion, but also of home. The despair of vast numbers of people somewhere not very far away as pain flies (the phrase came unsought) across the darkening plain was identified by him with his own sense of desolation, and thus made real imaginatively. (*BLSH*, p.347)

159

There is in this description, a very perceptive account of the way the mind is capable of blocking out and producing a sense of indifference to horrific events while also – when the events finally filter through, reinforced by his own despair – producing an imaginative empathy that has all the force of reality.

Writing this in the aftermath of the Kosovo conflict has brought home to me the accuracy of Stuart's account. Yet again the 'civilised' world found it necessary to unleash its weapons because 'an insane dictator' was encouraging one group to annihilate another, or in today's jargon 'engage in ethnic cleansing'. Most people, I suspect, realised that this was a very simplistic reading of a complicated history, and some had reservations about the tactic of nightly bombings on Belgrade and knew that a great deal of innocent suffering and indeed, killing, was being carried out in their name. But how many really felt guilty about it? How many tried to imagine what was going on in the make-shift bomb shelters; to experience, as Stuart had experienced:

> ... a turning of our dirty, pale face to the face of darkness beyond the cellar
> darkness; it was the feeling in the trembling of the cellar and the falling of
> the plaster the passing of the angel of death and the angel of the end.
> (R, p.43)

No, we did not seek out images of the suffering in Belgrade, we were content with official reports of legitimate targets and clean hits. We did, however, find the evidence of mass graves in Kosovo strangely reassuring because they restored our sense of moral righteousness. This is the way the human mind deals with suffering on such a scale; it distorts the actuality and distances itself. This is what Stuart did in Berlin; he could block out what was happening around him, until he found himself in some distress and then found he could not avoid imagining the suffering of others. But Stuart does not dwell voyeuristically or intellectually on the horror; instead, through his 'insignificant hero' H, he reports on his own experience, the way in which he, himself, coped with despair.

First he shows how this internalised desolation is transferred onto the outer world revealing the power of the imagination to shape reality.

> Back in Vienna he kept walking aimlessly through the streets that, unlike
> those in Berlin, remained lit until ten. He felt it here too: the city was

contaminated by the plague of despair that these lands were in the grip of. (*BLSH*, p.347)

Then, significantly H looks to literature for some understanding of his situation but, as always with Stuart, he questions the easy confirmation of his own stance, the refusal to be definite in his assertions.

> That night in bed he read in the Tauchnitz edition of *Death in Venice* that Susan had sent him to Munich a sentence or two that had a bearing on his thoughts of the evening. But he knew that when a state of mind becomes intense enough almost anything read has a special significance.
> (*BLSH*, p.348)

The first sentence to capture H's attention is one which reinforces the necessity of experience for the writer.

> Thomas Mann, more conscious than Yeats of the contradiction between his life and work, put the matter clearly: 'There he sat, the master: this was he who had found a way to reconcile art and honours; who had written "The Abject", and in a style of classic purity renounced Bohemianism and all its works, all sympathy with the abyss and the troubled depths of the outcast human soul'. (*BLSH*, p.348)

The second justifies H (and Stuart) in his decision not to take sides, and confirms that from this position, the writer can not only have compassion with the abyss, but experience the abyss itself.

> The next sentence that had caught H's tired attention – he read late because he feared the moment of turning out the light and laying his head on the pillow: 'Knowledge is all-knowing, understanding, forgiving; it takes up no position, sets no store by form. It has compassion with the abyss – it is the abyss.' (*BLSH*, p.348)

H, again like Stuart, does not dwell long in the abyss, instead he finds another image to convey a mood of slender optimism.

> One evening as he was crossing the square in front of the Café Mozart, he looked upward and saw in the deep incandescent blue, high above the weathered red roofs and the dome of the Opera House, a new moon. He used it, as he'd used the words in *Death in Venice*, as a confirmation of a certain consciousness in himself, this time one of very fragile hope. (*BLSH*, p.348)

Turning again towards life, H returns to Berlin and affirms life by beginning a sexual relationship with Halka, an affirmation that again includes a confirmation by literary reference and by a change in perspective.

> Afterwards they stayed on the couch while the water boiled on the much-patched electric ring in the corner ... he read her some of Keats's poems; raptly she listens, he reflected, his thoughts echoing the cadence of what he'd been reading out. Before she had to leave they made love again. In the hushed aftermath, for a little while, nothing is as it was before and objects are not quite set in their pre-orgasm outlines after their obscuration in the general physical melting. (*BLSH*, p.351)

Stuart therefore moves from the imaginative contemplation of suffering to a sliver of hope and then to the comfort of momentary union in which the perception of the world alters. He knows that the human mind is incapable of contemplating suffering on a vast scale so he turns towards the human, giving a disturbing yet convincing account of the struggle to survive. By refusing to intellectualise or politicise events and instead concentrating on the personal, the individual account, Stuart succeeds in revealing more powerfully the truth of the human condition and that there are humble virtues more precious than heroism. He shows how simple acts of human compassion hold out a frail, perhaps the only, hope against despair.

There is in this a simplicity which makes it difficult to argue with Terry Eagleton's assertion that this leaves the radical 'with nothing to pit against political barbarism but a change of heart'. But it also makes you aware how profoundly powerful 'a change of heart'[43] can be, not only personally, but politically. Despite his criticisms, Eagleton proclaims that Stuart has a claim to be 'the greatest revolutionary writer of modern Ireland'[44] revolutionary in that he is 'disruptively radical'.[45] Stuart's radicalism leads him to the brutal core of the human condition so that a journey with Francis Stuart is one that ultimately leaves you face to face with yourself, and those who shy away from his works are, in effect, shying away from themselves.

Postscript

... people will not like my work. This discovery is a shock but it is also a clarifying of the position. It will be hard for my novels to get themselves accepted. But if they are they will mean a great deal to a few.[46]

Endnotes

Introduction: Ní bhíonn saoi gan locht

1. Copeland, Rebecca, Introduction to Chiyo, Uno, *The Story of a Single Woman* (trans. Rebecca Copeland,) Charles E. Tuttle, Tokyo, 1993.
2. Stuart, Francis, letter to J.H. Natterstad, 6 October 1969, published in *The Journal of Irish Literature*, Vol.5, No.1, January 1976, p.98.
3. Burke, Bernard, *Irish Family Records,* Burke's Peerage Press, 1956.
4. In a letter to J.H. Natterstad, dated 6 October 1969, Stuart wrote 'He, and the circumstances of his end, were never mentioned to me as a child or youth. Even now I am not quite sure of them except that he suffered from prolonged and excessive drinking and possibly killed himself.' Published in *The Journal of Irish Literature*, Vol.5, No.1, January 1976, p.97.
5. Elborn, Geoffrey, *Francis Stuart: A Life*, Raven Arts Press, Dublin, 1990.
6. Ibid. p.14.
7. 'Iseult has been starved, kept without sleep & several times knocked down by her husband who is mad. His father died in a lunatic asylum and his mother's father died of drink. He has never given her any money – & Iseult from pride or from some more obscure impulse has not asked for any.' W.B. Yeats, letter to Lady Gregory, 1 August 1920 in Allen Wade (ed.), *The Letters of W.B. Yeats*, Rupert Hart-Davis, London, 1954.
8. Elborn, Geoffrey, *Francis Stuart: A Life*, p.60.

9. Stuart was awarded the Young Poets' Prize for 1923 awarded by Mrs Rockafeller McCormick for poems published in Harriet Monroe (ed.), *Poetry. A Magazine of Verse*, Chicago, 1923.

10. The address of The Oak Leaf Press was 13 Fleet Street, Dublin, the registered address of the General Advertising & Wood Printing Co., and also the registered address of the publishers of the first edition of *Tomorrow*, (the second edition having the registered address of Roebuck House, Maud Gonne's home in Dublin).

11. Stuart, Francis, *Nationalism and Culture*, Sinn Féin Árd Chomhairle, Baile Átha Cliath, 1924.

12. Con Leventhal, later to succeed Samuel Beckett at Trinity College Dublin and after 1963 acted as Beckett's secretary in Paris was, at that time, running a bookshop in Dawson Street in Dublin.

13. Cecil ffrench Salkeld, the son of Blanaid Salkeld, who enjoyed some success as a writer and actress at the Abbey Theatre, studied art in Germany, but is now best remembered as Brendan Behan's father-in-law, his daughter Beatrice having married the playwright.

14. 'A group of Dublin poets, a man called Higgins and the Stuarts and another, whose name I do not know, who were about to publish a review but it was suppressed by the printers for blasphemy. I got a bottle of Sparkling Moselle, which I hope youthful ignorance mistook for champagne, and we swore alliance. I saw a proof sheet marked by the printer 'with no mention meant to be made of the Blessed Virgin' – the good lady as we all know being confined to church. My dream is a wild paper of the young, which will make enemies everywhere and suffer suppression, I hope a number of times.' W.B. Yeats, letter to Olivia Shakespear, 21 June 1924, in Allan Wade (ed.), *The Letters of W.B. Yeats*, p.705.

15. 'The idea attracted Yeats and to our surprise and delight he offered to give us a new and unpublished poem of his to print in the first number. The poem was 'Leda and the Swan' and when I read it I realised that because of this poem our paper would be of importance. But Yeats's interest in the project went even further. He wrote an editorial for us, not, of course, to appear above his signature. In it he deplored the lack of any cultural standards in the new Irish State and in the Church in Ireland. I don't think we realised what a bombshell we were exploding when we printed this article, to say nothing of the poem with its strange, perverse eroticism. I know I didn't.' Francis Stuart in Francis MacManus (ed.), *The Yeats We Knew*, Mercier Press, Dublin, 1977.

16. In a letter to Lady Gregory, January 1925, Sean O'Casey tells her. 'There

is a very bitter article in this month's *Catholic Bulletin* about the recent happenings around the publication of *Tomorrow*. It is so vulgar in tone that I am reluctant to send it on to you.' In the article, the editor of the *Catholic Bulletin*, after a long tirade condemned 'the filthy Swan Song of Senator W.B. Yeats and the ribald obscenities and brutal blasphemies of the prose story signed Lennox Robinson.' The controversy led to the dismissal of Robinson from his position as secretary of the Carnegie Library Committee as a result of the protests of two clerical members of the committee, one Roman Catholic and the other Church of Ireland. Robinson said he found the 'whole thing inexpressibly painful. It alienated many of his friends and the breach was never healed'. Krause, David, *The Letters of Sean O'Casey, Vol.1, 1910–1941*, Macmillan, London, 1975, p.123.

17. Stuart, H., 'In the Hour Before Dawn', *To-morrow*, Vol.1, No.2, September 1924, p.4.

18. Edward Garnett was well known as the reader for Jonathan Cape from 1921 until his death in 1937. Garnett was the reader who turned down Beckett's *Dream of Fair-to Middling Women,* saying that he 'wouldn't touch it with a barge-pole. Beckett probably is a clever fellow, but here he has elaborated a slavish and rather incoherent imitation of Joyce, most eccentric in language and full of disgustingly affected passages – also indecent'. Garnett had the habit of closely tutoring his authors and O'Flaherty's correspondence with him shows that he had a tremendous influence on his thinking and writing, and indeed reading.

19. I am indebted to Mike Bott of the University of Reading Library for this information.

20. Yeats, W.B., dustjacket to *The Coloured Dome*, Victor Gollancz, London, 1932.

21. Hutchison, Percy, 'An Unusual Novel Out of Ireland: Mysticism and Colloquial Realism Combine to Make Mr. Stuart's *Pigeon Irish* an Out-of-the-Ordinary Work of Fiction', *New York Times*, 3 July, 1932.

22. Mackenzie, Compton, 'A Novel That Swept Me Off My Feet', *Daily Mail*, 16 February 1932.

23. O'Flaherty, Liam, Letters to Francis Stuart. 14 February 1932–July 1936 Manuscript 5/6. 29–36, Southern Illinois University Library, published in A.A. Kelly (ed.), *Letters of Liam O'Flaherty*, Wolfhound Press, 1996.

24. 'Summed up, the play seemed loosely written and loosely constructed; but Mr. Stuart can, of course, do better. He wouldn't have reached his present high rating in contemporary letters if he couldn't.' *Dublin Opinion*, April, 1933.

25. 'Mr. Brian Hearst, who produced the first modern Irish film, *Irish Hearts*, is about to begin work on the production of a paraphrased version of Synge's *Riders to the Sea*. The first shots will be made at the end of next month in Leenane, Connemara and Aran Island. The cast will be drawn from the Abbey and Gate Theatre Companies. Sara Allgood is to play the part of Moira, Ria Mooney that of Kathleen, her daughter; Duncan Guthrie, her son. The play is being adapted by Mr. Francis Stuart, Academy of Letters.' *Irish Press*, 28 May 1935.

26. Stuart, Iseult, letter to Francis Stuart, 15 May 1953, Manuscript 52 5/8.45 Southern Illinois University Library.

27. 'Plays of such merit are all too rare, and in this case Londoners had the advantage over Dubliners for "Glory" is not, I hear, to be staged at the Abbey Theatre. Glory is a play which gives a powerful dramatic presentation of Francis Stuart's "Testament of Beauty" – disillusionment follows the striving after beauty by means of territorial conquest.' *The Times*, 8 January 1936.

28. *Strange Guest*, Manuscript 52 2/4, Southern Illinois University Library.

29. Diary entry, 16 October 1942, Notebook III, Francis Stuart Collection, University of Ulster Library.

30. Diary entry, 25 September 1942, Notebook VIII, University of Ulster Library.

31. Diary entry, 20 August 1942, Notebook II, University of Ulster Library.

32. Diary entry, 25 September 1942, Notebook II, University of Ulster Library.

33. Diary entry, 25 September 1942, Notebook II, University of Ulster Library.

34. Ibid.

35. Diary entry, 9 April 1945, Notebook VII, University of Ulster Library.

36. *Sunday Independent*, November 1999.

37. Letter from Victor Gollancz, 14 April 1953, Manuscript 25.8, University of Ulster Library.

38. Letter from Victor Gollancz, 19 March 1948, Manuscript 5/2.5, Francis Stuart Collection, Southern Illinois University, Carbondale.

39. Reader's Report on *Danny Boy*, Manuscript 25.4, University of Ulster Library.

40. Letter from Sheila Hodge of Victor Gollancz, 28 September 1950, Manuscript 25.2, University of Ulster Library.

41. 'I would much like to see you and get away from this cotton wool fog, barrage of tact and money, solicitors… the devil. Don't know that I'd give you the money if I had it. I don't like to think of you so poor but we are

all poor together. You have disappointed me about your attitude over this house, but you poor old Grim, and you are as always very good in some ways, shockingly blind in other ways.' Iseult Gonne, letter to Francis Stuart, September (?), Manuscript 52, University of Ulster Library, also letters from Iseult Gonne, 17 October 1945, 27 October 1945, 1 November 1945 and 24 August 1951, Manuscript 5/8.40/43, Southern Illinois University Library.

42. Letter from Victor Gollancz, 17 February 1960, Manuscript 25.9, University of Ulster Library. 'A Trip Down the River', 1959, 556p. AMS, an unpublished novel begun November 15, 1959' Manuscript 2/5, Southern Illinois University.

43. Letters of rejection from David Higham Associates, 20 September 1967; McGibbon & Kee, 22 February 1968; A.P. Watt, 11 August 1969; Michael Gill, 4 November 1969, Andre Deutsch, 15 June 1970; Vernon Sternberg, 13 April 1972; Tom Stacey Ltd, 9 May 1972; Wm. Heinemann, 19 July 1972, Manuscript 27, University of Ulster Library.

44. O'Keefe, Timothy, letter to Francis Stuart, 22 February 1968, Manuscript 27, University of Ulster Library.

45. Arts Council News Release, 6 August 1980 Manuscript 167, University of Ulster Library.

Chapter One: The Reality of Unreality

1. The range of Stuart's reading is recorded in the Francis Stuart Special Collections held at the University of Ulster Library, Coleraine and at Southern Illinois University at Carbondale, in the correspondence, the manuscripts (Stuart had the habit of jotting down personal notes while writing which amount to a journal of progress and personal details), but mostly in the eighteen diaries held at Coleraine which date from March 1942 to August 1977.

2. Beckett, Samuel, 'Dante... Bruno... Vico... Joyce', *Disjecta: Miscellaneous Writings and a Dramatic Fragment*, John Calder, London, 1983, p.27.

3. Plato, *The Republic* (trans. Robin A.H. Waterfield) Book Vii (532c), Oxford University Press, Oxford, 1993.

4. Murdoch, Iris, *The Sovereignty of Good*, Routledge & Kegan Paul, London, 1970, p.93.

5. Plato, *Protagoras and Meno* (trans. W.R.C. Guthrie) Penguin Books, Harmondsworth, 1956, p.139.

6. Plato, *Philebus*, 51 (trans. Robin A.H. Waterfield) Penguin Books, Harmondsworth, 1982, p.121.

7. Ayer, Sir Alfred J., *Language, Truth and Logic*, Penguin, Harmondsworth, 1971, p.64.

8. Jaspers, Karl, *Man in the Modern Age* (trans. E. & C. Paul) G. Routledge & Sons, London, 1933.

9. Diary entry, 5 August 1942: Notebook II, August 42, Francis Stuart Collection, University of Ulster Library.

10. Natterstad, Jerry, 'Interview with Francis Stuart', in *The Journal of Irish Literature*, January 1976, Vol.5, No.1, p.17.

11. Diary entry 30 November 1942, Notebook IV, University of Ulster Library.

12. Eliot, Thomas S., 'Burnt Norton', *The Complete Poems and Plays*, Faber & Faber, London, 1970, pp11–43.

13. Stuart described *Black List, Section H* as 'autobiographical fiction' in a letter to Jerry Natterstad dated 6 October 1969, published in *The Journal of Irish Literature*, Vol.5, No.1, January 1976, p.98.

14. Ortega y Gasett, Jose, *The Modern Theme* (trans. James Cleugh) C.W. Daniel Co., London, 1931, p.26.

15. Jeans, Sir James H., *The Mysterious Universe,* Cambridge University Press, Cambridge, 1930, p.57.

16. 'What we observe is not nature in itself, but nature exposed to our method of questioning… in this way quantum theory reminds us, as Bohr has put it, that in the drama of existence we are both players and spectators.' Heisenberg, W., *Physics and Philosophy: The Revolution in Modern Science*, Harper & Row, New York, 1958, p.58.
'The traditional view that the world exists as a discrete, well-defined object, and that scientific representations effectively mirror the world as object, can no longer be maintained. The paradoxical *reality* of modern physics is inseparable from the manner in which the physicist experimentally interacts with phenomena.' White, Eric C., 'Contemporary Cosmology and Narrative Theory' in S. Peterfreund (ed.) *Literature and Science*, Northeastern University Press, Boston, 1990, p.98.

17. Stuart, Francis, 'Novelists on the Novel', *Crane Bag*, Vol.3, No.1, 1979.

18. Abrams, Meyer H., *The Mirror and the Lamp: Romantic Theory and the Critical Tradition*, Oxford University Press, Oxford, 1971, pp30–47.

19. McHale, Brian, *Postmodern Fiction,* Methuen, London, 1987, p.28.

20. Abrams, M.H., *The Mirror and the Lamp: Romantic Theory and the Critical Tradition,* p.47–70.

21. Paz, Octavio, *Children of the Mire: Modern Poetry from Romanticism to the Avant-garde* (trans. Rachael Phillips) Harvard University Press, Cambridge, Mass., 1974, p.60.

22. Berger, Peter and Luckman, Thomas, *The Social Construction of Reality: A Treatise in the Sociology of Knowledge*, Doubleday, New York, 1966, p.24–5.

23. Kearney, Richard, 'A Crisis of Imagination', *Crane Bag*, Vol.3, No.1, 1979, p.392.

24. Ibid.

25. Ibid. p.393.

26. de Mann, Paul, 'Action and Identity in Nietzche', *Yale French Studies*, No.52 , Fall 1975, pp16–30.

27. Nietzsche, Fredrich, *The Will to Power* (trans. W. Kaufmann and R.J. Hollindale) Weidenfeld & Nicolson, London, 1968, p.279.

28. See Introduction to Beckett, Samuel, *En Attendant Godot*, Harrap, London, 1966, p.xiii.

29. Beckett, Samuel, *Proust and Three Dialogues with George Duthuit*, John Calder, London 1987, p.13.

30. Ibid. p.103.

31. Ibid. p.125.

32. Beckett, Samuel, *The Unnameable,* in *The Beckett Trilogy*, Picador, London, 1979, p.381.

33. Stuart, 'Novelists on the Novel', p.410.

34. Reverdy, Pierre, *Le Gant de Crin*, Flammarion, Paris, 1968, p.52 (quoted in Bell, M., *Reverdy Translations*, Whiteknights, Reading, 1997).

35. de Nerval, Gerard, *Oeuvres* (1960) in *Selected Writings* (trans. Richard Sieburth) Penguin Books, Harmondsworth, 1999.

36. Hayter, Alethea, *Opium and the Romantic Imagination*, Faber & Faber, London, 1968. p.48.

37. Levi-Strauss, Claude, *The Savage Mind*, Weidenfeld & Nicholson, London, 1966, p.263.

38. Stewart, Kilton, *Pygmies and Dream Giants*, Harper & Row, New York, 1975, pp63–4.

39. Diary entry, June 1943, Notebook V, Francis Stuart Collection, University of Ulster Library, Coleraine.

40. Rilke, Rainer M., *New Poems [1907] (*trans. Edward Snow) North Point Press, San Francisco, 1987, p.214.

41. Paz, Octavio, *Configurations* (trans. M. Rukeyser et al), New Directions, New York, 1971, p.188.

Chapter Two: Images of Imagination

1. Hesiod, *The Works of Hesiod, Calimachus and Theognis* (trans. James Banks) G. Bell, London, 1914, p.305.

2. Donoghue, Denis, *Thieves of Fire*, Faber & Faber, London, 1973.

3. Ibid. p.26.
4. See Hassan, Ihab H., *The Dismemberment of Orpheus: Towards a Postmodern Literature,* Oxford University Press, Oxford, 1971.
5. Graves, Robert, *The Greek Myths*, Vol.1, Penguin Books, Harmondsworth, 1955, p.317.
6. Stuart Francis, 'Patrick Kavanagh: Earthly Visionary', *Hibernia*, July 1975, p.21.
7. Kant, Immanuel, *Critique of Pure Reason* (trans. Norman K. Smith) Macmillan & Co., London, 1934.
8. Ibid. (In B.138, Kant speaks of the transcendental imagination as an 'art concealed in the depths of the human soul'. It is that which grounds the objectifity of the object in the subjectivity of the subject – rather than in some 'transcendent' order beyond man. For Kant, then, imagination is a hidden condition of all knowledge.)
9. Ibid. p.146.
10. Kant, Immanuel, *The Critique of Judgement* (trans. James C. Meredith) Clarendon Press, Oxford, 1952, p.245.
11. Kearney, Richard, *The Wake of Imagination: Ideas of Creativity in Western Culture,* Hutchinson Press, London, 1988, p.175.
12. Kant, Immanuel, *The Critique of Judgement*, p.246.
13. Plato, 'Ion' in *Early Socratic Dialogues* (ed. Trevor J. Saunders), Penguin, Harmondsworth, 1987, p.55.
14. Aristotle, *Problemata*, Book XXX, *The Works of Aristotle*, Vol.Vii (trans. W.P. Ross) Clarendon Press, Oxford, 1929, p.953a (for a discussion of this problem and its background see Klibansky, Raymond, Panofsky, Erwin, and Saxl, Fritz, *Saturn and Melancholy: Studies in the History of Natural Philosophy, Religion and Art,* Nelson, London, 1964, pp15-41.)
15. Burton, Richard, *The Anatomy of Melancholy,* J. Peters (ed.) New York, 1979, p.115.
16. Ibid. p.44.
17. Ibid.
18. Browne, Ivor 'The Madness of Genius', *Irish University Review*, Vol.17, No.1, Spring 1987, p.129.
19. Ibid. p.132.
20. Ibid.
21. Ibid. p.133.
22. Ibid.
23. See Elborn, Geoffrey, *Francis Stuart: A Life*, Raven Arts Press, Dublin, 1990 and Natterstad, Jerry, 'The Artist as Outcast', *Studies in Anglo-Irish Literature* (edHeinz Kosok), Bouvier Verlag Hembert Grundman, Bonn, 1982.

24. Elborn, Geoffrey, *Francis Stuart: A Life*, p.20.
25. Natterstad, Jerry, 'An Interview with Francis Stuart', *The Journal of Irish Literature*, Vol.5, No.1, January 1976, p.20.
26. Natterstad, Jerry, 'The Artist as Outcast', p.339.
27. In a letter to Jerry Natterstad dated 6 October 1969, Stuart wrote 'He, and the circumstances of his end, were never mentioned to me as a child or youth. Even now I am not quite sure of them except that he suffered from prolonged and excessive drinking and possibly killed himself.' (Published in *The Journal of Irish Literature*, Vol.5, No.1, January 1976, p.97.)
28. Elborn, Geoffrey, *Francis Stuart: A Life*, p.11.
29. Jung, Carl G., 'Psychology and Literature', 1930 quoted in R. Selden, *The Theory of Literature*, Longman Press, London, 1988, p.23.
30. Natterstad, Jerry, 'An Interview with Francis Stuart', p.20.
31. Ibid. p.28.
32. Ibid, p.17.
33. Letter to J.H.Natterstad, 9 March 1970 (quoted in Jerry Natterstad, 'The Artist as Outcast', p.336).
34. Fisk, Robert, 'Interview with Francis Stuart', 13 June 1978 (published in Robert Fisk, *In Time of War: Ireland, Ulster and the Price of Neutrality*, Paladin, London, 1983, p.383).
35. Diary entry, 3 May 1945, Notebook VII, University of Ulster Library.
36. Diary entry, 9 April 1945 Notebook VII, University of Ulster Library.
37. Ibid.
38. Diary entry, 21 November 1945, Notebook IX, University of Ulster Library.
39. Stuart, Madelaine, *Manna in the Morning*, Raven Arts Press, Dublin, 1984.
40. Cronin, Anthony, Interview with Francis Stuart, 1979 (quoted in Robert Fisk, *In Time of War*, p.383).
41. Stuart, Francis, letter, *Irish Times*, January 1971.
42. Natterstad, Jerry, 'An Interview with Francis Stuart', p.19.
43. See Mandel, Eli, 'On Oscar Wilde and Jean Genet', *The Literature of Prison and Exile*, CBC Enterprises, Montreal, 1968.
44. Skvorecky, Josef, *The Writer and Human Rights*, Transcript of PEN Symposium (eds. Toronto Arts Group for Human Rights), Lester and Orpen Dennys, Toronto, 1983, p.134.
45. Davies, Ioan, *Writers in Prison*, Basil Blackwell, Oxford, 1990, p.25.
46. Havel, Václav, 'Stories and Totalitarianism', *Index on Censorship*, 17, 3, 1988, p.18.
47. Dostoevsky, Fydor M., *Notes from the Underground* (trans. Jessie Coulson) Penguin Books, Harmondsworth, 1972, p.16.

48. Bakhtin, Mikhail, *Problems of Dostoevsky's Poetics* (ed. and trans. Caryl Emerson) Manchester University Press, Manchester, 1984, p.234.

49. Letter to Ronald Hall, published in Elborn, Geoffrey, p.256.

50. Ms.27. 22 February 1968, letter from Timothy O'Keefe at McGibbon & Kee, Publishers, London, Francis Stuart Collection, University of Ulster Library.

51. Natterstad, Jerry, 'An Interview with Francis Stuart', p.29.

52. Poincare, Henri, 'Mathematical Creation', in Philip E. Vernon (ed.) *Creativity. Selected Readings,* Penguin Books, Harmondsworth, 1970, p.83.

53. Puskin, Alexander, 'The Poet' (trans. Tadeusz Rozewicz) quoted in 'Literature as Celebration: Four Papers from the First International Writers' Conference held in Dublin, May 1988' in *The Irish Review,* Autumn, 1988, p.90.

54. Rozewicz, Tadeusz, Paper given at the First International Writers' Conference, Dublin 1988, published in *The Irish Review,* No.5, Autumn 1988, p.91.

55. Hoyle, Fred and Wickramasinghe, N.Chandra, *Evolution from Space,* Dent, London 1981.

Chapter Three: An Analogy of Angels

1. Plato,'Symposium', *The Dialogues of Plato* (trans. B. Jowett), Clarendon Press, Oxford, 1964 (206a & 207a).

2. Plato, 'Pheadrus', *The Dialogues of Plato* (trans. B. Jowett), Clarendon Press, Oxford, 1964 (241d).

3. Plato, 'Symposium', 206a & 207a.

4. Ibid.

5. Daly, Mary, *Gyn/Ecology: The Metaethics of Radical Feminism,* The Women's Press, London, 1979.

6. Atwood, Margaret, *Surfacing,* McClelland & Stewart, Toronto, 1970.

7. Daly, Mary, *Pure Lust: Elemental Feminist Philosophy,* The Women's Press, London, 1984, p.x.

8. Donne, John, 'Aire and Angels', *The Complete English Poems of John Donne,* Penguin, Harmondsworth, 1971, p.41.

9. See Marks, Elaine and de Courtivron, Isabella, *New French Feminisms: An Anthology,* Harvester Press, Brighton, 1981.

10. Cixous, Helene, 'The Laugh of the Medusa' in Elaine Marks and Isabella de Courtivron, *New French Feminisms: An Anthology,* pp24–64.

11. Irigaray, Luce, *This Sex which is not one,* Cornell University Press, New York, 1985, p.85.

12. Cixous, Helene, 'The Laugh of the Medusa', pp245–64.

13. See Scott, Bonnie Kime, *James Joyce*, Harvester Press, Brighton, 1987, p.117.
14. Shelley, Percy Bysshe, 'Adonais', *Poetical Works*, Oxford University Press, Oxford, 1970, p.443.
15. See Daly, Mary, *Pure Lust*, pp.100–6.
16. Ibid. p.310.
17. King, Ursula, *Women and Spirituality: Voices of Protest and Promise*, Macmillan, London, 1989, p.199.
18. For a discussion of the double standards of morality see Thomas, K., 'The Double Standard', *Journal of the History of Ideas*, Vol.20, April 20, 1959, pp195–216.
19. Drysdale, George, *Physical, Sexual and Natural Religion: By a Student of Medicine*, Edward Truelove, London, 1855, pp172–3 (quoted in Linda Nead, *Myths of Sexuality*, Basil Blackwell, Oxford, 1988, p.21).
20. Marks, Elaine and de Courtivron, Isabella, *New French Feminisms: An Anthology*, p.36.
21. See Mallarme, Stephane, *Collected Poems* (trans. Fr. C.F. MacIntyre) University of California Press, Berkeley, 1957.
22. See Kristeva, Julia, *Revolution in Poetic Language* (trans. Margaret Waller) Columbia University Press, New York, 1984.
23. Kristeva, Julia, 'Polylogue' (quoted in A.R. Jones, 'French Theories of the Feminine' in G. Greene, and C. Kahn (eds), *Making a Difference,* Methuen, London, 1985, p.86
24. Olsen, Tillie, *Silences*, Virago, London, 1980.
25. Rich, Adrienne, *On Lies, Secrets and Silence*, p.68.
26. Harmon, Maurice, 'Francis Stuart' in R. Imhof (ed.) *Contemporary Irish Novelists*, Gunter, Narr Verlag Tubingen, 1989, p.15.
27. 'Feminist scholarship undertakes the dual task of deconstructing predominently male cultural paradigms and reconstructing a female perspective and experience in an effort to change the tradition that has silenced and marginalized us.' Green, G. and Kahn, C., 'Feminist Scholarship and the Social Construction of Woman', *Making a Difference: Feminist Literary Criticism*, p.1.
28. Rich Adrienne, 'Taking Women Students Seriously', *On Lies Secrets and Silence: Selected Prose 1966–1978*, p.245.
29. Cixous, Helene, 'The Laugh of the Medusa' p.245.
30. Fetterley, Judith, *The Resisting Reader, A Feminist Approach to American Literature*, Indiana University Press, Bloomington, 1981, p.viii.
31. Gardiner, Judith Kegan, 'On Female Identity', in Elizabeth Abel (ed.) *Writing and Difference*, Harvester Press, Brighton, 1982, p.184.

32. Ibid. p.185.
33. Spretnak, C. (ed.) *The Politics of Women's Spirituality*, Anchon Press, New York, 1982, p.60.
34. King, Ursula, *Women and Spirituality*, p.145.
35. *Story of a Soul: The Autobiography of St. Thérèse of Lisieux*, (trans. J. Clarke), ICS Publications, Washington DC, 1972.
36. Sackville-West, Violet, *The Eagle and the Dove*, Michael Joseph, London, 1944, p.148.
37. *Story of a Soul*, Manuscript B, pp190–200.
38. Ibid. p.168.
39. Sackville-West, Violet, *The Eagle and the Dove*, p.148.

Chapter Four: From Metaphysics to Metafiction

1. Stuart, Francis, letter to J.H. Natterstad, 22 November 1969, published in *The Journal of Irish Literature*, Vol.5, No.1, January 1976, p.99.
2. 'I have had the Gospel women in mind, or in the subconscious when depicting the main female characters in my fiction.' (Stuart, Francis, *The Abandoned Snail Shell*, p.46.)
3. Otto considers that the numinous experience of unseen presences provokes a reaction which is a mixture of 'awe, dread, mystery and fascination. It has its wild and demonic forms and can sink to an almost grisly horror and shuddering. It has its crude, barbaric antecedents, and early manifestations, and again it may be developed into something beautiful and pure and glorious. It may become the hushed, trembling, and speechless humility of the creature in the presence of – whom or what? In the presence of that which is a mystery inexpressible.' Otto, Rudolf, *The Idea of the Holy: An Inquiry into the Non-Rational Factor in the Idea of the Divine* (trans. John W. Harvey), Oxford University Press, Oxford, 1950, pp12–13.
4. 'One day I hope that You, the Adorable Eagle, will come to fetch me, Your little bird; and ascending with it to the Furnace of Love, You will plunge it for all eternity into the burning Abyss of this Lone to which it has offered itself as victim.' (Manuscript B), *The Story of a Soul: The Autobiography of St. Thérèse of Lisieux* (trans. J. Clarke), ICS Publications, Washington, 1972, p.22.
5. 'The *sambhoga-kaya* appears to indicate the aspect of 'awakenedness' or truth, as it is perceived in the realm of celestial bliss, that is the non-mortal realm.' *Dictionary of Religions* (ed. J. Hinnells) Penguin, Harmondsworth, 1984, p.70. 'There is a higher knowledge inaccessible to human understanding or through sense-experience, but attainable in expanded states of consciousness.' *Dictionary of Religions*, p.224.

6. Diary entry, 1 August 1942, Notebook II, Francis Stuart Collection, University of Ulster Library.

7. Shelley, Pearse Bysse, 'Adonais', *Poetical Works*, Oxford University Press, Oxford, 1970, p.443.

8. Diary entry, May 1945, Notebook VIII, University of Ulster Library.

9. See Bultmann, Rudolph, 'The New Testament and Mythology', in Hans W. Bartsch (ed), *Kerygma and Myth: A Theological Debate* (trans. Reginald H. Fuller), S.P.C.K., London, 1972.

10. See Tillich, Paul J.O., *The Dynamics of Faith*, George Allen & Unwin, London, 1957.

11. Bultmann, Rudolph, *The Theology of the New Testament* (trans. Kenrick Grobel), Scribner, New York, 1955, p.240.

12. Tillich, Paul, *The Dynamics of Faith,* p.42.

13. Ibid. p.43.

14. Heidegger, Martin, *Existence and Being* (trans. Scott Douglas), H. Regnery Co., Chicago, 1947, pp279–81.

15. Ibid. p.360.

16. Wright, Terence R., *Theology and Literature*, Basil Blackwell, Oxford, 1988, p.10.

17. Ibid.

18. Ricoeur, Paul, *Interpretation Theory, Discourse and the Surplus of Meaning*, Texas Christian University Press, Texas, 1976, p.61.

19. Wright,Terence R., *Theology and Literature*, p.140.

20. Ibid.p.142.

21. Jung, Carl G., *Psychology and Western Religion*, Ark Paperbacks, London, 1988, p.283.

22. Wright, Terence R., *Theology and Literature*, p.139.

23. Diary entry, September 1943, Notebook V, University of Ulster Library.

24. Blake, William, 'Augeries of Innocence', (ed. G. Keynes), *Complete Writings*, Oxford University Press, Oxford, 1969, p.431.

25. Ibid.

26. 'Yeats, William B., 'The Death of the Hare', *Collected Poems*, (ed. R.J. Finneran), Macmillan, London, 1989, p.238.

27. Yeats, William B., 'The Collar-Bone of the Hare', *Collected Poems* (ed. R.J. Finneran), Macmillan, London, 1989, p.136.

28. Lewis, Clive Staples, quoted in Terence R. Wright, *Theology and Literature*, p.47.

29. Eliot, Thomas S., *Selected Essays*, Faber & Faber, London, 1934, p.390.

30. Auerbach, Erich, *Mimesis: The Representation of Reality in Western Literature* (trans. Willard R. Trask) Princeton University Press, Princeton, 1953, p.6.

31. Barthes, Roland, 'The Structuralist Analysis of a Narrative', in A. Johnston (ed.), *Structuralism and Biblical Hermeneutics*, Pickwick Press, Pittsburgh, 1979, p.120.
32. Ibid.
33. Frye, Northrop, *The Great Code, the Bible and Literature*, Routledge & Kegan Paul, London, 1982, p.193.
34. Kermode, Frank, *The Genesis of Secrecy, On the Interpretation of Narrative*, Harvard University Press, Cambridge, Mass., 1979, p.89.
35. Kermode, Frank, *The Sense of an Ending, Studies in the Theory of Fiction*, Oxford University Press: New York, 1967, p.39.
36. Ibid.
37. Wright, Terence R., *Theology and Literature*, p.86.
38. Ibid. p.54.
39. Schneidau, Herbert, *The Sacred Discontent, the Bible and Western Literature*, University of California Press, Berkeley, 1976, pp4–12.
40. Crossan, John D., *In Parables: The Challenge of the Historical Jesus*, Seabury, New York, 1973, p.10.
41. See Wright, Terence R., *Theology and Literature*, p.55.
42. See Hutcheon, Linda, *Narcissistic Narratives: The Metafictional Paradox*, Methuen, New York, 1984, p.141.
43. O'Toole, Fintan, 'Stuart – Up to 90', *Irish Times*, April 29, 1992.
44. Ibid.
45. St Luke, 24:19.
46. St Luke, 24:29.
47. Ibid.
48. St Mark, 16:8
49. Kermode, Frank, *The Genesis of Secrecy*, p.68.
50. Wright, Terence R., *Theology and Literature*, p.82.
51. Ibid.
52. St Mark, 13:31.
53. Wright, Terence R, *Theology and Literature*, p.83
54. Ibid.
55. Natterstad, Jerry, 'Interview with Francis Stuart', p.16.
56. St Luke, 24:19.
57. Stuart, Francis, 'Literature and Politics', *The Crane Bag*, 1977, Vol.1. No.1, p.79.
58. Eliot, Thomas, S., *Selected Essays*, p.390.
59. O'Toole, 'Stuart – Up to 90'.

Chapter Five: The Significance of the Self

1. Stuart, Francis, 'Novelists on the Novel' *Crane Bag*, Vol.3, No.1, 1979, p.410.
2. Yeats, William B., *Autobiographies*, Macmillan & Co., London, 1955, p.106.
3. Natterstad, Jerry, 'An Interview with Francis Stuart', p.23.
4. Elborn, Geoffrey, *Francis Stuart: A Life*, p.88.
5. Natterstad, Jerry, 'An Interview with Francis Stuart' p.24.
6. King, Ursula, *Women and Spirituality*, p.106.
7. Natterstad, Jerry, 'An Interview with Francis Stuart', p.28.
8. Manning, Olivia, review of *The Pillar of Cloud*, Stuart Scrapbook, Francis Stuart Collection, University of Ulster.
9. Ibid.
10. Manuscript 17, Reader's Report on *The Pilgrimage*, Francis Stuart Collection, University of Ulster Library.
11. Manning Olivia, review of *The Pillar of Cloud*.
12. Elborn, Geoffrey, *Francis Stuart: A Life*, p.239.
13. Pascal, Roy, *Design and Truth in Autobiography*, Routledge & Kegan Paul, London, 1960.
14. Bruss, Elizabeth W., *Autobiographical Acts: The Changing Situation of a Literary Genre*, John Hopkins University Press, Baltimore, 1976, p.18.
15. Olney, James, *Metaphors of Self: The Meaning of Autobiography*, Princeton University Press, Princeton, 1972.
16. Wright, D.G., *Yeats's Myth of Self*, Gill and Macmillan, Dublin, 1987, p.6.
17. Burke, Bernard, *Irish Family Records*, Burke's Peerage Press, 1956.
18. Wright, D.G., *Yeats's Myth of Self*, p.5.
19. MacIntyre, Tom, 'Back to the Wall' in W.J. McCormack (ed.) *A Festschrift for Francis Stuart*, Dolmen Press, Dublin, 1972, p.46.
20. O'Toole, Fintan, 'Stuart – Up to 90'.
21. Myers, Kevin, 'Diary', *Irish Times*, March 1992.
22. Battersby, Eileen, 'Francis Stuart – An Icon of Hatred', *Irish Times*, 14 November 1996.
23. Myers, Kevin, 'Diary', *Irish Times*, 22 October 1997.
24. Natterstad, Jerry, 'An Interview with Francis Stuart', p.25.
25. O'Toole, Fintan, 'Stuart – Up to 90'.
26. O'Connor, Ulick, 'Interview with Francis Stuart', *Sunday Independent*, 13 November 1994.
27. O'Donoghue, David, 'Interview with Francis Stuart', 17 November 1989, O'Donoghue, David, *Hitler's Irish Voices: the Story of German Radio's Wartime Irish Service*, Beyond the Pale, Belfast, 1998, p.141.

28. Ibid.
29. Natterstad, Jerry, 'An Interview with Francis Stuart', p.25.
30. Diary entry, 18 February 1940, quoted in O'Donoghue, David, *Hitler's Irish Voices.*
31. O'Donoghue, David, 'Interview with Francis Stuart', 17 November 1989, p.141.
32. Ibid.
33. Radio broadcast, 17 March 1942, published in O'Donoghue, David, *Hitler's Irish Voices,* p.82.
34. Radio broadcast, 5 April 1942 published in O'Donoghue, David, *Hitler's Irish Voices,* p.83.
35. Diary entry, 1 August 1942, Notebook II, Francis Stuart Collection, University of Ulster Library.
36. Radio broadcast, August 1942, published in O'Donoghue, David, *Hitler's Irish Voices,* p.100.
37. O'Donoghue, David, *Hitler's Irish Voices,* p.43.
38. O'Donoghue, David, 'Interview with Francis Stuart', 17 November 1989, O'Donoghue, David, *Hitler's Irish Voices,* p.137.
39. O'Donoghue, David, *Hitler's Irish Voices,* p.x.
40. Ibid. p.141.
41. Natterstad, Jerry, 'An Interview with Francis Stuart', p.24.
42. Ibid., p.17.
43. Stuart, Francis, 'Literature and Politics', p.80.
44. Ibid.
45. Natterstad, Jerry, 'An Interview with Francis Stuart', p.30.
46. Freud, Sigmund, *On Creativity and the Unconscious,* Harper and Row, New York, 1958, p.12.
47. Hutcheon, Linda, *Narcissistic Narrative: The Metafictional Paradox,* Methuen, New York, 1980, p.141.
48. Wright, D.G., *Yeats's Myth of Self,* p.9.
49. Hutcheon, Linda, *Narcissistic Narrative,* p.139.
50. Iser, Wolfgang, 'Indeterminacy and the Reader's Response in Prose Fiction', in J. Hillis Miller (ed.) *Aspects of Narrative* New York, 1971, pp1–45.
51. Kermode, Frank, 'Novels: Recognition and Deception', *Critical Inquiry,* No.1, September 1974, pp.106–11.
52. Krieger, Murray, *A Window to Criticism, Shakespeare's Sonnets and Modern Poetics,* Princeton University Press, Princeton, 1964, p.3.

Chapter Six: Self Reflections

1. Banville, John, 'An Interview conducted by Rudolf Imhof', *Irish University Review*, Spring, 1981, p.10.
2. Diary entry, 13 November 1948, Notebook XII, University of Ulster Library.
3. Ibid.
4. Diary entry, May 1948, Notebook XI, University of Ulster Library.
5. Diary entry, 13 November 1948, Notebook XII, University of Ulster Library.
6. Ibid.
7. Eagleton, Terry, *Crazy John and the Bishop*, Cork University Press, Cork 1998, p.247.
8. Barthes, Roland, 'From Work to Text' in Joshue V. Harari (ed.) *Textual Strategies, Perspectives in Post-Structural Criticism*, Cornell University Press, New York, 1979, p.75.
9. Eagleton, Terry, *Crazy John and the Bishop*, p.245.
10. Fetterley, Judith, *The Resisting Reader, a Feminist Approach to American Fiction*, Indiana University Press, Bloomington, 1981, p.xx.
11. Ibid. p.xxi.
12. Eagleton, Terry, *Crazy John and the Bishop*, p.245.
13. Woolf, Virginia, *Orlando*, Hogarth Press, London, 1928, p.170.
14. Wittig, Monique, 'One is not Born a Woman', *Feminist Issues*, i, 1981, p.47.
15. Daly, Mary, *Pure Lust, Elemental Feminist Philosophy*, Women's Press, London, 1984.
16. Ests, Clarissa P., *Woman who Runs with Wolves. Contacting the Power of the Wild Women*, Rider, London, 1992.
17. McGahern, John, letter to Francis Stuart, Francis Stuart Collection, University of Ulster Library.
18. Diary entry, 13 November 1948, Notebook XIII, University of Ulster Library.
19. Ibid.
20. Kaplan, Sydney Janet, 'Varieties of Feminist Criticism', in Gayle Green, and Coppelia Kahn (eds) *Making a Difference: Feminist Literary Criticism*, p.40.
21. Irigaray, Luce, *The Sex which is not One* (trans. Porter, C.), Cornell University Press, New York, 1985, p.101.
22. Cixous, Helene, *To Live the Orange*, Cornell University Press, New York, 1979, p.10.
23. Cixous, Helene, 'The Laugh of the Medusa', p.253.

24. Kaplan, Sydney Janet, 'Varieties of Feminist Criticism', p.41.
25. Diary entry, 13 November 1948, Notebook XIII, University of Ulster Library.
26. Ibid.
27. Diary entry, 8 May 1948, Notebook XI, University of Ulster Library.
28. Diary entry, April 1951, Notebook XIV, University of Ulster Library.
29. Reader's report on *Danny Boy*, Manuscript, Manuscript 25.4, University of Ulster Library.
30. Wade, Allen (ed.), *The Letters of W.B. Yeats*, p.800.
31. MacKenzie, Compton, letter to Francis Stuart, 9 February 1932, Box 5/4, 52, Francis Stuart Collection, Southern Illinois University Library.
32. MacKenzie, Compton, review of *The Coloured Dome*, *Daily Mail*, 26 July 1932, Scrapbook, Francis Stuart Collection, University of Ulster Library.
33. Mannin, Ethel, letters to Francis Stuart, Francis Stuart Collection, University of Ulster Library.
34. Diary entry, November 1946, Notebook IX, University of Ulster Library.
35. Gollancz, Victor, letter to Francis Stuart, 17 February 1960, Francis Stuart Collection, University of Ulster Library.
36. 'A Trip Down the River', an unpublished novel, Manuscript 52 2/5, Southern Illinois University Library, Carbondale.
37. Gollancz, Victor, letter to Francis Stuart, 16 February 1960, Manuscript 25, University of Ulster Library.
38. Letters from John McGahern, October 1964–March 1978, Manuscript 78, University of Ulster Library.
39. Cronin, Anthony, *Identity Papers*, Lilliput Press, Dublin, 1979.
40. Diary entry, December 1948, Notebook XIII, University of Ulster Library.
41. Ibid.
42. (In *Situation II* (p.247) Sartre views torture not only as a kind of Black Mass in which both the torturer and the tortured commune in the destruction of humanity, but as a sexual relationship '... this moaning, sweating and polluted creature begging for mercy and surrendering with a swooned consent...').
43. Eagleton, Terry, *Crazy John and the Bishop*, p.245.
44. Ibid.
45. Ibid.
46. Diary entry , November 1947, Notebook X, University of Ulster Library.

Bibliography

Novels

Women and God, Jonathan Cape, London, 1931

Pigeon Irish, Victor Gollancz Ltd, London, 1932; Macmillan, New York, 1932

The Coloured Dome, Victor Gollancz Ltd, London, 1932; Macmillan, New York, 1933

Try the Sky, Victor Gollancz Ltd, London, Victor Gollancz Ltd, London, 1933; Macmillan, New York, 1933

Glory, Victor Gollancz Ltd, London, 1933; Macmillan, New York, 1933

In Search of Love, Collins, London, 1935; Macmillan, New York, 1935

The Angel of Pity, Grayson & Grayson London, 1935

The White Hare, Collins, London, 1936; Macmillan, New York, 1936

The Bridge, Collins, London, 1937

Julie, Collins, London, 1938; Knopf, New York, 1938

The Great Squire, Collins, London, 1939

Der Fall Casement: Das Leben Sir Roger Casement und der Verleum-dungsfeldzug des Secret Service (trans. Ruth Weiland), Hanseatische, Hamburg, 1940

A nagyur, The Great Squire, Szollosy Konyvkaido, Budapest, 1943

El gran senor, The Great Squire, de Caralt, Barcelona, 1945

The Pillar of Cloud, Victor Gollancz Ltd, London, 1948

Redemption, Victor Gollancz Ltd, London, 1949; Devin-Adair, New York, 1950

The Flowering Cross, Victor Gollancz Ltd, London, 1950

Good Friday's Daughter, Victor Gollancz Ltd, London, 1952

The Chariot, Victor Gollancz Ltd, London, 1953

Die Wolkensaule, The Pillar of Cloud, Drei Brucken Verlag, Heidelberg, 1953

The Pilgrimage, Victor Gollancz Ltd, London, 1955

La Porte d'esperance, The Chariot, Editions du Seuil, Paris, 1956

Victors and Vanquished, Victor Gollancz Ltd, London, 1958; Pennington Press, Ohio, 1959

Angels of Providence, Victor Gollancz Ltd, London, 1959

Black List, Section H, Southern Illinois University Press, Carbondale, 1971

Der weisse Hase, The White Hare, Manesse Verlag Zurich, 1972

Memorial, Martin Brian & O'Keeffe, London, 1973

Black List, Section H, Martin Brian & O'Keeffe, London, 1975

A Hole in the Head, Martin Brian & O'Keeffe, London, 1977

The High Consistory, Martin Brian & O'Keeffe, London, 1981

Black List, Section H, Penguin Books, Harmondworth, 1982

Faillandia, Raven Arts Press, Dublin, 1985

A Compendium of Lovers, Raven Arts Press, Dublin, 1990

The Pillar of Cloud, New Island Books, Dublin, 1994

Redemption, New Island Books, Dublin, 1994

Black List, Section H, Lilliput Press, Dublin, 1995

Black List, Section H, Penguin Classics, London, 1996

King David Dances, New Island Books, Dublin, 1996

Pamphlets

Nationality and Culture, Sinn Féin Árd Chomhairle, Baile Átha Cliath, 1924

Mystics and Mysticism, Catholic Truth Society of Ireland, Dublin, 1929

Racing for Pleasure and Profit in Ireland and Elsewhere, Talbot Press, Dublin, 1937

Prose

Things to Live For, Jonathan Cape London, 1934; Macmillan, New York, 1935

The Abandoned Snail Shell, Raven Arts Press, Dublin, 1987

States of Mind: Selected Short Prose 1939–1983, Raven Arts Press, Dublin /Martin Brian & O'Keeffe, London, 1984

Poetry

We Have Kept the Faith, Oak Leaf Press, Dublin, 1923

We Have Kept the Faith – new and selected poems, Raven Arts Press, Dublin, 1982

We Have Kept The Faith: Poems 1918–1992, Raven Arts Press, Dublin, 1992
Night Pilot, Raven Arts Press, Dublin, 1988
Arrows of Anguish: New Poems, New Island Press, Dublin 1996

Short prose

'A letter to a young lady, more sincere than most letters, yet not entirely so',
  Aengus, New Series, No.4, July 1920
'In Church', *Aengus,* New Series, No.4, July 1920
'A Note on Jacob Boehme', *Tomorrow,* ed. H. Stuart and Cecil Salkeld No.1
  August 1924
'In The Hour Before Dawn', *Tomorrow,* ed. H. Stuart and Cecil Salkeld No.2
  September 1924
'President de Valera', *Great Contemporaries: Essays by Various Hands,* Cassell,
  London, 1935
'Frank Ryan in Germany', *The Bell,* 16 No.2, November 1950
'Frank Ryan in Germany, Part II', *The Bell,* No.3, December 1950
'Extracts from the Journal of Apatriate', *Envoy: A Review of Literature and Art,*
  Vol.3, No.12, December 1950
'Minou, a Short Story', *Good Housekeeping,* March 1959
'Selection from Berlin Diary', *Journal of Irish Literature,* 5, January 1976
'A Minority Report: James Joyce', *Irish University Review,* No.12, 1982
'Introduction', *After the War is Over: Irish Writers mark the visit of Ronald
  Regan,* Raven Arts Press, Dublin, 1984
'Borges', *Antigonish Review* Vol.57, 1984
'Remembering Yeats', *Antigonish Review,* Vol.57, 1984
'Canto', *Southern Humanities Review,* 19, 1984
'Berlin in the Rare Oul' Times', *Irish Press,* 1 September 1989

Plays unpublished

Men Crowd Me Round, Abbey Theatre, Dublin, 1933
Glory, Arts Theatre Club, London, January 1936
Strange Guest, Abbey Theatre, Dublin, December 1940, Manuscript 52 2/4,
  Southern Illinois University Library, Carbondale
Flynn's Last Dive, Pembroke Theatre, London, March 1962, Manuscript 52
  2/2, Southern Illinois University Library, Carbondale
Who Fears to Speak, Liberty Hall, Dublin, 1970, Manuscript 11, University of
  Ulster Library
I Am Raftery: Radio play, Manuscript 23, University of Ulster Library
The Player King, written 1924, Manuscript 12, University of Ulster Library

Prose unpublished

'Early Story', a story written by Francis Stuart 'Aged 7', Manuscript 1, University of Ulster Library

'A Trip Down the River', an unpublished novel, Manuscript 52 2/5, Southern Illinois University Library, Carbondale

'Back to Suffer', begun 19 June 1960, an unpublished novel, Manuscript 52 1/1, Southern Illinois University Library, Carbondale

'The Water Gardener', fragment of an unpublished novel, Southern Illinois University Library, Carbondale

Interviews and articles

'De Valera', *Great Contemporaries – Essays by Various Hands*, Cassell & Co., London, 1935

'The Irish Novelist', *Irish Times*, 1 December 1972

'A Just Society in the North', *Irish Times*, 12 November 1974

'Patrick Kavanagh: Earthy Visionary', *Hibernia,* 25 July 1975

'An Interview' conducted by J.H. Natterstad, published in *Journal of Irish Literature,* Vol.5, No., 1976

'Literature and Politics', *Crane Bag*, Vol.1, No.1, 1977

'Novelists on the Novel', *Crane Bag*, Vol.3, No.1, 1979

'Interview with Denis O'Donoghue', 17 November 1989, O'Donoghue, David, *Hitler's Irish Voices: the Story of German Radio's Wartime Irish Service,* 1998

'A Conversation with Francis Stuart', in Bill Lazenbatt (ed.) *Writing Ulster, Francis Stuart Special Issue*, No.4, 1996

Books and articles on Francis Stuart

Barnwell, William C., 'Looking to the Future: The Universality of Francis Stuart', *Eire-Ireland: A Journal of Irish Studies,* Vol.12, No.2, 1977

Battersby, Eileen, 'Ever the outsider, still unrepentant', *Sunday Tribune*, Dublin 11 February 1990

Bolger, Dermot, 'A Memory of Madeleine', in Bill Lazenbatt (ed.) *Writing Ulster, Francis Stuart Special Issue*, No.4, 1996

Caterson, Simon, 'Stuart, Yeats and the Artist's Self', in Bill Lazenbatt (ed.) *Writing Ulster, Francis Stuart Special Issue*, No.4, 1996

Caterson, S., 'Joyce, the Kunstlerroman and Minor Literature, Francis Stuart's *Black List, Section H*, in *Irish University Review: A Journal of Irish Studies*, Spring/Summer, 1997

Corcoran, Neil, *After Yeats and Joyce: Reading Modern Irish Literature,* Oxford University Press, 1997

Cronin, Anthony, 'Religion Without Revelation', *Heritage Now*, Brandon Press, 1970

Cunningham, V., '*The High Consistory*', *Times Literary Supplement*, 1981

Deane, Seamus, *A Short History of Irish Literature*, Hutchinson Publishing, London, 1986,

Deane, Seamus, *Strange Country*, Oxford University Press, 1997

Donovan, Stewart, 'Remembering Yeats', *The Antigonish Review*, Vols. 71–72, 1987–1988

Eagleton, T., *Crazy Jane and the Bishop*, Cork University Press, 1998

Elborn, G., *Francis Stuart: A Life*, Raven Arts Press, Dublin, 1990

Garfitt, R., 'Contemporary Irish Literature', in D. Dunn (ed.) *Two Decades of Irish Writing*, Carcanet Press, 1975

Garfitt, R., 'Outside the Moral Pale: The Novels of Francis Stuart', *London Magazine*, October/November 1976

Greene, D.H., 'The Return of Francis Stuart', *Envoy*, April/June, 1951

Hamilton, H., 'Understand Francis Stuart', in Bill Lazenbatt (ed.) *Writing Ulster, Francis Stuart Special Issue*, No.4, 1996

Harmon, M., 'Francis Stuart', in R. Imhof (ed.) *Contemporary Irish Novelists*, Gunter Narr Verlag Tunbingen, 1989

Harmon, M., 'The Achievement of Francis Stuart', in Bill Lazenbatt (ed.) *Writing Ulster, Francis Stuart Special Issue*, No.4, 1996

Hazeldine, Peter, 'Private Lives' *PN Review*, Vol.15, No.1 63, 1988

Honan, K., 'Refloating the Ark', *The Irish Review*, Spring, 1988

Kiely, B., *Modern Irish Fiction – A Critique*, Dublin, 1950

Joannon, P., 'Francis Stuart of the Spy of Truth', in P. Rafroidi (ed.) in *The Irish Novel in our Time*, Publications de L'Universite de Liffe, 1975

Kennelly, Brendan, 'Teacher in the Joy', in Bill Lazenbatt (ed.) *Writing Ulster, Francis Stuart Special Issue*, No.4, 1996

Kilroy, Thomas, 'The Irish Writer: Self and Society' in P. Connolly (ed.) *Literature and the Changing Ireland*, Colin Smythe, 1982.

Lazenbatt, B. (ed.) 'Francis Stuart's Outrageous Fortune: A Reading of Arrow of Anguish', *Writing Ulster, Francis Stuart Special Issue*, No.4, 1996

Melmoth, J., '*Faillandia*', *Times Literary Supplement*, January 17 1986

Molloy, F.C. 'A Life Reshaped: Francis Stuart's *Black List, Section H*', *Canadian Journal of Irish Studies*, 14: 2, 1984

Molloy, F.C., 'Autobiography and Fiction: Francis Stuart's *Black List, Section H, Critique*', *Studies in Contemporary Fiction*, Vol.25, No.2, Winter, 1984

Molloy, F.C., 'Francis Stuart's Australian Connection: The Life and Death of Henry Irwin Stuart', *Irish University Review*, Vol.16, No.1, Spring 1986

Molloy, F.C., 'The Life of Francis Stuart', *Biography*, Vol.10, No.2, Spring 1987

Molloy, F.C., 'Francis Stuart, W.B. Yeats and *Tomorrow*', *Yeats Annual*, Vol.8, 1991

Murphy, D., *Imagination and Religion in Anglo-Irish Literature*, Irish Academic Press, Dublin, 1987

Murphy, H., 'Case for the Cause of Francis Stuart', *New Edinburgh Review*, Spring, 1984

McCartney, A., 'Sharing the Leper's Lair: Francis Stuart and Religion', in R. Welch, (ed.) *Irish Writers and Religion*, Colin Smythe, 1992

McCartney, A., 'The Impact of Reality: Francis Stuart's Narrative Theology' *Religion and Literature*, University of Notre Dame, 1996

McCartney, A., 'The Significance of the Self in Francis Stuart's Work', in Bill Lazenbatt (ed.) *Writing Ulster, Francis Stuart Special Issue*, No.4, 1996

McCartney, A., 'Transported into the Company of Women: A Feminist Critique of Francis Stuart', *Irish University Review*, Spring/Summer 1997

McCormack, W.J., *A Festschrift for Francis Stuart on his Seventieth Birthday*, Dolmen Press, Dublin, 1972

McCormack, W.J., 'Francis Stuart: The Recent Fiction', *Cahiers Irlandais*, Vol.4–5, 1976

McCormack, W.J., 'Francis Stuart: The Recent Fiction' in P. Rafroidi (ed.) *The Irish Novel in our Time*, Publications de L'Universite de Liffe, 1975

McCracken, Kathleen, 'Talking to one of the Old Masters: Paul Durcan's Response to Francis Stuart', in Bill Lazenbatt (ed.) *Writing Ulster, Francis Stuart Special Issue*, No.4, 1996

McGuckian, Medbh, 'Poet on Poet: McGuckian reads Stuart', in Bill Lazenbatt (ed.) *Writing Ulster, Francis Stuart Special Issue*, No.4, 1996

Natterstad, J.H. *Francis Stuart*, Bucknall University Press, 1974

Natterstad, J.H., 'Francis Stuart: At the Edge of Recognition', *Eire Ireland*, No.9, Autumn 1974

Natterstad, J.H. 'Francis Stuart: A Voice from the Ghetto', *The Journal of Irish Literature*, January 1976

Natterstad, J.H., 'Francis Stuart: The Artist as Outcast', in in P. Rafroidi (ed.) *The Irish Novel in our Time*, Publications de L'Universite de Liffe, 1975

Natterstad, J.H., 'The Artist as Rebel: Some Reflections on Francis Stuart, *ICarbs*, Vol.1 No.1.

Natterstad, J.H., 'Francis Stuart: From Laragh to Berlin', *ICarbs*, Vol.4, 1978

Natterstad, J.H., 'Locke's Swoon: Francis Stuart and the Politics of Despair', *Eire-Ireland: A Journal of Irish Studies*, Vol.26, No.4., 1991

O'Brien, R.J. 'Francis Stuart's Cathleen Ni Houlihan', *The Dublin Magazine*, Summer 1971

O'Donoghue, David, *Hitler's Irish Voices: the Story of German Radio's Wartime*

Irish Service, Beyond the Pale, Belfast, 1998

O'Toole, F., 'Stuart – Up to 90', *The Irish Times,* 29 April 1992

O'Toole, F., 'The Survivor', in Bill Lazenbatt (ed.) *Writing Ulster, Francis Stuart Special Issue,* No.4, 1996

Rafroidi, P., '*Black List, Section H*', *Etud Irlandaises,* 7, 1982

Welch, R., 'Francis Stuart: We are all one flesh', *Changing States: Transformations in Modern Irish Writing,* Routledge, London, 1993

White, T.D., '*States of Mind*', *Times Literary Supplement,* 1984

Unpublished sources

The Francis Stuart Collections at the University of Ulster Library at Coleraine and Southern Ilinois University Library at Carbondale are rich in material relating to the author. The Stuart Papers at Carbondale (Manuscript 52) consist of three series: manuscripts, workbooks and letters and clippings. This collection mainly covers the author's work from 1940 to 1975 with manuscripts for *Victors and Vanquished, Black List, Section H* and three unpublished novels, 'The Water Gardener', 'A Trip Down the River' and 'Back to Suffer'. The Letters and Clippings Series includes letters from Stuart's family, friends and other writers such as Ezra Pound, George Bernard Shaw, Compton Mackenzie and Heinrich Boll. The Francis Stuart Collection in Coleraine includes the manuscripts and notebooks for *Pillar of Fire (A Pillar of Cloud), A Hole in the Head, The High Consistory, Faillandia and Memorial.* Also 'A Novel Not Written' and playscripts for *Who Fears to Speak* and *The Player King.* The collection also includes the two editions of *To-Morrow* as well as original poems and letters from friends and family. Most importantly, the collection also includes eighteen Notebooks which constitute his diaries from March 1942 to August 1977.

Index